RED Hot & Blue

A SMITHSONIAN SALUTE TO THE AMERICAN MUSICAL

AMY HENDERSON and DWIGHT BLOCKER BOWERS

THE NATIONAL PORTRAIT GALLERY and
THE NATIONAL MUSEUM OF AMERICAN HISTORY

in association with the SMITHSONIAN INSTITUTION PRESS • Washington and London

An exhibition at the National Portrait Gallery, October 25, 1996, through July 6, 1997

"Red, Hot & Blue" is sponsored by Discover® Card

This exhibition has been jointly organized by the National Portrait Gallery and the National Museum of American History. Additional support has been provided by The Shubert Foundation, the Ira and Leonore Gershwin Philanthropic Fund, Harold and Judy Prince, and the Smithsonian Institution Special Exhibition Fund. In-kind support was provided by Red, Hot & Blue Limited Partnership.

Library of Congress Cataloging-in-Publication Data
Henderson, Amy.
    Red, hot & blue : a Smithsonian salute to the American musical / Amy Henderson and Dwight Blocker Bowers.
        p. cm.
    "An exhibition at the National Portrait Gallery, October 25, 1996, through July 6, 1997"
    Includes bibliographical references (p.   ) and index.
    ISBN 1-56098-698-0 (alk. paper)
    1. Musicals—United States—Exhibitions. 2. Musical films—United States—Exhibitions. I. Bowers, Dwight Blocker. II. National Portrait Gallery (Smithsonian Institution).   III. National Museum of American History (U.S.). IV. Title.
ML141.W3N38   1996
782.1'0973'074753—dc20   95-51339

British Library Cataloguing-in-Publication Data is available

Manufactured in Italy, not at government expense
03 02 01 00 99 98 97 96   5 4 3 2 1

∞ The paper used in this publication meets the minimum requirements of the American National Standard for Information Sciences—Permanence of Paper for Printed Library Materials ANSI Z39.48-1984.

FRONTISPIECE: Robert Preston in *The Music Man* (1957). By Eliot Elisofon for *Life* magazine, 1958. © Time, Inc.
FRONT COVER: Gene Kelly (Academy of Motion Picture Arts and Sciences. © Turner Entertainment Co., all rights reserved); human fountain from *Footlight Parade*, 1933 (Warner Bros. Archives, Wisconsin Center for Film and Theater Research, Madison. © Turner Entertainment Co., all rights reserved).
BACK COVER, CLOCKWISE FROM BOTTOM: Judy Garland and Mickey Rooney by Harold Edgerton, 1985, from 1940 negative (National Portrait Gallery, Smithsonian Institution. © 1940 The Harold E. Edgerton 1992 Trust, courtesy of Palm Press, Inc.); A *Chorus Line* company, 1975, by Martha Swope (© Time, Inc.); Eddie Cantor by Frederick J. Garner, 1933 (National Portrait Gallery, Smithsonian Institution); detail of Bert Williams, from "It Was Me," from *Ziegfeld Follies of 1911* sheet music (National Museum of American History, Smithsonian Institution); poster for *The Jazz Singer*, 1927 (Michael Kaplan Collection); Carol Channing in *Hello, Dolly!* by Mark Kauffmann for *Life* magazine, 1964 (© Time, Inc.); Bill "Bojangles" Robinson stair-dancing with Shirley Temple in *The Little Colonel*, 1935 (Photofest).

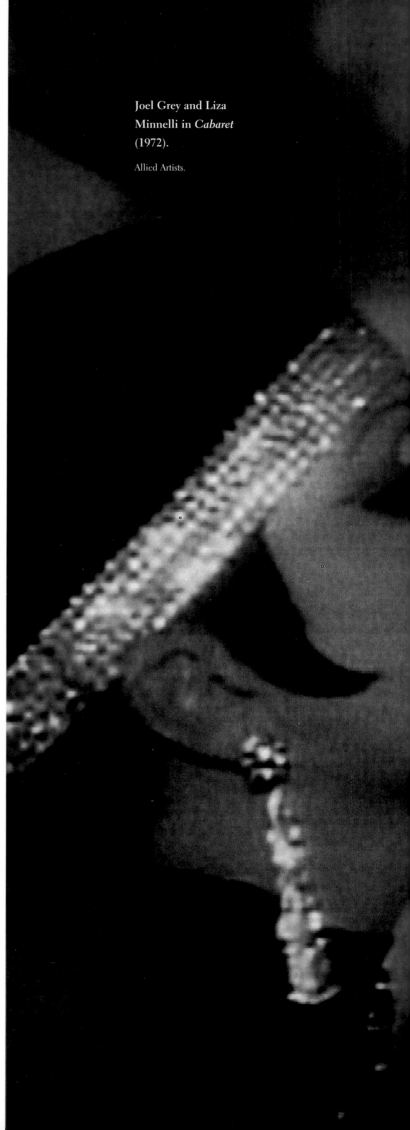

Joel Grey and Liza Minnelli in *Cabaret* (1972).

Allied Artists.

Bill Robinson stair-dancing with Shirley Temple in *The Little Colonel* (1935).

Photofest.

Gene Kelly in *Singin' in the Rain* (1952).

CONTENTS

Judy Garland, Jack
Haley, and Ray Bolger
in *The Wizard of Oz*
(1939).

Alice Becker Levin.
© Turner Entertainment
Co. All rights reserved.

INTRODUCTION

Did the citizens of Athens in the era of Pericles *know* that they were living in a Golden Age? I certainly didn't know that I was growing up in the Golden Age of American musicals, as I lived my teenage years in New York City in the forties and my law-student days a decade later in the "tryout city" of New Haven, Connecticut. Only now, after reading this lively history of one of America's most popular art forms, do I realize how remarkable an era it was.

I may even have taken for granted the fact that each season brought to Broadway a range of hits such as *Oklahoma!, South Pacific, Kiss Me, Kate,* and *Guys and Dolls,* and the stage power of the likes of Mary Martin and Ethel Merman. It all seemed natural and inevitable, that energy and talent. Even the availability of cheap seats to see world-class shows seemed part of the natural order of things.

When I was a student at Yale Law in New Haven, I had the chance to see musicals that are now classics, even before they reached Broadway. But I must admit my judgment was not always the best. I remember passing up one show because I didn't like its premise. Who wanted to see that wonderful story *Pygmalion* ruined? By the time it reached Broadway, I had come to my senses. But by then I had to pay a fortune to see *My Fair Lady.*

I went to see it the night before my bar exam. That was the best thing I ever did.

Everyone who picks up this book will have their own memories of the great musicals of Broadway and Hollywood. The authors, Amy Henderson and Dwight Blocker Bowers, have done us all a favor by convening once again the great talents of stage and screen who wrote the music and penned the words, who staged and choreographed the productions, and who gave voice and presence to emotion and drama and impossible grace.

They have focused on the individuals who arose out of what they call our "commotion of cultures" to create a form that owes something to the operettas of Europe but which has been transformed by the rhythms of our national life. There are echoes of all of our origins here, the mix and match of who we are and what we have formed together.

It's time that the Smithsonian put the spotlight on this energetic tradition and a nice coincidence that we do it in our 150th anniversary year. It took two of our great museums, the National Portrait Gallery and the National Museum of American History, to make it happen, and I congratulate them for the success of their collaboration. It is a gift to all of us.

I. MICHAEL HEYMAN
Secretary
Smithsonian Institution

Robert Coote, Julie
Andrews, and Rex
Harrison in *My Fair
Lady* (1956). By
Leonard McCombe
for *Life* magazine,
1956.

© Time, Inc.

xiii

FOREWORD

The Smithsonian keeps putting me in its debt. This is the second time I have been obliged to make a deep bow in its direction and say, "Thank you!" *Red, Hot & Blue* is a compendium of musical theater that anyone interested in the medium must be grateful for. Amy Henderson and Dwight Blocker Bowers have an encyclopedic grasp of the art form that we in this country had the wit to invent—the American musical theater. When I was reading this splendid book, I felt as if I were being led through the story of my own very long life because I knew most of the "greats" who are in its pages. In fact, I am one of the few people left who *did* know them.

The first time the Smithsonian did me a service was some years ago when Roger Kennedy, then director of the Smithsonian's National Museum of American History, asked me to speak on the American musical theater. Now, that was not something that I normally did; as an actress and a singer, I was used to speaking other peoples' lines. So I went to my husband, Moss Hart, and I said, "What on earth would I talk about?" And he said, "Well, you knew everyone in the American musical theater, and you knew most of them before you knew me. You knew Jerome Kern, Cole Porter, and Oscar Hammerstein, Irving Berlin, George Kaufman—and me. As well as Dietz and Schwartz, and Leonard Bernstein and Comden and Green, and Kurt Weill. My dear, I think you will find that your friends *are* the American musical theater."

LEFT: "Give My Regards to Broadway." Sheet music.

National Museum of American History, Smithsonian Institution, Washington, D.C.

RIGHT: Cole Porter (right) and Moss Hart (far right) breakfasting in Panama on their world tour in 1935.

Wisconsin Center for Film and Theater Research, Madison.

Indeed, I did know Frederick Loewe in my first Broadway show, called *Champagne Sec*, which was really *Die Fledermaus*. Fritz, as he was called, was playing the piano in the pit orchestra. And every evening he would come up to my dressing room and he would stand behind me while I was making up and say, with his strong Austrian accent, "Someday I am going to wrrrite the best musical on Brrroadway." And I would think—how many pit pianists, at this very moment, are saying the same thing!

Well, Lap dissolve—as they say in the movies—to opening night of *My Fair Lady*, for which Alan Jay Lerner and Frederick Loewe wrote the music and lyrics, and which Moss directed. We were all standing against the back wall in the theater. Moss and Alan Jay Lerner began pacing, and Fritz came up to me and whispered in my ear, "Tell Moss and Alan to stop vurrrying—this is the musical I prrromised 25 years ago. I told you I would wrrrite the best musical on Brrroadway."

My marriage to Moss brought me closer to that charmed circle of gifted composers, lyricists, directors, and designers—all of the artists who form that incredible collaboration that creates theater.

Moss said, "A musical is like a mosaic; if one tiny piece is missing, the picture is incomplete and the show cannot be a hit." Some of the highlights of Moss's career span the golden age of the American musical theater. This entertaining and informative book features this amazing period, which includes Moss's book for Irving Berlin's *Face the Music* and sketches for *As Thousands Cheer*. He and Cole Porter wrote *Jubilee* while on an around-the-world cruise. (Those were the days!) Then there was *I'd Rather Be Right* with George F. Kaufman and Rodgers and Hart. Moss directed *Camelot* with Lerner and Loewe. Then came the trek to Hollywood. He wrote *A Star Is Born* for Judy Garland, with music by Harold Arlen and lyrics by Ira Gershwin. And *Hans Christian Andersen* for Danny Kaye, with music by Frank Loesser.

Once again, I say, dear National Portrait Gallery, dear National Museum of American History, dear Smithsonian, and dear, dear Amy Henderson and Dwight Blocker Bowers, I thank you with all my heart for this wonderful tribute to a unique art form and the people who created it, the American musical theater.

KITTY CARLISLE HART

ACKNOWLEDGMENTS

The explorations that took us from Forty-second Street, to Kansas in August, to the wonders of Oz have been eased considerably by those who provided enormous assistance at every stage of this hydra-headed project.

For their enthusiastic support of this project—as their contributions to this volume warmly attest—we first wish to thank I. Michael Heyman, Secretary of the Smithsonian Institution, and Kitty Carlisle Hart, theater legend and longtime chairman of the New York State Council on the Arts.

We owe much to Tom L. Freudenheim and Barbara Schneider, who administered the Smithsonian Special Exhibition Fund that allowed this project to develop; to Harold S. Prince; to Mr. and Mrs. Michael S. Strunsky of the Ira and Leonore Gershwin Philanthropic Fund; to the Shubert Organization; and to Rob Wood, Bill Walsh, and Benedicta Lawrence of our principal funder, Discover Card, for bringing *Red, Hot & Blue* to fruition.

At the National Portrait Gallery, we are grateful to Alan Fern, director; Carolyn Carr, deputy director; Frederick S. Voss, historian, and Dorothy Moss of the Historian's Office; Frances Stevenson, publications officer, and Dru Dowdy, managing editor; Cecilia Chin, chief librarian, and Pat Lynagh, Jill Lundin, and Kim Clark; chief photographer Rolland White and photographer Marianne Gurley; the Office of Exhibitions staff, including Claire Kelly, Liza Karvellas, and Heather Donaldson; Deborah Berman, development officer; exhibition designers Nello Marconi and Al Elkins; Wendy Wick Reaves, curator of prints and drawings, and Ann Wagner, curatorial assistant; Mary Panzer, curator of photographs, and Ann Shumard, assistant curator; Suzanne Jenkins, registrar, and Molly Grimsley, associate registrar.

At the National Museum of American History, we are grateful to Spencer Crew, director; Martha Morris, deputy director; James Weaver, chairman, Cultural History; Lonnie Bunch, associate director for historical resources; Lonn Taylor, historian; John Fleckner, chief archivist, Archives Center; Robert Harding, deputy archivist; Elizabeth Greene, associate director for development opportunities; David Shayt; Kristin Felch; Robert Selim; and former director Roger G. Kennedy.

Our interns have been terrific, and we want to thank Eric Aron, Lynn Colton, Amy Featherstone, Andrea Ferretti, Sharon Lanza, James Loeffler, Heidi Lutz, Matthew MacArthur, Emily Smachetti, Heather Sullivan, and Ellen Weiss.

At the Library of Congress, we would like to thank Samuel Brylawski of Recorded Sound, Elena Millie of Prints and Photographs, and Mark Horowitz, Ray White, and most especially Walter Zvonchenko of the Performing Arts Research Center. The research staff at Howard University's Moorland-Spingarn Collection has been extremely helpful, as has that of Maryland Historical Society's Special Collections, and Geraldine Duclow of the

Free Library of Philadelphia. We are especially grateful to Liza Minnelli, Ginger Rogers, Roberta Olden, Mrs. George Abbott, Mrs. Boris Aronson, Tony Walton, Geoffrey Holder, Jo Sullivan Loesser, Chita Rivera, and Betty Kern Miller. George Feltenstein at MGM/UA has been inspirational, and we are extremely grateful for the assistance of Linda Mehr and Sam Gill at the Academy of Motion Picture Arts and Sciences; to Ned Comstock at the University of Southern California; and to Beth Werling at the Los Angeles County Museum of Natural History. We thank as well our film researchers Grace Barnes and X. Ted Barber, and our costume researcher Louise Coffey-Webb. At the Harry Ransom Research Center at the University of Texas at Austin, we are delighted to thank Melissa Miller-Quinlan; at the Marion Koogler McNay Art Museum in San Antonio, we are grateful to Robin Tobin, and to Linda Hardberger, curator of the Tobin Collection. In New York, Bob Taylor at New York Public Library's Billy Rose Theatre Collection has been invaluable; we are grateful as well to Marty Jacobs at the Museum of the City of New York. At the Shubert Archive, we are indebted forever to Brooks McNamara, Maryann Chach, Reagan Fletcher, and Mark Swartz. We are also indebted to Martha Swope, Ray Wemmlinger at The Players, Richard Barrios at Photofest, Michael Kerker and Karen Sherry of ASCAP, and Arlene Caruso of Harold S. Prince Productions. At the State Historical Society of Wisconsin (SHSW), we send heartfelt thanks to H. Nicholas Muller and Betsy Torrison, and to Maxine Fleckner Ducey at the Wisconsin Center for Film and Theater Research; we are also very grateful to Harry Miller of the manuscripts collection at SHSW.

We wish to thank our incredible audiovisual production team, including Mickey Green, Al Hillman and Michael Carr, Eric Kulberg and John Paige, Carolyn Lawrence, Pat Liebert, and John Meehan, as well as Robert Winter and Jay Heifetz of Calliope Media, who worked so closely with the inexhaustible Caroline Newman of the Smithsonian Institution Press. We also want to thank various Press staff for their enthusiastic support: Daniel Goodwin, director; Amy Pastan, acquisitions editor; Duke Johns, assistant managing editor; Ken Sabol, production manager; and Janice Wheeler, designer. Our copy editor, Vicky Macintyre, has been terrific throughout, and we thank her enormously.

Very special thanks go to Marc Pachter, who enthusiastically supported this project from its inception, and to Hap Erstein, Pie Friendly, Ellen Roney Hughes, Margo Kabel, Everett Raymond Kinstler, Russell Lehrer, Alice Becker Levin, Ken Ludwig, Mrs. Vincente Minnelli, Ann Morgan, Jim Morris, Dane Penland, Jack Raymond, Charles Sachs, and Hugh Talman.

And most of all, great thanks to our compatriot in tap dancing, National Portrait Gallery curator of exhibitions Beverly Jones Cox.

AMY HENDERSON
Historian
National Portrait Gallery

DWIGHT BLOCKER BOWERS
Historian
National Museum of American History

LENDERS TO THE EXHIBITION

Mrs. George Abbott

Academy of Motion Picture Arts and
Sciences, Beverly Hills, California

American Society of Composers, Authors
and Publishers, New York City

Rita Arlen

Lisa J. Aronson

Ray Avery Jazz Archives, Los Angeles,
California

Dwight Blocker Bowers

Center for Creative Photography,
The University of Arizona, Tucson

Chicago Historical Society, Illinois

Robertson E. Collins

Rare Book and Manuscript Library,
Columbia University, New York City

Condé Nast, New York City

Megan Cox

Eileen Darby

Frank Driggs

The Margo Feiden Galleries Ltd., New
York City

Sara and Armond Fields

Robert Galbraith

Judy Gershwin

Philippe Halsman Estate, New York City

Kitty Carlisle Hart

Amy Henderson

Jerry Herman

Geoffrey Holder

Moorland-Spingarn Research Center,
Howard University, Washington, D.C.

Steve and Nancy Ison

Michael Kaplan Collection

John Kisch Separate Cinema, Hyde Park,
New York

The Kobal Collection, New York City

Eric and Constance Kulberg

Eugene Lee

Annie Leibovitz

Alice Becker Levin

Library of Congress, Washington, D.C.

The Live Entertainment Corporation of
Canada, Inc., Toronto, Ontario

Jo Sullivan Loesser

Los Angeles County Museum of Art, Los
Angeles, California

Roddy McDowall

Maryland Historical Society, Baltimore

Metropolitan Opera Archives, New York
City

Liza Minnelli

Mrs. Vincenté (Lee) Minnelli

Museum of the City of New York, New
York

National Museum of American History,
Smithsonian Institution, Washington,
D.C.

National Portrait Gallery, Smithsonian
Institution, Washington, D.C.

Natural History Museum of Los Angeles
County, Los Angeles, California

New York Public Library for the
Performing Arts, New York City

Roberta Olden

The Paper Mill Playhouse, Millburn,
New Jersey

Photofest, New York City

The Hampden-Booth Theatre Library at
The Players, New York City

Harold Prince

The Rodgers and Hammerstein
Organization, New York City

Philip Samuels

Ken Schultz

Robert Seymour

The Shubert Archive, New York City

William L. Simon

Time-Life, New York City

Robert L. B. Tobin

Turner Entertainment Company, Los
Angeles, California

Harry Ransom Humanities Research
Center, The University of Texas at
Austin

Tony Walton

Wisconsin Center for Film and Theater
Research, Madison

Saul Zalesch

Mrs. Patricia Stephenson Ziegfeld

Richard Ziegfeld

PREFACE

"A Fine Romance"

Fred and Ginger, gliding cheek to cheek across an Art Deco floor . . . Bill "Bojangles" Robinson stair-dancing with Shirley Temple . . . Judy Garland, skipping over a rainbow and down a yellow brick road . . . Gene Kelly, romping gleefully in the rain . . . Robert Preston, warning about trouble in River City . . . Ethel Merman, nagging her daughter to "Sing out, Louise!" . . . Joel Grey, bidding us "Willkommen" . . .

The fleeting images of Broadway and Hollywood musicals are frozen in our national psyche. From the days when "the Great White Way" blazed along Broadway, through the "all singing! all talking! all dancing!" days of early Hollywood, to a Technicolor heyday when movie musicals sprawled across the silver screen, these venerated images have captivated American popular culture. Energized by the words and music of, among others, Jerome Kern, George and Ira Gershwin, Irving Berlin, Cole Porter, Rodgers and Hammerstein, and Leonard Bernstein, we have happily conducted—in the words of lyricist Dorothy Fields—"a fine romance" with our musical icons for most of this century.

Earlier, before movies and recordings gave musicals a degree of permanence, all that existed was live performance. People streamed into vaudeville houses, theaters, and concert halls for their musical entertainment. But by the late nineteenth century, a nascent mass entertainment industry was appearing. In 1877 Thomas Alva Edison invented a cylinder "talking machine," advertising that "it talks, it laughs, it plays, it sings!" By 1889 he had devised a "kinetoscope," a machine in which fifty feet of 35-mm positive film revolved on a spool: when a coin (a nickel) was dropped in a slot, an electric light flashed on the film; a tiny motor moved the film frame by frame

LEFT: Fred Astaire and Ginger Rogers dancing to "Night and Day" in the *Gay Divorcee* (1934).

Photofest.

RIGHT: George M. Cohan. By Walter K. Kinstler, 1923.

National Portrait Gallery, Smithsonian Institution, Washington, D.C.

1

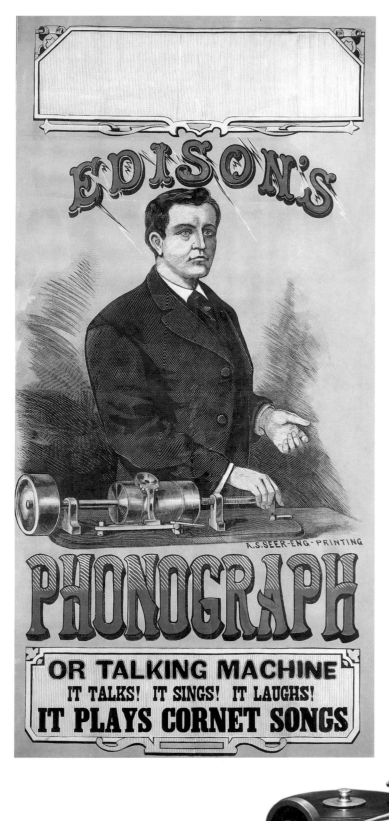

Poster advertisement
for the Thomas
Edison Phonograph,
circa 1878.

National Portrait Gallery,
Smithsonian Institution,
Washington, D.C.

RIGHT: The Edison
Automatic
Phonograph, 1897.

National Museum of
American History,
Smithsonian Institution,
Washington, D.C.

Emile Berliner's disc
talking machine,
1897.

National Museum of
American History,
Smithsonian Institution,
Washington, D.C.

so that a viewer looking through the peephole would see a cavalcade of images in motion. Musical performers were among the first filmed, their movements flickering across tiny screens. Their voices, recorded scratchily on Edison's early cylinder machines and on Emile Berliner's disc talking machine, a gramophone patented in 1887, could be heard by the end of the century on the Edison Automatic Phonograph in penny arcades and exhibition parlors; musical performers could also be seen in nickelodeons on such large-scale motion picture projections as the Vitascope.[1] The era of technology's linkage to the rise of popular culture—of which musical theater served as a prime example—had begun.

Streetside life in the late nineteenth century nourished a musical theater that spoke for the new American mosaic. The result was a celebration of diverse urban cultures, including the Irish-tinged vaudeville routines of Harrigan and Hart, the "Dutch" acts of Weber and Fields, and the minstrelsy of Williams and Walker. But it was only after the turn of the century that the American musical began to evolve its own particular character. As the entertainment industry became centralized in New York, musical theater developed strong commercial underpinnings. And with the growing emphasis on the "business" side of the show, impresarios such as Florenz Ziegfeld and the Brothers Shubert forged a musical theater dependent on the star system—a constellation in the 1910s and 1920s that included Al Jolson, Fanny Brice, Eddie Cantor, and Marilyn Miller.

During the peak 1927–28 season, Broadway marquees glittered with over fifty musicals, including Fats Waller in the all-black revue *Keep Shufflin'*, Fred and Adele Astaire in the Gershwins' *Funny Face*, and Marilyn Miller in *Rosalie*. But the milestone musical that year—one that marked the emergence of the modern American musical—was the Jerome Kern–Oscar Hammerstein II production, *Show Boat*. Here, wonderful songs—including "Ol' Man River," "Bill," and "Why Do I Love You?"—combined with a strong narrative and carefully drawn characters to create an American classic.

At almost the same time, the premiere of *The Jazz Singer* ushered in the era of talkies; capitalizing on the popularity of Broadway shows, Hollywood soundstages

were soon overtaken by a musical mania. Much of Broadway virtually moved west, including such performers as Ginger Rogers and Fred Astaire, and songwriters like George and Ira Gershwin, Jerome Kern, Cole Porter, Rodgers and Hart, and Irving Berlin. Busby Berkeley brought his Machine Age choreography to the big screen, while Fred and Ginger created a gossamer world of silvery Art Deco glamour. Even during the Depression, people continued to flock to their neighborhood movie theaters, welcoming the respite provided by Shirley Temple chirruping about "The Good Ship Lollipop," or Nelson Eddy and Jeanette MacDonald crooning "Indian Love Call" on a moonlit lake. Fantasies about a better world over the rainbow peaked with the 1939 *Wizard of Oz*—but this film's ultimate message, after all, was "there's no place like home."

The era launched by Rodgers and Hammerstein's *Oklahoma!* in 1943 was the Golden Age of the American stage and movie musical, yielding the genre's most enduring works. While film, recording, and broadcast technologies allowed musicals to reach their widest audience to date, the themes of both Broadway and Hollywood musicals of the 1940s and 1950s often reflected divergent views of the American character: where *Oklahoma!*, *Meet Me in St. Louis*, and *The Music Man* celebrated a nostalgia for small town America, *On the Town*, *Guys and Dolls*, and *West Side Story* exploded with urban energy. Broadway pulsated with the music of Rodgers and Hammerstein, Leonard Bernstein and Comden and Green, Lerner and Loewe, and Jule Styne, while the glamorous MGM musicals—spearheaded by producer Arthur Freed and director Vincente Minnelli—created a uniquely "American" portrait on film.

By the late 1950s American society, like the Sharks and the Jets in *West Side Story*, was beginning to rumble with dissonance. Years of enormous cultural and social change would clearly affect the American musical: the vast middle-class, mainstream audience that had always supported the musical dissolved, and without a center, musicals became as disparate as the rest of American culture. The traditional musical survived in such works as Jerry Herman's *Hello, Dolly!* and *Mame*, but the last thirty years have been more a period of redefinition and revival, better characterized by Joseph Papp's search for broader, more diverse audiences through such productions as *Hair* and *A Chorus Line*, by Stephen Sondheim's theatrical experimentation in such shows as *Company* and *Sweeney Todd*, and by Harold Prince's astonishing feats of stagecraft, particularly in the 1994 revival of the Kern-Hammerstein classic, *Show Boat*.

Show Boat, along with new versions of Frank Loesser's *Guys and Dolls*, Cole Porter's

Anything Goes, and Ken Ludwig's *Crazy for You* "revisal"
of the Gershwins' *Girl Crazy*, indicates the current repertory nature of the modern musical. Although musical
theater continues to be redefined, the essential core of
the American musical remains with its past. No matter
how extravagantly refashioned, there is a "ghost in the
machine" quality to modern musical theater that, while
redefining itself in a thoroughly contemporary context,
harkens back to its origins—to earlier images flickering
on a Vitascope screen, raspy voices rolling out of Victro-
las, and silvery figures dancing across a Bakelite set.

   We have written this book as a cultural history rather
than as a comprehensive history of American musicals—
although we did decide early on that instead of discussing
two separate spheres known as Broadway and Hollywood
it made more sense to consider American musicals as part
of an ongoing cultural continuum. As each quantum leap
in technology—recordings, movies, radio, and television—vastly broadened access to entertainment for an
ever-widening audience, key figures in the musical industry crossed freely from one
medium to another. And it is these key figures who form the core of this book, for although
we discuss a variety of cultural issues that have fascinated us along the way, *Red, Hot &
Blue* is essentially a collective biography focusing on some of the personalities—performers, composers, directors, choreographers, set and costume designers, impresarios—who
helped to create the Broadway and Hollywood musical.

   "A fine romance," indeed.

Give my regards to Broadway,
Remember me to Herald Square.
Tell all the gang at Forty-second Street
That I will soon be there.

GEORGE M. COHAN, "GIVE MY REGARDS TO BROADWAY," 1904

Setting the Stage

Before the gang congregated at Forty-second Street, America's musical voice reverberated through the Bowery, lower Broadway, and Union Square. In the 1870s and 1880s this ethnic crossroads was a veritable commotion of cultures, with the sound of music cascading in a jumble of minstrelsy, musical extravaganzas, opera, songs from German beer gardens, Irish brass bands, and tinny pianos plunking out sentimental ballads and curbside Gilbert and Sullivan. Amid the sweatshops, pushcarts, "temples of love," and tenements, the street boasted a cultural life that coursed from dime museums to a "paradise of beer saloons, barrooms, concert and dance halls, cheap theatres, and low-class shows."[1] The Bowery at night was "in its glory . . . a blaze of light from one end to the other. . . . There is nothing in this glare of light, nothing in this swarming pavement, to indicate that midnight is passed. The windows gleam, the saloons are all aglare, a half-score pianos and violins . . . blend into . . . the roysterer's song, the brawler's oath and the hundred strange voices of the night."[2]

Immigration and an urban setting had produced a highly fragmented culture, with audiences divided by race and ethnicity, social class, and gender. Nor was there any centralized entertainment industry: organized theatrical circuits such as the Keith-Albee, Loew's, or the Shuberts had yet to appear, and only a few theatrical agents and sheet-music publishing houses were established.[3] An emerging entertainment district took root in the Bowery in the 1880s, moved with vaudeville to Union Square in the 1890s, and then, by the early 1900s, to West Twenty-eighth Street between Broadway and Sixth Avenue, where the

LEFT: Interior view of Niblo's Theatre, from *Ballou's Pictorial*, February 24, 1855.

The J. Clarence Davies Collection, Museum of the City of New York.

RIGHT: The Thalia Theatre rose above the elevated tracks at Canal Street in New York, 1879.

Museum of the City of New York.

din of pianos clanging out new tunes led songwriter-journalist Monroe Rosenfeld to compare the cacophony to clashing tin pans, thereby inventing the sobriquet Tin Pan Alley.[4]

The most popular entertainment of post–Civil War New York was a musical extravaganza called *The Black Crook*, which opened at Niblo's Garden in 1866. A bizarre hybrid that combined a heavy-handed adaptation of Carl Maria von Weber's 1821 opera *Der Freischütz* with dance featuring the Great Parisian Ballet Troupe, *The Black Crook* came about only because the theater where the ballet had planned to open, the Academy of Music, burned down; the manager of Niblo's was persuaded to blend the ballet into the melodrama, and the result was a five-hour spectacle that succeeded largely because the ballet featured 100 chorines in flesh-colored tights. It was the first major production on an American stage to spotlight seminudity, prompting the *New York Tribune* to report that "though we cannot say that anything has been done for the dramatic art . . . we can heartily testify that Scenic Art has never, within our knowledge, been so amply and splendidly exemplified." *The Black Crook* appealed to the audience's appetite for spectacle. Playwright-producer Dion Boucicault, one of the brightest luminaries of the era, once said that "sensation is what the public wants, and you cannot give them too much of it."[5] Sensation is what *The Black Crook* served up to its audience, and annual productions of the show took place into the 1880s.[6]

Star ballerina Maria Bonfanti is featured on the cover of the sheet music for the "Transformation Polka," from *The Black Crook*, 1866.

Museum of the City of New York.

The Black Crook had been a fluke that magically worked, but it had little direct effect on the immediate evolution of American musicals. Blackface minstrelsy, which had achieved widespread popularity in the 1840s, continued to have a dominant presence after the Civil War. Variety, a theater of pastiche that largely grew out of minstrelsy in the 1860s–80s, also offered absurdly exaggerated skits and parodies of current topics, always performed at a gallop; like minstrelsy, which had played well to illiterate audiences in the antebellum years, variety's large gestures appealed to non-English-speaking immigrant audiences. Yet because it was performed in beer halls and "concert saloons," variety suffered from a lack of respectability, thereby limiting its potential drawing power.

When a middle class with the leisure to be amused emerged in the 1880s, show business entrepreneurs saw the financial logic of broadening entertainment's appeal to a wider audience. A first step was to purge variety of its licentious reputation—to remove its saloon atmosphere of general sleaze and give it a sheen of respectability that would draw middle-class men and women within its doors.[7]

Pioneering this theatrical reform was impresario Tony Pastor, who refined variety away from its origin as saloon fare and helped transform it into the phenomenally successful commercial enterprise known as vaudeville. Vaudeville was similar to variety, presenting a series, or "olio," of specialty acts and skits drawn from blackface minstrelsy and the circus, but it sought to enlarge its audience by presenting itself as "a crazy-quilt form of family entertainment."[8]

Tony Pastor's Music Hall on Fourteenth Street, 1886.

Harry Ransom Humanities Research Center, The University of Texas at Austin.

Born in New York around 1834, Pastor grew up in show business, singing at temperance meetings as a child in the mid-1840s, then moving on to become a tambourine player and singer with the minstrel show at Barnum's American Museum in New York. P. T. Barnum was the self-styled "Prince of Humbug," a calling he described as someone who advertises

Impresario Tony Pastor. By Matlinger, circa 1900.

Harry Ransom Humanities Research Center, The University of Texas at Austin.

P. T. Barnum, the "Prince of Humbug." Attributed to Max Rosenthal, 1851.

National Portrait Gallery, Smithsonian Institution, Washington, D.C.

OUR MANAGERS.

MR. TONY PASTOR.

his wares in an outrageous manner, but who gives his customers their money's worth. His "museum" was a bedazzling netherworld, where twenty-five cents afforded entrée to a land of dwarfs, mermaids, and giants, as well as concerts, juggling acts, ventriloquists, and blackface minstrels. Fascinated by burnt cork and sawdust, Pastor said late in his life that he would have worked for free: "How much do you suppose I got for singing and thumping the tambourine? Two dollars a week. . . . Yes, indeed, I'd have sung . . . for nothing."[9] In addition to minstrelsy, he also performed in circuses as a singer, acrobat, and ringmaster until, by the late 1850s, he turned to comedy and became recognized as "the great American clown." Armed with what one reporter called a "witchery of personality" and outfitted in a baggy polka-dot costume, Pastor would barrel into the circus ring, twirl his mustache, stumble, execute a backflip or somersault, and launch into such audience favorites as "Teetotal Society" or "Wedlock Is a Ticklish Thing."[10]

Eventually, Pastor tired of the rigorous life of circus touring and in the early 1860s settled in New York, where he began to appear as a comic singer. Some of his songs—including "We Are Coming, Father Abraham," which parodied a popular recruiting song and the 1863 draft riot in New York City—were published in "songster" books such as *Tony Pastor's "Own" Comic Vocalist*. A contemporary account conveys a vivid image of Pastor in performance:

Beautiful women danced upon the stage. Amazing negro comedians created much laughter, and dextrous acrobats held me in breathless yet fearsome delight. After a while a movement in the audience presaged the coming of the principal attraction—Tony Pastor. Can I ever forget my sensations? I had read of Tony Pastor, had purchased his song books and essayed to sing his songs, and indeed had created an ideal. Fancy my surprise when a dapper little chap of about 110 pounds came on the stage dressed in the garb of a circus clown, and sang "Everything Is Lovely and the Goose Hangs High," a satire on current events.[11]

In 1865 Pastor took over Volk's Garden in the Bowery and renamed it Tony Pastor's Opera House, intending to make it, as one of his playbills proclaimed, a "Temple of Amusement" that would serve as "The Great Family Resort of the City where heads of families can bring their Ladies and children, and witness unexceptionable entertainment—one that will please the most fastidious."[12] The *New York Herald* reported that "rowdyish and troublesome elements" were being eliminated, and that Pastor's Opera House was presenting not only good-natured "mirth" but "histrionic art, and music, and the ballet." There were tightrope acts, jugglers, Carrie Austin "in her lightning Zouave drill," gymnasts, and "a comic pantomime, *The Magic Flute*." Good order was strictly observed, as well as "the absence of peanut feasts and boisterous applause."[13]

Broadside advertising "Tony Pastor's Troupe," circa 1880.

Harry Ransom Humanities Research Center, The University of Texas at Austin.

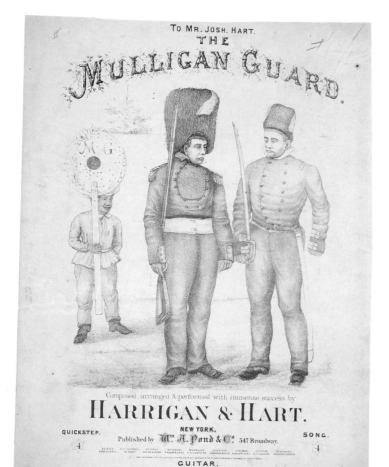

The Mulligan Guard.
Sheet music, 1879.

National Museum of
American History,
Smithsonian Institution,
Washington, D.C.

**Edward Harrigan and
Tony Hart, 1872.**

Albert Davis Collection,
Harry Ransom Humanities
Research Center, The
University of Texas at
Austin.

For the next forty years Pastor would oversee the enormous success of vaudeville as it moved from the Bowery to Broadway. He is credited with discovering many of the leading entertainers of the late nineteenth century, from such great two-man acts as Harrigan and Hart or Weber and Fields to important individual stars such as Lillian Russell and George M. Cohan. His own theaters, from the Opera House at 201 Bowery to his Music Hall on Fourteenth Street, registered the march of respectability—a trek that also chronicled the path of immigrant cultures as well as the coalescing of a formative period in American musical theater.

Performers trodding the boards of Pastor's or other vaudeville houses radiated an overwhelming ethnicity, with Irish, "Dutch" (i.e., Deutsch [German]), and African American acts predominating. And while some theaters aimed at only a single ethnic element, most of the major houses tried to offer the broadest range of acts to attract the largest audience. Leading teams of the era likewise presented themselves not simply in the guise of one particular ethnicity but cheerfully changed from "Dutch" to blackface minstrel to Irish.

Edward "Ned" Harrigan, the playwright half of the great Irish act Harrigan and Hart, once explained how the team spotlighted this diversity when it launched its career in the early 1870s with the hugely successful *The Mulligan Guard*, a musical focusing on Bowery denizens: "It began with the New York 'boy,' the Irish-American, and our African brother. As it grew in popularity, I added the other prominent types which go to make up life in the metropolis . . . Englishmen, German, Low German, Chinese, Italian, Russian."[14] As contemporary journalist Richard Harding Davis wrote in 1891, "Mr. Harrigan has taken his material from around about him, and his cast of characters on the programme reads like a selection from the names in the New York directory."[15] Harrigan's daughter Nedda recalled that her father "would ride the streetcars. . . . He would go and sit in Battery Park. He'd follow people around, learn their walks, see where they lived. He would buy clothes off people's back to use for costumes, so they would look authentic."[16]

Harrigan and Hart's shows were farces that relied on the

re-creation of local color to convey the vitality of Bowery life in the streets. As a playwright, Harrigan couched difficult ethnic jealousies on stage in a variety-style setting. Outrageous exaggerations transformed dialect humor into popular parodies, and, at least while the audience remained in the theater, defused the bitterness of everyday life. In *McSorley's Inflation* (1882), one of the songs characterized the ethnic elbowing of tenement life:

> It's Ireland and Italy, Jerusalem and Germany,
> Oh, Chinamen and naygroes, and a paradise for rats,
> All jumbled up togayther in the snow or rainy weather,
> They represent the tenants in McNally's row of flats.[17]

Harrigan quit school at fourteen and worked as an errand boy, shipyard apprentice, and printer's devil before turning to acting. In the 1860s he performed in minstrel shows from San Francisco to Chicago, there becoming associated with another young trouper, fifteen-year-old comic actor Tony Hart. In 1872 Harrigan and Hart took up residence at the Theatre Comique on lower Broadway, where they were joined by composer David Braham. Working with Braham, Harrigan began to add songs to his sketches; the two would compose more than two hundred songs over the next twenty years. Their greatest success was

**"Baxter Street" scene
designed by Charles
W. Witham in 1888
for Harrigan's play
The Leather Patch.**

Museum of the City of
New York; gift of William
Seymour.

The Mulligan Guard, first performed in 1873. More than a musical sketch, but not yet a full-scale play, it was straight out of variety. The protagonist was Dan Mulligan, an Irish immigrant who, to one critic, became "more than a symbol of Irish ascendancy in the seventies and eighties; he grew into the hero of a minor American saga." It would be through Dan's eyes that Harrigan described life in the Bowery—among "the shanties, the mud-scows . . . the politicians of New York . . . the secret societies of the Full Moons and the *Turnvereine* of his German cadets, the clothes stalls of his Jews."[18] Set in "Mulligan's Alley," the action often took place at McSweeney's Wee Drop Saloon. Across the street was an Italian junk shop and Ah Wung's Chinese laundry and roominghouse; next door was an African American social club, the Full Moon Union. The stories, heavily laced with ethnic humor, slapstick, and enthusiastic singing and dancing, depicted neighborhood rivalries that centered on such conflicts as that of competing marching bands—the Irish American "Mulligan Guards," for example, versus the African American "Skidmore Guards"—or on politics, perhaps posing Dan Mulligan against the German butcher Gustave Lochmuller in some local political battle.[19]

Harrigan felt that "haste and strife" were the two words that most characterized his New York, and he adhered to their staccato rhythm in all of his work. The plot lines of his sketches—including *The Mulligan Guard's Picnic* (1878), *The Mulligan Guard's Ball*

(1879), *The Mulligan Guard's Surprise* (1880), *Cordelia's Aspirations* (1883), and *Dan's Tribulations* (1884)—delineated the everyday lives of Dan Mulligan; his wife, Cordelia; and his marching band. The *Boston Herald* said Harrigan's productions depicted "the war of the races in cosmopolitan New York," and there is little question that the proximity of clashing cultures formed the nucleus of Harrigan's work. One of the most popular scenes occurred at the second-act curtain of *The Mulligan Guard's Ball*, which took place in a dance hall where an absentminded German proprietor had inadvertently rented the place out to two intensely rival social clubs, one Irish and one African American. The resulting chaos—a convention in every Harrigan play that he called "the Tumult"—featured a ferocious fight scene that left the gallery stomping and screaming in appreciation.[20]

Using his plays to highlight the Irish–German–black rivalry that he saw as central to urban immigrant life in the 1870s and '80s, Harrigan created a Hogarthian realism then unknown on the American stage. As he stated in his programs, his objective was "to catch the living manners as they rise."[21] Indeed, he presented a theatrical prelude to the later emerging realist literary works of such novelists as Theodore Dreiser and Frank Norris. But however prescient Harrigan was in his dramatic sensibilities, it is more difficult to credit the songs he wrote with David Braham, none of which have proved enduring—even though, in their own time, they were internationally famous, winning praise from such writers as William Dean Howells, who characterized Harrigan as America's Dickens, and Rudyard Kipling, who quoted *The Mulligan Guard* in his 1901 novel, *Kim:* "At the far end of the plain a heavy, dusty column crawled in sight. Then the wind brought the tune: 'We crave your condescension / To tell you what we know / Of marching in the Mulligan Guards / To Sligo Port below.'"[22]

The team of Harrigan and Hart dissolved in 1885, following a disastrous fire at the Theatre Comique. Harrigan continued to produce new shows until his farewell tours of 1908 and 1909, but the times had passed him by; his plays came to be viewed as period pieces. Yet in the 1870s and '80s he had provided a vital step in the creation of an American musical theater: he infused his depictions of immigrant life with a new realism, emphasizing local color and topical songs and turning the urban hero into a Broadway staple.

Like Harrigan and Hart, the vaudeville team of Joe Weber and Lew Fields began in the Bowery. They both grew up in Polish Jewish immigrant families in the 1870s and as schoolboys often escaped to the Bowery Theater to soak up the "glamorous life" of show business. At nine and ten years old, they were trying out their own act, performing in blackface at local Elks Clubs and dime museums, imitating the leading two-man teams of the day. In the 1870s ethnic acts dominated popular theater, with blackface acts predominant, Irish acts next, and "Dutch" third. As one vaudeville historian has written, the original two-man acts "worked as blackface comic and straight man. The next teams to win favor were the double Irish, with exaggerated make-ups; later . . . came the double Dutch. . . . You will notice that the comic characters followed the pattern of our immigration."[23]

Young Weber and Fields would hang out at a neighborhood sa-

Joseph Weber and Lew Fields in character as a pair of German army deserters in *Twirly-Whirly.*

Billy Rose Theatre Collection, New York Public Library for the Performing Arts, New York City.

loon, not to drink but "to hear the talk of the Germans who frequented it." Like Harrigan and Hart and later vaudevillians George M. Cohan and Bert Williams, Weber and Fields collected ideas from their everyday experience, then shaped their act to suit their immediate audience. Working as "small-timers" in their teens in the 1880s, Weber and Fields were successful enough to open their own Music Hall in 1896; for the next eight years, they created the standard for an incipient American musical comedy. Their act combined "Dutch knockabout"—that is, slapstick—and burlesque, not as "striptease" but as parody or comic imitation. It was a rambunctious, physical act, involving a lot of pushing and shoving, and, in what is said to be original with them, custard pies in the face.

Weber and Fields's "Pool Room Sketch" was one of their most famous and illustrated two-man ethnic comedy at its best. Tall, thin Fields and short, hefty Weber appeared here as Mike and Meyer—with Meyer/Fields serving as the pool-hall hustler trying to victimize the mild-mannered and naïve Mike/Weber. Amid the slapstick confusion of the sketch, a basic affection between the two was clear, thereby giving a more gentle sensibility to what was often, in the world of the streets, a far harsher reality. "Don't poosh me, Meyer!" Mike would plead as Meyer shoved him around the stage; Meyer would then tell Mike (while choking him), "If you luffed me like I luf me, no knife could cut us togedder."[24] Throughout the sketch, an ersatz German dialect was used—one the audience found hysterically funny despite its close-to-the-bone familiarity. But that was the point: to illustrate the tougher side of immigrant life in a way that made people laugh.

When "Weberfields," as they were known, opened the doors to the Weber and Fields Music Hall in the summer of 1896, America's popular theater was at a turning point.

Poster advertising Weber and Fields's *Re-united*, c. 1923.

The Shubert Archive, New York City.

While Tony Pastor still worked to introduce vaudeville to a widening audience of middle-class consumers, such leading performers of the immediate past as Harrigan and Hart had become passé. But Broadway itself was now moving uptown and emerging as a definable area: in 1901, it was christened "The Great White Way" by an advertising genius named O. J. Gude, the so-called Napoleon of publicity, whose passion for electrical signboard advertising left Broadway studded with what he described as "the phantasmagoria of the lights and electric signs."[25] In 1902 *New York Times* publisher Adolph S. Ochs bought and demolished the Hotel Pabst on the point between Broadway and Seventh Avenue, clearing the way for "Times Square," the theoretical heart of Broadway. Legitimate theaters moved into the area from Thirty-ninth Street to Forty-fifth, including the New Amsterdam on Forty-second—the site of Florenz Ziegfeld's first *Follies* in 1907. Lobster houses such as Rector's and Delmonico's opened to provide an extended nightlife scene, while support businesses such as wig and costume shops sprang up throughout the theater district. And as the area grew and centralized, so did the entire music and theater industry, from the music publishers of Tin Pan Alley, to the new business elements that emerged to promote Broadway itself—an entire commercial culture of publicity wizards, theatrical agents, and booking entrepreneurs. Times Square became a "staggering machine of desire."[26]

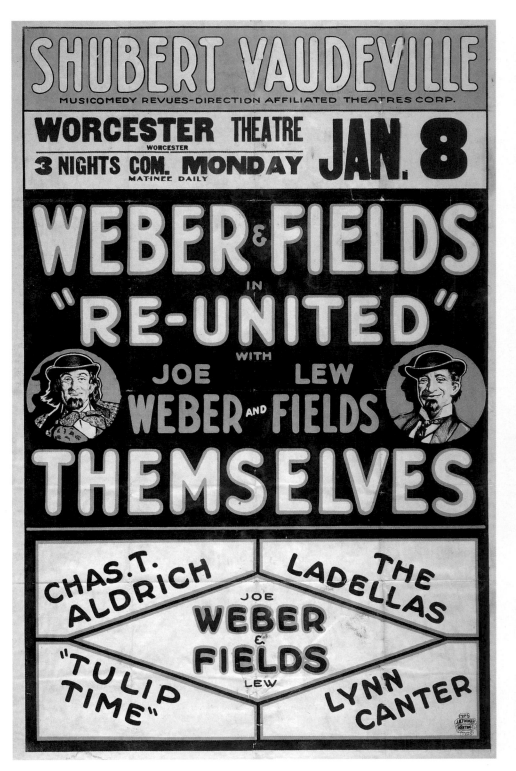

In the midst of this transformation, musical theater itself changed, turning away from ethnic caricature and taking a fond look at politics and current events. Weber and Fields capitalized on this trend when they decided not to continue to present burlesques of immigrant life but to focus instead on such new targets as impresario David Belasco, the so-called Bishop of Broadway, whose melodramas were the rage of the legitimate stage. All-star vaudeville acts were also featured on the Weber and Fields bill, along with topical parodies performed by Weber and Fields as Mike and Meyer. But most important was their adaptation of a new format of musical revue that they took straight out of George Lederer's productions of *The Passing Show* at the Casino Theater.

Opening in 1894, *The Passing Show* has been called the prototypical musical revue. Productions at the Casino featured musical burlesques of current Broadway shows, but Lederer's style was far more static—coming from the "legitimate stage"—than musical revues would become in the Weberfieldsian world. Where Lederer's actors held to theatrical convention and kept to their scripts, the vaudevillians over at Weber and Fields's Music Hall performed at a breakneck pace and flung themselves into the give-and-take of ensemble improvisation.

Impresario David Belasco. By the Misses Selby (Emily and Lillian), c. 1923.

National Portrait Gallery, Smithsonian Institution, Washington, D.C.

Aside from this kind of energized, helter-skelter performance style, a whole new dimension was added to musical burlesques in 1897 when Fields hired Julian Mitchell as dance director. Mitchell, who later worked on Ziegfeld's *Follies*, established the importance of the dance director in his work at the Weber and Fields Music Hall: he is credited with being the first to integrate dance and story line, and he set rigorous standards for the appearance and training of his dancers. "They are," he said, "a part of the play." In a typical production, the first act would consist of musical numbers and comic routines, loosely basted together by a plot; a dance would be offered during the entr'acte, while the second and final act would be an extended burlesque/satire of a particular current Broadway hit. Unlike earlier variety revues that used songs by any number of composers, the Weber and Fields shows were written by a single "voice," notably John Stromberg, who wrote the music for twenty-eight of their shows. Yet music continued to play second fiddle to "spectacle": Mitchell and Fields gave priority to the visual impact of the show, bragging to the press that the sets and costumes for one production cost $10,000.[27] The suggestion of integrated story, dance, and book, along with lavish sets, trained chorus lines, and well-honed comedy routines made the Music Hall productions a major advance in musical theater production: they were both an immediate precursor to the "book" musicals seen in the works of Jerome Kern and later of Rodgers and Hammerstein, and a bridge to the full-fledged musical revues seen in the *Ziegfeld Follies* and in Broadway shows well into the thirties.[28]

In 1904 this most beloved of vaudeville teams separated, undone by the exhaustion of success: the previous year, Weber and Fields's production of *Twirly-Whirly* had concluded a phenomenal run of 247 performances; while some of the company went off on tour, Weber and Fields not only filled the bill at their Music Hall but bought the West End Theater in Harlem. Tempers stretched with the growth of empire, and a distinct difference of opinion arose about future ventures. Weber saw no reason to change the magic formula of their success: "I believe it is a good thing to stick to success," he said, "and not go experimenting. . . . Our style of show has made us a good deal of money and a big reputation. Why shouldn't we stick to it?" Fields, however, wanted to "make a decided change in the style of entertainment. . . . I think the public has got sick of sidewalk conversation. . . . I tell you the public is educated beyond that sort of stuff."[29]

As a team, Weber and Fields had been part of the transformation of musicals from a loosely organized world of dime museums, minstrelsy, circuses, variety, and vaudeville on the Lower East Side to a centralized industry dominated by Broadway. After the dissolution of Weberfields in 1904, Lew Fields continued to be a major player, this time as one of the preeminent impresarios of the emerging Broadway. Between 1904 and 1916, he produced, and at times appeared in, forty shows, ranging from musical comedies to vaudeville. His objective was to create a "typically American" musical voice, not something derived from Europe or England; as he had begun with his Music Hall productions, Fields continued to develop shows that had coherent plots, songs that advanced the story line, and characters drawn from the American grain.[30]

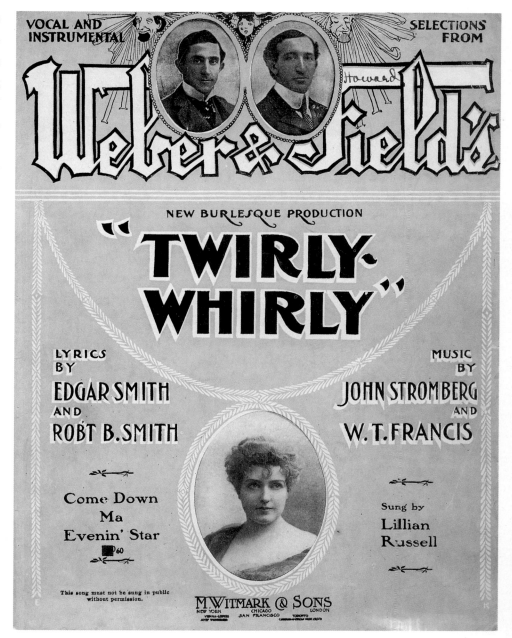

"Come Down, Ma Evenin' Star," from Weber & Fields's *Twirly-Whirly* (1902). Sheet music.

William L. Simon.

Among the stars that appeared in his productions after 1904 were headliners Nora Bayes and Marie Dressler, and newcomers Helen Hayes and Vernon Castle. Fields would lose his dance director, Julian Mitchell, to Ziegfeld, but would gain Ned Wayburn—who had not only invented "tap dancing" by attaching metal plates to dance shoes, but would raise the chorus line to even greater heights than had Mitchell. Fields would also team with such other leading Broadway lights of the day as operetta composer Victor Herbert and Lee and J. J. Shubert, who acted as his coproducers and booking agents. The Shuberts even built Winter Garden Theater for Fields in 1911, hoping to extend the summer schedule of his highly profitable musical revues to year-round box office. In the words of the *New York Globe*, Lew Fields ruled the boards as the "King of Musical Comedy."[31]

As Harrigan and Hart had been in the forefront of the "Irish" teams, and Weber and Fields the preeminent "Dutch" act, Williams and Walker were the leading African American minstrels from the 1890s to 1909, when illness forced Walker to retire. Minstrelsy had

Julian Mitchell rehearsing the Ziegfeld chorus for the *Follies of 1907.* Although deaf, Mitchell staged more than eighty musicals in his career.

Byron Collection, Museum of the City of New York.

Ned Wayburn is credited with inventing tap dancing in 1903.

Byron Collection, Museum of the City of New York.

originated in the antebellum era when white entertainers "blacked up" and performed caricatures of African Americans in song and dance. A leading popularizer was Thomas D. Rice, whose novelty act as "Jim Crow" helped to spark a great vogue for blackface minstrelsy before the Civil War. Radiating from a northeastern base, minstrel troupes also webbed out in a Southern circuit that included Baltimore, Charleston, Mobile, and New Orleans and reached across the Midwest and as far west as San Francisco. These shows found great favor with working-class audiences by presenting stage extravaganzas with set skits, large numbers of performers, and such sentimental ballads as Stephen Collins Foster's "Old Black Joe," "Old Folks at Home," and "My Old Kentucky Home." The presentation was formalized into three acts: following an opening "walk-around" by the entire company—garbed in blackface masks and flashy costumes—the rest of the first act was taken up with a comic dialogue between the "interlocutor" and a pair of endmen known as "Mr. Tambo" and "Mr. Bones," named after the instruments they played. The second act consisted of the olio, or variety segment, and featured burlesques of topical songs or events performed in some kind of dialect—Irish, Dutch, or African American—that relied heavily on malaprops and puns. The final act was often a farce about plantation life, or, after the Civil War, a parody of Shakespeare or a current serious drama.[32]

After the war, minstrel troupes, along with other forms of popular entertainment, sought to broaden their audience to appeal to the middle-class consumer. The growth of a diverse urban culture after 1865 forced all entertainment to expand its ethnic appeal and scope by offering a greater variety of amusement to an ever-widening audience—one that, in the case of impresarios such as Tony Pastor and Lew Fields, even included women and children.

But minstrelsy itself also changed, for it was in these years that African Americans took advantage of minstrelsy's popularity to gain access to mainstream entertainment, joining these troupes, performing in blackface themselves, and forming their own troupes. By the mid-1870s, as white performers began to concentrate on caricaturing the ethnic foibles of Irish and German immigrants pouring into New York, minstrelsy became more and more the focus of African American entertainers. By the 1890s black artists were slowly omitting the remnants of a white minstrelsy that had caricatured plantation life; increasingly, African Americans moved to create a more authentic reflection of their experience—one that blended survivals from folklore with shards of everyday urban life.[33] Black minstrelsy became the road for African Americans' entrance into mainstream entertainment: it was virtually the only way to gain recognition on the American stage, and nearly all of the important black performers who succeeded in the early twentieth century grew out of its tradition.

Williams and Walker were the most popular of the blackface minstrels at the turn of this

century. Egbert "Bert" Williams was born in the West Indies in the mid-1870s and moved with his family to California in 1885. He briefly attended Stanford University before moving to San Francisco and working as an entertainer in saloons, restaurants, and road shows. In 1893 he met George Walker, a performer from Kansas who had worked his way west in minstrel troupes and medicine shows. They decided to form a team and for the next two years put together an act in which Williams was the straight man and Walker the comedian. Working in street clothes and without blackface, they appeared in Victor Herbert's musical *The Gold-Bug* (1896), where they captured popular attention by their performance of "the cakewalk," a dance that became a national craze. This syncopated dance, possibly a West African survival that became a part of plantation life, had appeared in earlier vaudeville acts, including Harrigan and Hart shows. Beginning with a promenade, the cakewalk proceeded with a high-stepping dance that slaves had performed in a competition for cakes or other prizes. It would be Williams and Walker, however, who gave it such vogue in the 1890s; the cakewalk became a part of popular culture in stage revues and early motion pictures and was even adapted as an alternative to the waltz.[34]

Williams and Walker worked at the top-ranked Koster and Bial's Music Hall in New York for a couple of years before going out

on their own and establishing a reputation as one of the leading comedy-dance acts in vaudeville. In 1901 they recorded for the Victor Talking Machine Company, becoming the first African American artists to record on disc.[35] The following year, they starred in a musical they had written with composer Will Marion Cook and African American dialect poet Paul Laurence Dunbar, *In Dahomey*—a major development in the evolution of the black musical.[36] A huge success, this show not only took them to Broadway but to England, to a command performance at Buckingham Palace for Edward VII and then to a seven-month tour of the British Isles. Returning to the United States, they next produced and starred in *Abyssinia* (1906) and *Bandanna Land* (1908), both co-written by Will Marion Cook.

The team broke up when Walker became terminally ill in 1909, and Williams performed alone on the vaudeville circuit before starring in the 1910 *Mr. Lode of Koal*. Florenz Ziegfeld then asked him to join the *Follies*, and until 1919 Williams became one of Ziegfeld's featured performers. Considered a comic genius, he was nevertheless criticized both for choosing to appear in an all-white revue and for continuing to perform in blackface. His colleague Paul Laurence Dunbar had written in 1896:

> We wear the mask that grins and lies,
> It hides our cheeks and shades our eyes—
> This debt we pay to human guile;
> With torn and bleeding hearts we smile,
> And mouth with myriad subtleties.

But Williams had come to feel that this was a compromise worth making and instilled his *Follies* performances with a dignified humanity. Writing about the universal focus of his humor in an article entitled "The Comic Side of Trouble," Williams said: "The sight of other people in trouble is nearly always funny. . . . Nearly all of my successful songs have been based on the idea that I am getting the worst of it." He was probably best known for the song "Nobody," whose lyrics epitomized Williams's own struggle as an African American performer in an increasingly segregated society:

> When life seems full of clouds and rain,
> And I am full of nothin' but pain,
> Who soothes my thumpin', bumpin', brain?
> Nobody!

Williams's *Follies* colleague W. C. Fields once said: "He was the funniest man I ever saw and the saddest man I ever knew." Upon his death in 1922 during the tryout run of *Under the Bamboo Tree*, Williams was eulogized as one of the truly great comics of his day.[37]

Bert Williams was one of the few African American artists who performed on Broadway for white audiences after 1910. In New York, the generation of black performers who had grown up after the Civil War was uniquely optimistic, born free and believing in the possibility of progress and racial accessibility in education,

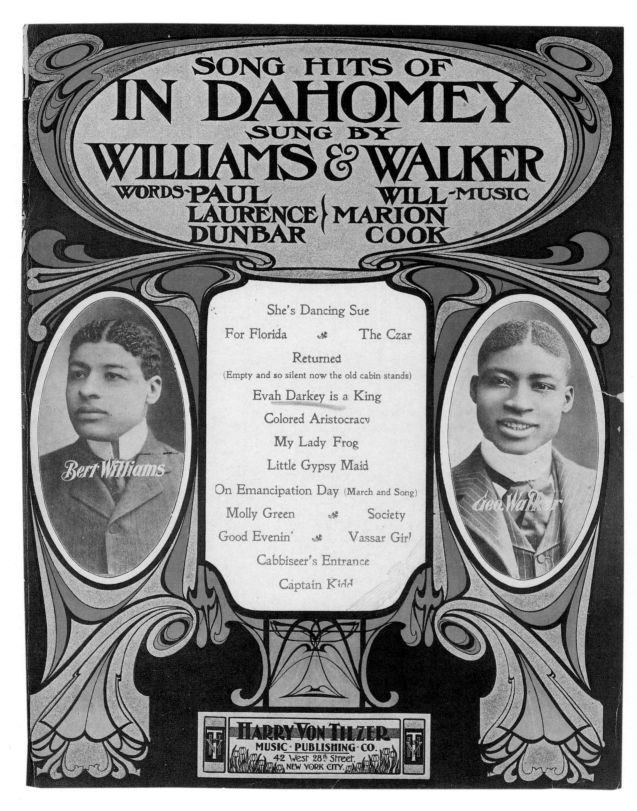

business, law, and the arts. At the turn of the century, New York was a magnet for black entertainers, and some thirty African American shows were staged on Broadway and in black New York neighborhoods between 1890 and 1915. But thereafter, as Jim Crowism took root, Broadway came to represent, literally, "The Great White Way."[38]

Will Marion Cook exemplified the limits of African American accessibility to Broadway

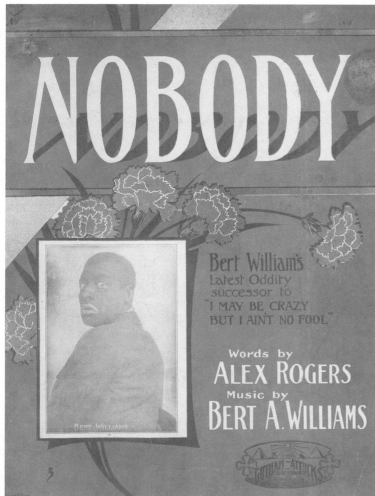

in this era. A musician and composer classically trained in Europe, Cook had returned to the United States in the 1890s. Finding it impossible to have a career in the States as a concert violinist, he "threw these European standards over" and turned to popular music, achieving success in 1898 with the musical *Clorindy, or The Origin of the Cakewalk*. With lyrics by Paul Laurence Dunbar, *Clorindy* was a series of skits performed in ragtime and using a large chorale and flashy dancing; emphasis was not on caricatures of plantation life but on themes and idioms derived from black folk traditions and sketches of African American life in the city. Housed in the roof garden of the Casino Theater on Broadway, *Clorindy* launched Cook's career and led to his highly successful collaboration with Williams and Walker in the next decade. The night *Clorindy* opened, Cook later wrote, "I was so delirious that I drank a glass of water, thought it wine and got gloriously drunk. Negroes were at last on Broadway, and there to stay. Gone was the uff-dah of the minstrel! Gone was the Massa Linkum stuff! We were artists and we were going a long, long way. We had the world on a string tied to a runnin' red-geared wagon on a downhill pull. Nothing could stop us, and nothing did for a decade."[39]

By the mid-teens, the wagon had rolled to a stop, and the African American presence in big-time Broadway productions had been greatly reduced. At the same time segregation was

LEFT: Composer
Will Marion Cook.

Moorland-Spingarn
Research Center, Howard
University, Washington,
D.C.

RIGHT: Poet and
lyricist Paul Laurence
Dunbar. By William
McKnight Farrow,
1934.

National Portrait Gallery,
Smithsonian Institution,
Washington, D.C.

becoming institutionalized in show business, some of the biggest stars of the earlier generation had either retired or died. When Bert Williams moved over to the *Follies* in 1910, he
did so because he found "colored show business . . . at a low ebb just now."[40] Rampant dis-
crimination led producers to create black shows for Harlem rather than for Broadway, and
on the road black touring companies were handled by the Theater Owners Booking Association, or TOBA, rather than by white booking agents such as the Shuberts.[41]

Like Bert Williams and Will Marion Cook, Sissieretta Jones grew up in a generation
optimistic about African American accessibility to mainstream American society. She
was born in Portsmouth, Virginia, in 1869, as Matilda Sissieretta Joyner, daughter of an
African American Methodist minister; her mother was an accomplished soprano, and
when the family was transferred to a Providence, Rhode Island, church in 1876, encouraged her daughter's music studies. An unfortunate youthful marriage to a gambler named
Richard Jones did not prevent eighteen-year-old Sissieretta from enrolling as a voice student at the New England Conservatory in Boston. She made her debut in New York at
Steinway Hall in 1888 and was soon performing up and down the East Coast. In a reference to the renowned Italian American diva Adelina Patti, the *New York Clipper* called her
"the Black Patti"—a well-intentioned but condescending sobriquet that would hauntingly
identify her throughout her career. Typical reviews raved about the way she "rendered a
piece by Verdi, called 'Sempre libera.' . . . [I]f Madame Jones is not the equal of Patti, she
at least can come nearer than anything the American has heard. . . . Her notes are as clear

as a mocking bird and her enunciation perfect." Another described how "Carnegie Music Hall presented an animated appearance Monday night, when the brilliant audience hung with breathless stillness upon the clarion notes of the most gifted singer the age has produced. . . . It was the first time any company of colored artists has ever occupied the hall." In 1892 she was invited to perform for President Benjamin Harrison at the White House and later that year was the star attraction at the Grand Negro Jubilee at Madison Square Garden. She also made a highly successful appearance at the 1893 Chicago World's Fair and undertook a European concert tour that included a command performance for the Prince of Wales.[42]

In 1896 Sissieretta Jones organized an African American vaudeville troupe—the Black Patti Troubadours—with which she toured across the nation for the next twenty years. Her company provided one of the most significant training grounds of the era for African American performers and was important as well for popularizing a repertoire that reflected the transition away from old style minstrelsy.[43] According to James Weldon Johnson in his 1930 chronicle of black theater history, the troupe followed a vaudeville pattern that started with a sketchy farce interspersed with songs and dances; then came the olio (medley), with a finale entitled an "Operatic Kaleidoscope," in which Mme. Jones performed a selection of arias from well-known operas. Alone among the larger African American shows, Johnson suggested, the Troubadours enjoyed great popularity in the South—a factor that accounted for their overall longevity.[44] Before Sissieretta Jones retired in 1916, the troupe was able to produce a number of full-length musical comedies—*A Trip to Africa* (1910), *In the Jungles* (1911), *Captain Jaspar* (1912), and *Lucky Sam from Alabam* (1914)—that advanced the African American contribution to a modern musical theater.

Although Sissieretta Jones shared a background of classical

training with Will Marion Cook—and, like Cook, had to resort to minstrelsy and vaudeville to succeed in the musical mainstream—she was never able to cross over into recordings as had Bert Williams. There was actually a Black Patti recording label, and although her name appeared on each disc, she herself was never recorded. There is no way to confirm contemporary accounts, in which her voice was repeatedly described as lustrous and rich. Will Marion Cook said she had "the finest voice and largest range of any Negro voice I've ever heard, and I don't except Marian Anderson."[45] James Weldon Johnson wrote that

"she had most of the qualities essential in a great singer: the natural voice, the physical figure, the grand air, and the engaging personality."[46] Such written records will have to suffice, because Sissieretta Jones belonged only to the world of live performance.

Until the end of World War I, few African American vocalists, choral groups, or orchestras made recordings. Yet black music earned widespread popularity because of the recordings of major white stars such as Al Jolson, May Irwin, and, especially, Sophie Tucker. Born in Poland in either 1884 or 1888, Sophie Tucker grew up in Hartford, Connecticut, where she sang as a child to attract customers to her parents' restaurant. Her roots were in Yiddish theater, but early on she rejected that direction for her career. When offered the opportunity to tour with such stars of the Yiddish stage as Jacob Adler and Boris Thomashefsky, she declined, explaining in her memoir, *Some of These Days*, that "I wasn't keen for it. I had seen how hard it was to make the Jewish plays a success even for one night," whereas "American shows" succeeded.[47] When she left Hartford for New York in 1906 to make her way in vaudeville, she again opted against Yiddish theater, choosing instead to build her career by singing the songs coming out of the music publishing houses of Tin Pan Alley.[48]

Armed with an overpowering voice and broad vibrato, Tucker originally performed in blackface and was billed as the "World-renowned Coon Shouter," but she soon abandoned this to perform and record ragtime and blues. She appeared briefly in the 1909 *Ziegfeld Follies*, winning enthusiastic reviews: to one newspaper critic, Sophie Tucker could be heard "as far away as Harlem, for she has a voice like a steam siren." Another noted that "the feminine voice that takes best with the

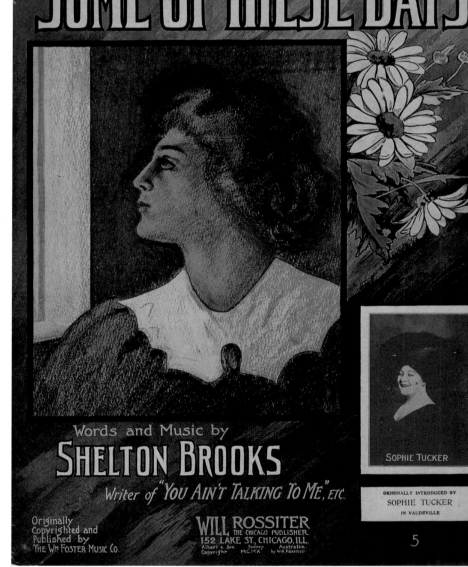

"Some of These Days" became Sophie Tucker's theme song. Sheet music, 1910.

William L. Simon.

Nora Bayes (1880–1928)

Self-proclaimed as "The Greatest Single Woman Singing Comedienne in the World," Nora Bayes (née Dora Goldberg) was among the most accomplished theatrical figures of her generation, amassing numerous credits as a performer, writer, and producer. Petite in stature but towering in talent, she earned her first successes as a singer in Chicago vaudeville houses. Her husky contralto voice—which could reach the back row of the largest theater—and her confident, energetic performance style eventually established her as a headliner in variety shows both in New York and London.

In 1907 Bayes joined the cast of Florenz Ziegfeld's inaugural *Follies* at Manhattan's Jardin de Paris rooftop theater. The following season, in the *Follies of 1908*, she and her husband Jack Norworth introduced their song "Shine On, Harvest Moon," which became her signature tune. She signed with impresario-comedian Lew Fields in 1910 and appeared in several shows produced under his supervision. Perhaps the most notable was *The Jolly Bachelors* (1910), which contained several hits written by Bayes and Norworth, including the lively "Young America," which reveals Bayes's penchant for Cohanesque patriotism:

Their daddies may be English, Irish,
German, French, or Dutch,
But if the kids are born in Yankee Land
The rest don't count for much.
We'll put them in our melting pot
Teach them the golden rule.
Then we'll hatch our future presidents
In any public school!

NORA BAYES AND JACK NORWORTH,
"YOUNG AMERICA," 1910

In 1917 Cohan asked Bayes to promote his stirring wartime anthem "Over There" in her vaudeville act at the famed Palace Theatre. One year later, in the musical comedy *Ladies First*, she introduced "The Real American Folk Song (Is a Rag)," the first professional collaboration of George and Ira Gershwin, with George acting as her onstage accompanist.

Above all, Nora Bayes quite literally lived to be on stage. Much-married and possessed with legendary volatility, she seemed happiest when reaching out over the footlights to join in a spiritual embrace with her audience. In reviewing one of her performances in 1918, the critic of the *New Republic* reported favorably on "the tone of her speaking voice . . . the camaraderie of her smile, and . . . the beauty of her gesture and dress," praising her ability to project "a thorough artist's taste in every spacing and movement."

Nora Bayes.

Photofest.

Bayes and Jack Norworth wrote the lyrics to and sang "Shine On, Harvest Moon" in Ziegfeld's *Follies of 1908*. They were married that same year.

William L. Simon.

audience this week is owned by Sophie Tucker. . . . Her stage presence and powerful, mellow voice are well worthy of recognition." Indeed, her success was so great that the two *Follies* principals, Nora Bayes and Lillian Lorraine, forced Ziegfeld to fire her.[49]

Tucker recovered quickly, going on tour and adding a tantalizing new twist to her act—what she called a "double-entendre" song—that caused a sensation. In the *Chicago Examiner* Ashton Stevens wrote: "And speaking of elephants and ladies, there is Sophie Tucker. . . . Some of her songs are red, white, and blue, and some omit the red and white. But they are never quite dark navy blue." She returned to New York triumphantly and became a headliner at the Plaza Music Hall. Hailed as "The Singing Sensation of the Year," she was twitted by *New York Variety* for the "curiously risqué songs with which she has chosen to identify herself. The Plaza audience is not particularly keen in the appreciation of this sort of thing, but Miss Tucker makes her odd ragtime music unmistakable in its import. Her 'Soul Kiss' ditty stunned by its clever daring, but at the finish there was applause to shake the building." The *New York Evening Journal* reported that "Sophie Tucker is the name of a loud, cheerful noise. . . . There's a fine, buxom, happy-go-lucky girl for you."[50]

She would begin her act with "a lively rag, then would come a ballad followed by a comedy song and novelty number. And finally the hot song. In this way I left the audience laughing their heads off."[51] Touted both as "the Mary Garden of Ragtime" and "the Goddess of Ragtime," she was signed to an exclusive Edison recording contract. Her first record was "The Lovin' Rag," and within a year she recorded what became her theme song, "Some of These Days," written by the African American composer Shelton Brooks:

> And when you leave me,
> You know it's gonna grieve me,
> You're gonna miss your red, hot mama,
> Some of these days.[52]

Over the years, she would become one of the great mainstream popularizers of black music. In a career that extended into the 1960s, she would remain a headliner on the nightclub and theater circuits, billed as "the last of the red hot mamas."

Despite the rough-and-tumble of life in vaudeville, especially on tour, women such as Sissieretta Jones and Sophie Tucker were able to carve out successful careers. One newspaper of the day vouched that "a woman is as free and independent as a man," and was "usually able to take care of herself."[53] That was certainly true as well of Lillian Russell, who rose to enormous popularity in the vogue for European light opera that swept America from the late nineteenth century to the First World War. The public could not get enough of French opéra bouffe, British comic opera, and Viennese operetta—of Offenbach, Gilbert and Sullivan, and Lehár. Gilbert and Sullivan had provoked near mania with *H.M.S. Pinafore*, which opened in New York in December

Lillian Russell was discovered by Tony Pastor in 1881. By Benjamin J. Falk, c. 1886.

National Portrait Gallery, Smithsonian Institution, Washington, D.C.

By 1885, when this poster was produced, Lillian Russell had become known as the "Queen of Broadway."

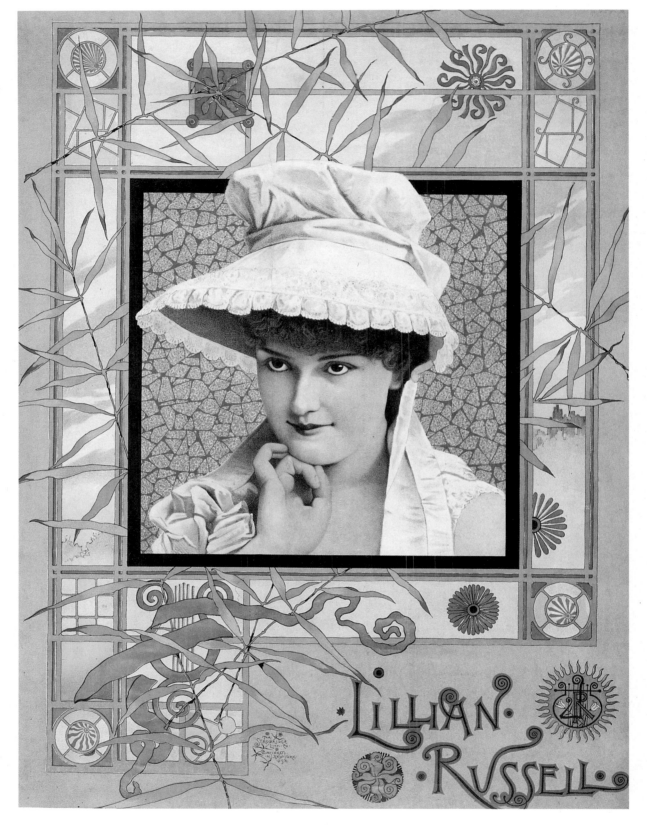

Victor Herbert,
c. 1910 (detail).

Prints and Photographs
Division, Library of
Congress, Washington,
D.C.

1879, a year after a pirated American production had swept the country. Lillian Russell—born Helen Leonard in Iowa, but rechristened with the help of impresario Tony Pastor—made her debut in Boston in that production and was "discovered" by Pastor. She made her earliest New York appearances in 1880 at Pastor's Music Hall, performing a burlesque of Gilbert and Sullivan's *Patience*. She was billed as "Lillian Russell, the English Ballad Singer," and soon reigned as what one critic called the "bright particular star" of operetta and opéra bouffe in this country.[54] Perhaps her greatest success came in February 1890, when she starred in Jacques Offenbach's *The Grand Duchess*. She made her entrance in this operetta draped in ermine, wearing an enormous fur hat, and driving a sleigh on stage in a snowstorm. At intermission, she was chosen to participate in the first public use of Alexander Graham Bell's long-distance telephone: she sang the "Sabre Song" into a large metal funnel, while, at the other end of the line in Washington, President Grover Cleveland happily listened. Soon thereafter, the *New York World* reported that Thomas Alva Edison was going to visit Miss Russell to "bottle up her voice in a phonograph. . . . He will send her a piece of her preserved voice in the shape of a roll of foil."[55] The parlor song for which this popular lyric soprano is best remembered, "Come Down, Ma Evenin' Star," was introduced in *Twirly-Whirly* (1902) and revived for her in her last musical show, *Hokey-Pokey* (1912).

Another major figure in the American craze for light opera at the turn of the century was Victor Herbert. Born in Dublin in 1859 and trained in Germany as a cellist, Herbert immigrated to the United States at the age of twenty-seven to play cello in the Metropolitan Opera orchestra. Yet he was intrigued more by the "folk theater" of Harrigan and Hart, the Irish American musical farceurs, and by the potential market for an *American* operetta. In 1893 he wrote his first light opera, designed for Lillian Russell. This was never produced, however, and Herbert's earliest known operetta, *Prince Ananias*, opened at the Broadway Theater on November 20, 1894—a season in which operetta's popularity saw fourteen light opera companies on tour in America.[56] Herbert specialized in romantic music and exotic settings, such as Venice, Persia, and Egypt. Of his two greatest hits, the 1903 *Babes in Toyland* was set in "The Land of Mother Goose," while the 1910 *Naughty Marietta* found itself in late eighteenth-century Spanish New Orleans. In both of these operettas, Herbert's integration of music and story set a new standard for American musicals.

It is also a mark of Herbert's importance as a composer that he actually changed the role of music in American musicals: before him, music was little more than window dressing; with Herbert, the music became central. His highly success-

ful recording career also allowed him to reach a far wider audience than composers had reached previously, as the newly burgeoning recording industry—one of the avatars of the mass entertainment media—carried his music from Broadway theaters to living rooms. *Naughty Marietta* in particular was received as the "classic American operetta" and contained such still-familiar songs—thanks also to the 1935 MGM film that first paired Jeanette MacDonald and Nelson Eddy—as "Tramp! Tramp! Tramp!," "I'm Falling in Love with Someone," and "Ah! Sweet Mystery of Life."

Popular as light opera was in America from the late nineteenth century to the years of the First World War, it was a tradition that retained a distinctive "European" edge, unlike the immigrant strains heard in Bowery music halls, vaudeville theaters, and the publishing houses of Tin Pan Alley. The late nineteenth century's great vogue for Gilbert and Sullivan was followed in 1907 by the opening of Franz Lehár's *The Merry Widow*, a Viennese

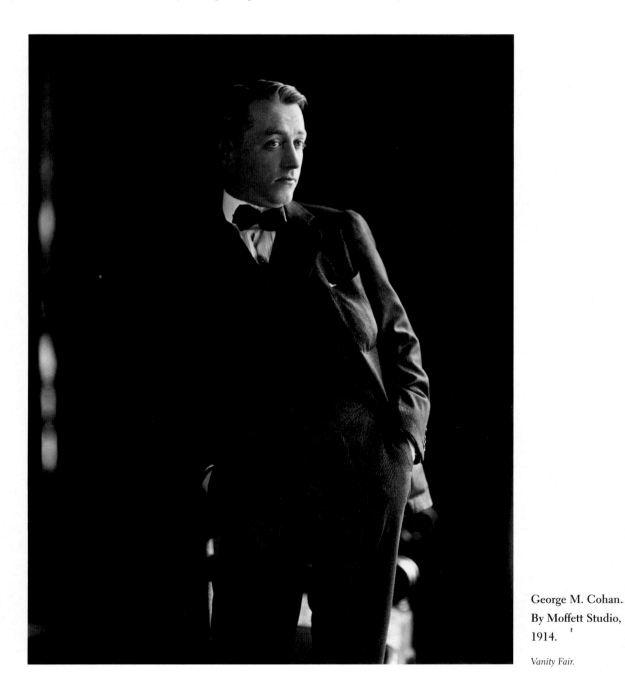

George M. Cohan.
By Moffett Studio,
1914.

Vanity Fair.

This poster promoted the Cohan family in *Widow McCann's Trip*, **c. 1891.**

Billy Rose Theatre
Collection, New York
Public Library for the
Performing Arts, New York
City.

George M. Cohan on stage in the original 1904 Broadway production of *Little Johnny Jones*, singing "Give My Regards to Broadway."

Harry Ransom Humanities Research Center, The University of Texas at Austin.

operetta that proved colossally successful. Victor Herbert was the leading American exponent of operetta, and his emphasis on a strong book and integration of music and story would be apparent within a generation, notably in the works of Jerome Kern.

Another strain in the development of an American musical theater—the music-hall tradition presided over by Tony Pastor that spotlighted a virtual "melting pot" of such vaudevillians as Weber and Fields and Harrigan and Hart—took a slightly different form with the emergence of George M. Cohan at the turn of the century. Originally part of the Four Cohans, a leading act on the vaudeville circuit, Cohan ventured off alone in his early twenties, becoming the librettist, composer, producer, and star of his own productions. Beginning with his first Broadway musical in 1901, *The Governor's Son*, Cohan was as far removed from the romantic gentility of the operetta craze as it was possible to be. His models were the farces of Harrigan and Hart, with their vaudevillian zest for the "grand melee" and their relish for incorporating the staccato rhythms of urban immigrant life. He even wrote a rousing popular song for his hero, Ned Harrigan: "H–a–double r–i–g–a–n spells Harrigan."

Cohan gave musicals a coherence they had lacked outside of operetta simply by making "the entire production an extension of his brash, electrifying personality."[57] But there would be no confusing his shows with anything coated with Viennese schlag: with Cohan, as with his earlier Bowery mentors, the focus was on the vernacular culture of the streets—in words, music, and character. In the 1904 *Little Johnny Jones*, this focus is discernible in two of his songs that became classics, "Give My Regards to Broadway" and "Yankee Doodle Boy," where the hero—Yankee Doodle—represents an all-American goodness: "I'm a Yankee Doodle Dandy, Yankee Doodle do or die, / A real live nephew of my Uncle Sam, Born on the Fourth of July." The twin themes of urban heroism and fundamental patriotism emerged as quintessential Cohan motifs in his most successful musicals, including *Forty-five Minutes from Broadway* and *George Washington, Jr.*, especially in such songs as "Mary's a Grand Old Name" and "You're a Grand Old Flag." His biggest hit, "Over There," was written not for a Broadway show but as a patriotic song during the First World War.

The electric Cohan persona embodied the America of urban industrialism, of a "melting pot"—in the words of Israel Zangwill's hit 1908 play—of ethnic cultures forging a new America. What Cohan did was to infuse the emerging American musical voice with the energy of vaudeville, and to bring that vernacular culture into the mainstream.[58] If it was not "high art," it was nevertheless widely accessible to a broadly based audience—the audience necessary to support musical theater commercially. Indeed, one of the defining characteristics of American musical theater would be its connection to the rise of popular culture. Playwright-actor Edwin Milton Royle wrote in 1899 that, like vaudeville, the developing musical theater belonged to "the era of the department store and the short story. It may be a kind of lunch-counter art, but then art is so vague and lunch is so real."[59]

"Give My Regards to Broadway," from *Little Johnny Jones* (1904). Sheet music.

Dwight Blocker Bowers.

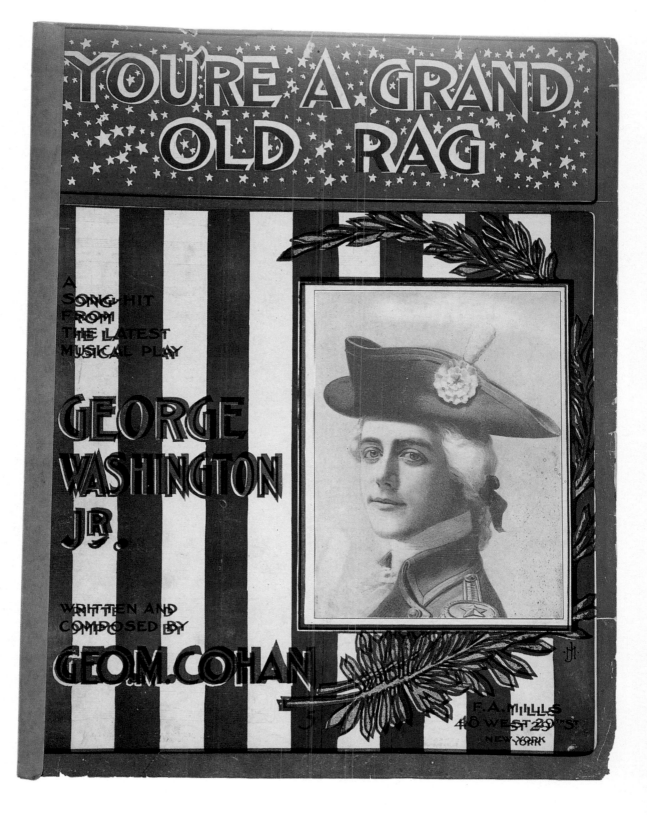

Just you watch my step
I've got push and pep
I'll win fortune and renown.

P. G. WODEHOUSE AND JEROME KERN,
"JUST YOU WATCH MY STEP"

In the score of years that passed between 1907 and 1927, the American musical theater brazenly marched forward, establishing the elements and standards that would give it a uniquely native voice. The strong, varied elements of ethnicity and immigrant culture, as evidenced in the work of Weber and Fields, Harrigan and Hart, and Williams and Walker, were swiftly synthesizing themselves into a central, mainstream perspective that depicted a romanticized, idealized view of American life.

With New York City firmly established as the national heart of the popular entertainment industry, an organization known as the Theatrical Syndicate charted national circuits for touring productions, introducing clever marketing strategies to American theater management and touting their productions as being "direct from Broadway with the Original New York Cast." Tin Pan Alley publishers widely distributed song sheets of musical comedy songs with the catchphrase "try this on your piano." Technological innovations brought the voices and sounds of the musical theater into American homes through recordings and, a decade later, through radio and early sound films.

The refinement of a common artistic vision for the American musical theater was the result of ongoing collaborations among producers, performers, directors, authors, and designers. However, the role of the impresario was paramount in the assembly of all the elements of production into a seamless entity. Although there were others, two entrepreneurial forces dominated the musical theater in this era: Florenz Ziegfeld Jr. and the Shubert Brothers. These showmen redefined the theatrical producer, from simply being a funding source to being a strong, abiding influence in establishing styles of production that set enduring standards for the American musical theater.

Florenz Ziegfeld Jr., a self-proclaimed "impresario extraordinaire," matched his penchant for theatrical grandeur with an autocratic, flamboyant persona that his friend and associate Harry B. Smith described as "Napoleonic, even in trifles."[1] Between 1907 and 1933 "the Great Glorifier" presented over sixty musical productions on Broadway, ranging from lavish, star-bedecked revues and giddy musical comedies to the epochal American operetta, *Show Boat* (1927). Whatever the conceptual framework, each show was hallmarked by Ziegfeld's instinctive talent for infusing the crowd-pleasing aspects of mainstream popular entertainment with the more sublime aesthetic sensibilities of high culture.[2] As observed by his widow, actress Billie Burke, "the things

LEFT: Built in 1903, the New Amsterdam Theatre was called "The Grandest in the World." Ziegfeld's *Follies* ran here from 1913 to 1927.

Wisconsin Center for Film and Theater Research, Madison.

RIGHT: Impresario Florenz Ziegfeld Jr. By Cesare Stea, c. 1927.

National Portrait Gallery, Smithsonian Institution, Washington, D.C.; gift of Mrs. A. Sandor Ince.

Florenz Ziegfeld with Anna Held in their private train car, c. 1900.

National Portrait Gallery, Smithsonian Institution, Washington, D.C.

Flo cherished as a showman were color, music, spectacle, and fun."[3] In doing so, he asserted new criteria for the American musical theater in terms of theatrical production.

Ziegfeld's circuitous path to Broadway began on the streets of his native Chicago. The oldest child of European immigrants, he first witnessed the art of the impresario under the tutelage of his father, an accomplished concert pianist and the esteemed director of the Chicago Musical College.[4] Ziegfeld père, an astute businessman as well as a musician, often engaged internationally acclaimed musicians to perform at his conservatory. Well-versed in the traditions and disciplines of European music, young Florenz became, at the age of sixteen, irrevocably smitten with the zestful glitter of American popular entertainment when he attended a performance of Buffalo Bill's Wild West Show. In the fall of 1892, with the opening of the Chicago World's Fair imminent, he cajoled his father into hiring him as a talent scout to search for entertainers to perform at the Trocadero, an old armory that the elder Ziegfeld had converted into a nightclub. Although his first group of performers was an unmitigated disaster, he scored a decided coup by hiring German strongman Eugene Sandow, known as "the modern Hercules." Sandow, clad in as little as the law would allow, was Ziegfeld's first experiment with "artful" nudity. Ziegfeld's success propelled him to New York City, where in 1896 he launched his career as a Broadway producer. Securing the rights to a comedy called *The Parlor Match*, he sailed to England in search of the perfect leading lady. In London he discovered Anna Held, a wide-eyed, curvaceous music hall performer of humble Polish Jewish heritage whose stage image was "the incarnation of Gallic vivacity."[5] Infatuated with her porcelain beauty and piquant demeanor, Ziegfeld brought her to New York and soon established her as a top box office attraction through a series of largely undistinguished stage vehicles and a relentless, ingeniously designed publicity campaign.

In 1897 Ziegfeld and Held began a common-law union, which endured, with tumultuous interludes, until 1912. During this period, Held proved greatly influential in the formation of Ziegfeld's unique theatrical perspective. In their annual trips abroad, she cultivated in him a deep appreciation for the graciousness of European culture, particularly with regard to high fashion and its central role in the overall effectiveness of commercial entertainment. Moreover, it was Held who urged him to adapt the Parisian genre of the revue for Broadway audiences, retaining its emphasis on feminine beauty and embellishing it with the distinctly American taste for topical humor. Her suggestion, driven by Ziegfeld's inherent flamboyance and ambition, provided the impetus for the creation of the *Ziegfeld Follies,* the series of shows that undisputedly defined the look and sound of the American musical revue.

The premiere edition of the series, *Follies of 1907,* began as an inconsequential summer entertainment. Theatrical Syndicate chieftains Abraham Erlanger and Marc Klaw hired Ziegfeld to develop a bill of vaudeville entertainers that would attract audiences to their nightclub, Jardin de Paris, an open-air performance space perched atop the roof of the New York Theatre. Recalling Held's idea of borrowing the format of a French music hall revue, Ziegfeld set to work to make the show more than just a hodgepodge of variety acts. He engaged Harry B. Smith, perhaps the most prolific librettist of the era, to devise a skeletal narrative that would connect the parade of disparate vaudeville performers.[6] Smith's libretto, which he openly admitted was equipped with "just enough story to hold the scenes together," used the characters of Captain John Smith and Pocahontas, a barbed reference to the year's observation of the Jamestown Tercentenary, as the evening's master and mistress of ceremonies.[7] The script was peppered with topical satire, poking fun at the foibles of such notables as Teddy Roosevelt, John D. Rockefeller, grand opera producer Oscar Hammerstein, and grand opera divo Enrico Caruso. Smith also supplied the show's name, which he appropriated from the byline of his *Chicago Daily News* column, "Follies of the Day." Ziegfeld took immediately to the title, primarily because its number of characters totaled thirteen, which the cocky impresario considered his lucky number. If the sets, costumes, and continuity lacked the distinction of later editions, the show did introduce one

"The Peacock Girls" stood behind star Emma Carus as she sang an operatic version of Oscar Wilde's *Salome* in Flo Ziegfeld's first *Follies,* in 1907.

Harry Ransom Humanities Research Center, The University of Texas at Austin.

"Lovie Joe" was a hit song from the *Follies of 1910*. Sheet music.

National Museum of American History, Smithsonian Institution, Washington, D.C.

significant Ziegfeld trademark: a large ensemble of revealingly dressed beautiful women, in this instance called the Anna Held Girls, in a variety of ingenious precision dance routines and sumptuous tableaux. The *Follies of 1907* continued through the summer and transferred briefly indoors to Erlanger's Liberty Theatre (with vaudevillian Nora Bayes added to the cast) before embarking on a tour to Washington, D.C., Baltimore, Chicago, and Philadelphia.

If Ziegfeld did not, as he later claimed, introduce the revue genre to Broadway, he was pivotal in establishing its popularity with audiences and enhancing its image in the theater community, turning the vagaries of the vaudeville stage into the stuff and substance of the legitimate theater. Over the next eight seasons, he continually experimented with the form, reshaping its presentational methods and imprinting them with his own taste and vision. Gradually, he freed the revue from the rough-and-tumble approach of Weber and Fields and substituted a sleek, sophisticated elegance in movement and decor. Building

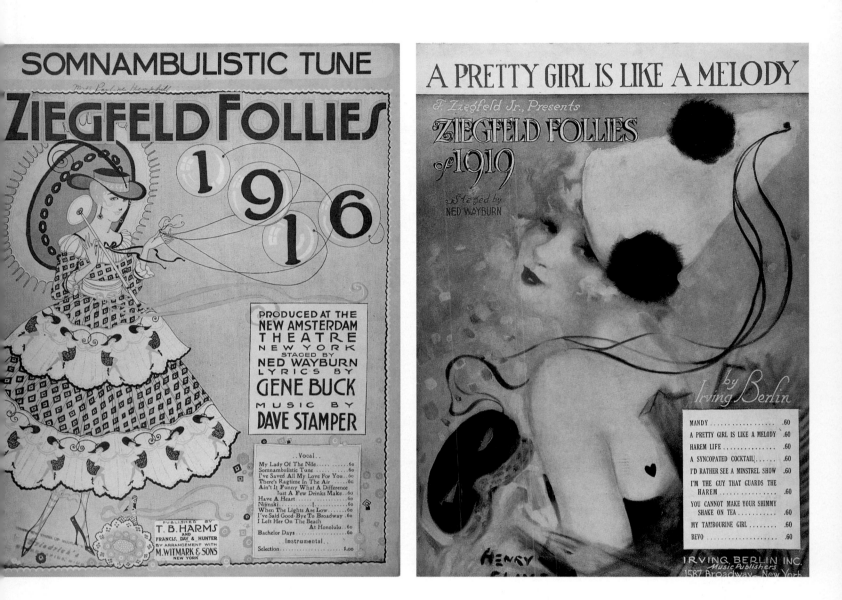

upon his reputation as a starmaker, he used the annual editions of the *Follies* as a showcase
for a multitude of rising luminaries, including Fanny Brice, Eddie Cantor, and Marilyn
Miller. Tin Pan Alley's leading composers and lyricists were commissioned to contribute
such memorable songs as "Shine On, Harvest Moon," "Hello, Frisco," "My Man," and the
revue's song of songs, "A Pretty Girl Is Like a Melody."

In 1911, justifiably proud of his product, he added his own name to the title, making its
official name the *Ziegfeld Follies.* Two years later he persuaded Erlanger to move the *Follies* to the New Amsterdam Theatre, an Art Nouveau structure in the heart of Times
Square that was touted in publicity releases as the "grandest in the world." The series
reached its zenith in its thirteenth edition, *Follies of 1919,* which brilliantly brought together all the elements of "the Ziegfeld Touch": a seemingly endless display of tastefully
sumptuous settings and costumes, graceful staging techniques, a glittering roster of star
personalities, witty topical comedy, beguiling melodies, and above all, a stageful of feminine pulchritude. Through sheer perseverance and experimentation, Ziegfeld had become the first aesthetic prophet of the modern American musical theater, having "lifted,
with sensitive skill, a thing that was mere food for smirking bald heads and downy college
boys out of its low estate and into a thing of symmetry and bloom."[8]

Fanny Brice sang "Second Hand Rose" in Flo Ziegfeld's *Follies of 1921*. Sheet music.

William L. Simon.

As team members in his efforts toward formalizing the elements of the American musical revue, Ziegfeld assembled a superior staff of theater professionals. Among them were songwriter-amanuensis Gene Buck, director-choreographers Julian Mitchell and Ned Wayburn, couturiers Lucile (Lady Duff-Gordon) and John Harkrider, and artist-tableaux vivantes specialist Ben Ali Haggin. But perhaps the most significant addition to the Ziegfeld stable was scenic designer Joseph Urban. Urban's elegant, impressionistic settings, a fusion of modern stagecraft and commercial art, brought a new visual brilliance to the American musical theater and contributed immeasurably to the glamour that is synonymous with Ziegfeld productions.

Carl Maria Georg Joseph Urban, an Austrian by birth, studied art and architecture in Vienna at the Academy of Fine Arts. There, he was a protégé of instructor Karl Freiherr von Hasenauer, the noted Ringstrasse architect.[9] Following graduation and a brief apprenticeship with von Hasenauer, he became a founding member of the Hagenbund, a

Bessie McCoy Davis sits in a moon designed by Joseph Urban for Ziegfeld's *Miss 1917.*

Harry Ransom Humanities Research Center, The University of Texas at Austin.

With World War I as its theme, Ziegfeld's *Follies of 1918* featured chorus girls in an armored tank.

Harry Ransom Humanities Research Center, The University of Texas at Austin.

collective of progressive Viennese artists and architects that soon won favor from both the government and the aristocracy. As one of his earliest commissions, Urban designed the interiors of the Austrian Art Pavilion at the St. Louis World's Fair, which brought him briefly to America in 1904. While a member of the Hagenbund, he created his first professional scenic designs for the Vienna Court Opera and the Hofburg Theatre. His blossoming career was cut short in 1909, when his mismanagement of funds for the Imperial Jubilee of 1908 forced him to resign his post and seek employment elsewhere. Shortly thereafter, he became a theatrical designer in earnest, working with provincial opera troupes throughout Europe. By 1912 Urban had immigrated to America, assuming the post of director of productions at the Boston Opera. His daring, unconventional settings proved shocking to those who were more comfortably acquainted with the traditional two-dimensional realism then dominant in the settings of American opera companies. Urban's work, dominated by vivid color and architectural detail, clearly reflected the avant garde aesthetics of the "new stagecraft," a design trend that arose in Europe in the early twentieth century through the work of Edward Gordon Craig, Adolphe Appia, and Max Reinhardt.

Although Urban's initial Broadway effort, an Edward Sheldon melodrama called *Garden of Paradise*, was a commercial failure, his contribution to the proceedings received critical acclaim that brought him to the attention of Gene Buck, Ziegfeld's right-hand man. Ziegfeld immediately recognized Urban's prodigious talent and hired him to redesign the New Amsterdam Theatre's rooftop cabaret. Shortly thereafter, he offered the designer the opportunity to create the settings for his next edition of the *Follies*. Urban accepted the impresario's offer only after issuing an ultimatum: "I do not make the scenery to fit your material. I design scenery first and then you fit material to it."[10]

In previous editions of the *Follies*, Ziegfeld had engaged various visual artists and construction companies to contribute settings of wildly different and unrelated character to each production. However, with Urban at the helm as sole designer, all the elements of scenic decor were blended to create a visual statement reflective of a single artistic perspective. The *Ziegfeld Follies of 1915*, Urban's first assignment in the series, presented a progression of unfailingly beautiful stage pictures, each seemingly more captivating than its predecessor. Because of subtle, recurrent uses throughout of shades of blue, reportedly the favorite color of both the designer and his producer, the 1915 edition became known as the "Blue Follies." In this production, Urban brought a number of scenic innovations to the commercial musical theater. To achieve the iridescent hues and soft pastels so vital to his work, he projected sophisticated patterns of white and colored light onto canvas drops painted in an approximation of the French impressionist technique of pointillage, which used multihued layers of stippled paint to create the illusion of texture and depth. Also, he consistently made use of visual leitmotifs in his designs for the *Follies*,

Set designer Joseph Urban worked for Flo Ziegfeld from 1914 until 1931.

Wisconsin Center for Film and Theater Research, Madison.

Joseph Urban's rendering for the opening scene of Ziegfeld's *Follies of 1916.*

Joseph Urban Collection, Rare Book and Manuscript Library, Columbia University, New York City.

Joseph Urban designed the Ziegfeld Theatre, which was built in 1927 at the corner of Sixth Avenue and Fifty-fourth Street.

Wurts Collection, Museum of the City of New York.

instilling a sense of unity to the otherwise episodic nature of the revue genre. Finally, his training as an architect equipped him with the skills to manipulate the rhythms and dynamics of the stage environment, supporting his philosophy that "speed is the essential of the musical show."[11] He designated the shallow forestage or apron in front of the theater's proscenium as a space for solo performers and backed the area with an inner proscenium and a drop curtain that could be raised to reveal a more spectacular setting. While the apron was in use as a performance space, behind the drop curtain the stage crew could simultaneously shift the setting for the next sequence, allowing for more fluid transitions from scene to scene. Moreover, he made frequent use of platforms, creating multiple playing areas within a single setting.

Although he would work for other producers, most notably Guilio Gatti-Casazza at the Metropolitan Opera, Urban acted as Ziegfeld's principal designer until 1931, ingeniously creating scenic decor for over sixty productions. These ran the gamut from the breathtaking and often exotic spectacles in the annual editions of the *Follies* to the striking evocations of late nineteenth- and early twentieth-century America fashioned for the original Broadway presentation of the musical play *Show Boat.* The effect of Urban's vision on the American musical theater was extraordinary and enduring. Other producers clamored for his services and other, less skillful designers slavishly imitated, or simply stole, many of his effects for their scenery.

In 1926 Ziegfeld commissioned Urban (in collaboration with

Thomas Lamb) to create a new theater at Fifty-fourth Street and Sixth Avenue. Opening to the public on February 2, 1927, the Ziegfeld Theatre, as it was called, became the flagship for the best of the impresario's subsequent productions. Urban asserted that in developing his plans for the building, "the whole idea back of the Ziegfeld Theatre is the creation of an architectural design which shall express in every detail the fact that here is a modern playhouse for modern musical shows."[12] The exterior facade, made of tan stone, was dominated by a bowed window flanked by pilasters, which matched the semiovid shape of the stage and proscenium within the theater. The interior walls were wrapped in a mural (created by Urban's protégée Lillian Gaertner) that used fanciful medieval images as its organizing motif. The theater outlived both its designer and the producer who commissioned it, functioning as an active Broadway house until it was closed and demolished in 1967.

Ziegfeld continued to produce revues and musicals until his death in 1932. Throughout most of the 1920s he had a near-perfect record for theatrical success, presenting such well-remembered musicals as *Sally* (1920), *Rio Rita* (1926), *Show Boat* (1927), and *Whoopee* (1928). He was, like so many of his contemporaries, financially devastated by the effects of the 1929 stock market crash and thereafter struggled in vain to keep his footing on the ever-moving escalator of the commercial theater. His final shows—the musical comedies *Show Girl* (1929), *Smiles* (1930), and *Hot-Cha!* (1932) and a 1931 edition of the *Follies*—were commercial and artistic disappointments, bearing only the fleeting glimmer of his former brilliance. Perhaps his final blaze of glory was his supervision of the 1930 motion picture version of *Whoopee*. Boasting evocative Joseph Urban settings, original star Eddie Cantor, and a bevy of tastefully dressed and undressed showgirls in intricate dance routines patterned by Busby Berkeley, the film survives as a enduring example of the Ziegfeld touch.

Ziegfeld's chief rival in the presentation of musical shows was a theatrical force known professionally as "the Messrs. Shubert." Envious of Ziegfeld's success, they often imitated his style of production in their various series of revues, and after Ziegfeld's death they cagily secured the rights that enabled them to produce posthumous editions of the *Ziegfeld Follies* in 1934, 1936, and 1943. Aside from a sincere ongoing commitment to the Viennese operetta and its American descendants, the Shuberts sponsored productions that were thoroughly professional if predictable and workmanlike, often seeming to be gaudy cartoon redactions of Ziegfeld's flawless taste and theatrical innovation. However, the Shuberts made no pretenses or concessions to art; their approach to theatrical production was more akin to the order, discipline, and commercial viability of industry and corporate organization. To them, shows were commodities for barter and profit and the theater "a machine that makes dollars."[13] In their work, they distinguished themselves as savvy businessmen who determined management procedures that enthroned them as the most powerful impresarios of their generation.

At the start, "the Messrs. Shubert" were a theatrical Cerberus consisting of brothers Sam S., Lee (for Levi), and J(acob) J. Little is known about their earliest years, and what exists is wildly contradictory, with conflicting birthdates, birthplaces, and surnames. It was as if they spent much of their lives inventing and reinventing themselves and their background to suit the whims of their public and private lives. According to records in the Shubert

Archive in New York City, all three brothers were born in the East Prussian town of Neustadt. Lee, the oldest, was born in 1875 and Sam and J. J. were born in 1877 and 1879, respectively.[14] With their resourceful mother, they immigrated to America in the mid-1880s to join their father, an alcoholic peddler who had settled in Syracuse, New York. As a means of escape from the relentless poverty and despair at home, Sam was the first to find a future in the theater. At the age of ten, he finagled a walk-on role, for which he received one dollar per week, in a production of David Belasco's melodrama *May Blossom*. Then, he held various backstage jobs until, at seventeen, he had become box office manager at Syracuse's Weiting Opera House. Impelled by hard-driving ambition and a precocious understanding of the business of the theater, Sam set about acquiring the touring rights to a number of Broadway plays and used his profits to lease a string of theaters in upstate New York. With the pugnacious J. J. exiled as manager of his Rochester theater and with Lee on board as general factotum, Sam set his sights on a venue in Manhattan. He realized his dream in 1900 by leasing the Herald Square Theatre and two other minor Broadway houses. In little more than a decade, the Brothers

J. J. and Lee Shubert on board ship, c. 1910.

The Shubert Archive, New York City.

J. J. Shubert's dragon chair.

The Shubert Archive, New York City.

Shubert had soared phoenix-like out of the ashes of a Syracuse ghetto and asserted themselves as a Manhattan theatrical power to be reckoned with.

At the beginning of the twentieth century the American theater was trapped in the talons of the Theatrical Syndicate.[15] The goal of the Syndicate was to apply the streamlined management tactics of industry to the commercial stage. In theory, the organization was to blaze a transcontinental trail for touring Broadway productions and thus allow theatrical managers across the country to set up their seasons by dealing with one central booking agency. In fact, the Syndicate quickly established a ruthless monopoly, systematically destroying the careers of all who refused to cooperate with it. In less than a decade, the Syndicate had crushed all opposition and had become "the unseen monster that hovered over Broadway and preyed on theatre people."[16]

Initially, Sam Shubert maintained a healthy working relationship with the Syndicate. But as he continued to amass his own national circuit of theaters, he rejected the organization's strictures and policies. In 1905 he and Lee formed the Shubert Theatrical Corporation to protect their interests and then, joining with a group of fellow theater professionals—including his idol, producer-director-author David Belasco—he launched a counterattack against the Syndicate. Sam, "an electric battery when set in motion," immediately discontinued all advertising in the Syndicate-managed newspaper, the *Morning Telegraph*, and in 1905 created the *Show*, a modest, one-cent news magazine that promoted theatrical issues from the perspective of the Shuberts.[17] In various editorials he called on the American theater to free itself from such stringent control. Just as his press war was launched, Sam was killed in a freak train accident on May 11, 1905, while en route to Pittsburgh to investigate the acquisition of yet another theater. If, in life, Sam's relationships with his brothers were far more complex than simply fraternal, his sudden death proved unequivocally devastating to Lee and J. J. For a moment, they considered dissolving their theatrical interests but soon rallied to pick up the battle with Erlanger and his cohorts. With Lee at the helm, the brothers established the newspaper the *New York Review*, a more elaborate vehicle of theatrical propaganda than their earlier magazine, the *Show*. For the rest of the decade and into the next, the Shuberts steadily charged at the managerial fortress walls constructed by the Syndicate, acquiring or building theaters in key cities across the country and establishing stockades of their own. By 1920 Lee and J. J. had successfully crushed the Syndicate's stranglehold on the American theater. Ironically, their efforts replaced that organization's monopoly with an even more intricate and ruthless one of their own.

First and foremost, the Shuberts' interests in the world of show business were financial. Of all their various theatrical endeavors, musicals consistently yielded the biggest box-office bonanzas. Their association with the musical theater began in 1902, when Sam, an avowed Anglophile, scored a hit with his New York production of the London musical *A Chinese Honeymoon*. Until his death three years later, he continued to import, by and large with success, several British musicals per season. In 1906 Lee and J. J. acquired the

Program for the Shuberts' Lyric Theatre, New York, 1910.

The Shubert Archive, New York City.

PASSING SHOW
1918

ADELE ASTAIRE
"I Just can't make my
feet behave" number 9
PASSING SHOW
1918

**Costume designs by
Cora MacGeachey
for *The Passing Show
of 1918*. The pilgrim
costume was designed
for Adele Astaire.**

The Shubert Archive, New
York City.

5,000-seat Hippodrome Theatre in New York City, and for the next nine seasons they used its cavernous auditorium to mount annual seasons of musical extravaganzas. Featuring elaborate ultrarealistic scenery, gargantuan casts, dance routines, incidental song elements, and a chorus of women in abbreviated costumes, these shows revived briefly the mid-nineteenth-century vogue for romantic spectacle, as evidenced in *The Black Crook* (1866) and its many descendants. But both the English imports and the homegrown extravaganzas were a mere prologue to the Shuberts' long association with the Broadway revue and operetta genres.

The Mimic World, the Shuberts' 1908 foray into the world of the Broadway revue, was, as its title ironically implies, a derivative retort to the Ziegfeld-Erlanger-Klaw *Follies of 1907*. Ziegfeld reportedly threatened a lawsuit when he learned of their plans to use the term "Follies" in their show's subtitle.[18] Produced in tandem with veteran Lew Fields, the show was swiftly trounced by critics and rejected by audiences.

Nonplussed by its failure and eager to come up with a competitive vehicle that would steal some of Ziegfeld's thunder, Lee and J. J. unveiled *The Passing Show* in 1912 at their newly redecorated theater, the Winter Garden. The show's name represented yet another manifestation of the Shuberts' tendency to "borrow" selectively from the achievements of others for their own benefit. It was lifted verbatim from an 1894 variety entertainment of the same title.[19] Like the earliest editions of the *Follies*, the *Passing Show of 1912* was concocted as an easy-to-take summer entertainment boasting an assortment of comics, singers, dancers, and the inevitable chorus line of beauties.

If the ingredients of *The Passing Show* echoed the Ziegfeld model, the matrix was somewhat different, recalling the tried-and-true two-part structure of a Weber and Fields show. The first half, a prologue of sorts, consisted of "The Ballet of 1830," an excessively arty British dance piece that depicted *la vie bohème* in nineteenth-century Paris. The second portion used the Weberfieldsian strategy of presenting an assemblage of raucous lampoons of current plays. As staged by Ned Wayburn, these burlesques of contemporary theater proved the highlight of the show. The Shuberts assembled a fine company of entertainers who rivaled, and perhaps even surpassed, Ziegfeld's current cast and revealed their skills as talent scouts. But at its heart this and subsequent installments of *The Passing Show* were "unabashedly girlie revues, full of low comedy and novelty effects, and produced with an eye to the budget and to the taste of the Tired Businessman in the audience."[20]

Although it returned to Broadway with altered casts and new material for the next twelve seasons, *The Passing Show* never really succeeded in supplanting the *Ziegfeld Follies* in the hearts of theatergoers. Nor for that matter did any of the Shubert-sponsored series of revues the followed, including *The Greenwich Village Follies* and *Artists and Models*, both of which wallowed in blatant nudity and sophomoric humor.

Infinitely more valuable to the evolution of the American musical theater was J. J. Shubert's unparalleled ardor for the lush, romantic sensibilities of European operetta. As was so often the case, his commitment to the genre was fueled initially by the white-hot blaze of professional jealousy. In 1907 Austrian composer Franz Lehár's continental confection *The Merry Widow* waltzed onto Broadway and into archenemy Abraham Erlanger's New Amsterdam Theatre. The staggering popularity and quick financial success achieved by the production fired the Shuberts to purchase the rights to similar Viennese works and assert themselves as the nation's preeminent purveyors of European-styled operetta. Their method of development and production was one of formulaic efficiency, much as the procedures of factory line assembly. They bought, as cheaply as possible, all performance rights for presentation on Broadway and on tour, commissioned an English adaptation of the script and lyrics, interpolated a new song or two by one of their stable of house composers, hired designers to swiftly and thriftily construct sets and costumes that would then be recycled repeatedly from show to show, and controlled all subsequent stock and amateur productions through their leasing agency, the Century Library.

Despite their stern management methods, the Shuberts were synonymous with the operetta genre, having sponsored the New York premieres of works by such European exponents as Oskar Straus, Leo Fall, and Emmerich Kalman. When anti-Viennese sentiments prevailed during World War I and anything remotely of Graustarkian in milieu proved a commercial failure, they sought out and promoted indigenous incarnations of the form. The finest of the latter sprung from the fertile imagination of Hungarian émigré Sigmund Romberg, a long-suffering, long-term contractee of the Shuberts. Although dismissed by drama critics for his pedestrian progression of production numbers for various Shubert ex-

Composer Sigmund
Romberg.

Van Damm Collection,
New York Public Library
for the Performing Arts,
New York City.

travaganzas, Romberg surprised one and all with his graceful, melodious scores for such Shubert-sponsored operettas as *Maytime* (1917), *Blossom Time* (1921, adapted from music by Franz Schubert), and *The Student Prince* (1924). The last-named work, a bittersweet romance between a royal and a barmaid, contains some of the finest compositions in the operetta mold, including "Drinking Song," "Serenade," and "Deep in My Heart, Dear." In its initial Broadway engagement, *The Student Prince* enjoyed a run of 608 performances, earning status as the longest-running musical play of the 1920s.

With skillful management, these romantic musical shows became the Shuberts' greatest annuities. After long runs on Broadway, the productions were scaled down in size of cast, scope of talent, splendor of decor, and, ultimately, costs of operation and then sent out on seemingly endless national tours in the hinterlands that continued, with changes in personnel if not in production, for decades. "Like a touring production of *Blossom Time*" was a simile that the theatrical wags soon adopted to denote a production's unrelieved shabbiness and lackluster casting.

Bound by the memory of Sam Shubert's gentle dynamism and a shared jungle instinct, Lee and J. J. maintained a civil but cool distance from each other throughout much of their joint careers. Most of their communication was through messengers who carried their notes back and forth on Forty-fourth Street between Lee's office above the Shubert Theatre and J. J.'s apartment atop the Sardi's Building. On those rare occasions when they both needed to attend an out-of-town meeting, they would always travel separately, as if they were independent representatives of a royal or presidential family. In their public personae, they seemed the embodiment of the ancient Greek masks of comedy and tragedy.

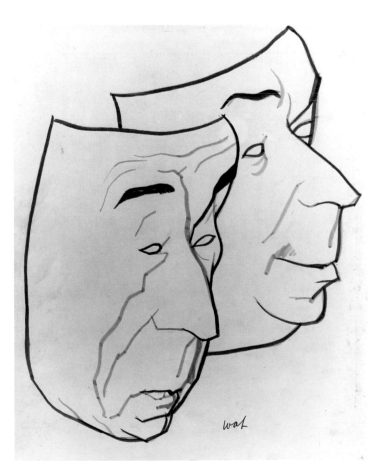

Lee and J. J. Shubert. By William Auerbach-Levy, 1939.

National Portrait Gallery, Smithsonian Institution, Washington, D.C.

Lee was shy with a pronounced tendency to stammer when excited. He would often shield his insecurities with a "menacing politeness."[21] J. J., on the other hand, was menacing, period, and prone to violent outbursts among his associates. They remained czars of Broadway until the late 1940s and continued to rule their national circuit of theaters until 1956, when the federal authorities forced J. J. to sell many of their theaters across the country because ownership constituted violation of antitrust laws. Their legacy lives on today in a number of ways: in many of the theaters that they built in cities across the country that are still in use; in the short Manhattan block known as Shubert Alley, which parallels Broadway and connects Forty-fourth and Forty-fifth streets in the heart of the theater district; and, finally, in the Shubert Organization, a production and management corporation that still ranks as one of the most powerful empires in the American theater.

Along with their other contributions to the creation of the modern American musical theater, both Ziegfeld and the Brothers Shubert promoted the development of distinctly native performance styles in the entertainers they discovered and nurtured into stardom. Ziegfeld always professed (and often displayed) an innate ability to spot an entertainer with potential, boldly asserting that "stardust is immediately apparent to the seeking eye."[22] The

Shuberts also were astute in discovering promising performers, especially if they had already exhibited some degree of drawing power under the aegis of other producers.[23] A handful of some of the era's leading entertainers, such as Al Jolson, built their stage careers on an exclusive commitment to a single management. Curiously enough, some of the brightest luminaries of the era, including Fanny Brice, Marilyn Miller, and Eddie Cantor, ricocheted between the Ziegfeld and Shubert camps, seeking the best showcase for their bright, particular talents.

"I could never write the story of my life without half of it being Ziegfeld," observed Fanny Brice in an interview.[24] Indeed, Brice's schizophrenic stage images of melancholy torch singer and raucous dialect comedienne never had finer, more bejeweled showcases than those offered under the Ziegfeld banner. Although she was far removed from the classic long-stemmed beauties that the flamboyant impresario traditionally favored, she was his urban Rose, whether her guise was the broad humor of "Second Hand Rose" or the tear-stained pathos of "Rose of Washington Square." Handsome and elegant, with an appealing sense of the absurd and "the soul of a peasant," Brice, more than any other of her generation, proved that a woman did not require the facade of a femme fatale in order to exude femininity and sex appeal.[25]

The youngest daughter of Jewish immigrant saloonkeepers, Brice (née Borach) was a natural mimic at a tender age, easily absorbing the myriad accents and attitudes around her in the streets of New York and reproducing them with warmth and humor. Her earliest brush with show business occurred in 1906 in an amateur contest at a Brooklyn theater. Her vibrant performance of sentimental ditties and "coon songs" brought down the house. In less than a year, the tyro turned pro, earning a spot in a George M. Cohan–sponsored revue called *The Talk of Broadway.* Her victory was short-lived, however, for she was fired before the production reached Broadway, with the producer citing her inability to blend into the anonymity of chorus as just cause for her dismissal. Eventually, Brice found employment in the world of burlesque. There, amid the rowdy, predominantly male audiences, she honed her way with a ballad as well as with the pratfall. One of her *specialités du jour* was a trifle entitled "Sadie Salome, Go Home."[26] Its composer, a twenty-year-old dynamo named Irving Berlin, persuaded her to deliver the song with a broad Yiddish accent, thereby establishing one of her most identifiable characteristics as a performer. On reflection she asserted, "In anything Jewish I ever did, I wasn't standing apart making fun. I was the race and what happened to me on stage is what could happen to my people. They identified with me, which made it alright to get a laugh."[27]

After a three-year tenure on the various burlesque circuits, Brice was tapped by Ziegfeld himself to become a featured player in the *Follies of 1910,* joining a cast that included Bert Williams and luscious Lillian Lorraine, the producer's latest inamorata and his leading showgirl. Brice's performance of two dialect numbers—Berlin's "Goodbye Becky Cohen" and "Lovie Joe" by Will Marion Cook and Joe Jordan—along with a brilliant display of her gifts for improvised eccentric comedy, won praise from both critics and public. In subsequent *Follies,* she perfected several of her stock of comic characters, including the inept Pavlova disciple in the song "Becky Is Back in the Ballet" and the buckskin-clad whirlwind equipped with a hilariously incongruous Yiddish accent in the madcap "I'm an Indian" ("Oi! Oi! Oi! I'm a terrible squaw"). And yet, one of her finest moments in the *Follies* had

Fanny Brice. By William Sharp, c. 1940–41.

National Portrait Gallery, Smithsonian Institution, Washington, D.C.

nothing at all to do with humor. In the *Ziegfeld Follies of 1921* she introduced one of her signature pieces, the *cri de coeur* "My Man" ("Mon Homme"). The heartbreak described in the lyric obviously limned a very public parallel to her own personal grief as the wife of shady gambler Nick Arnstein:

What's the difference if I say
I'll go away
When I know I'll come back
On my knees some day
For whatever my man is
I am his
Forevermore!

MAURICE YVAIN AND CHANNING POLLOCK,
"MY MAN" ("MON HOMME"), 1921

Perhaps more than any of her contemporaries, Fanny Brice was the performer most associated with the *Follies*. She appeared in seven Ziegfeld-supervised editions, starred in two posthumous Shubert-sponsored installments in 1934 and 1936, played herself in the fictionalized 1936 film biography of the great impresario, and headlined a glossy, mid-1940s MGM technicolor screen adaptation.

In direct contrast to Brice's earthy urban ethnicity, Marilyn Miller was the quintessential Broadway ingenue—a petite pink-and-blonde sprite who was as dainty as a Dresden china figurine and, at least in outward appearances, just as exquisitely fragile. Easily one of the greatest stage stars of the twentieth century, Miller was pivotal in redefining the image of the leading lady in the American musical theater, transforming it from the stately turn-of-the-century Art Nouveau voluptuousness of a Lillian Russell into the more animated but streamlined Art Deco sensibilities of the Jazz Age.

Identified only as "Mademoiselle Sugarlump," Marilyn Miller was already pirouetting *en pointe* in vaudeville at the age of five as part of an act known as the Columbians, headed by her stagestruck mother and ambitious stepfather.[28] To skirt the rules of the Gerry Society for the Prevention of Cruelty to Children, an American organization that placed restrictions on child performers, the Columbians embarked on a series of lengthy international tours. During this period, Marilynn, as she was then known, perfected her imitations of such prominent entertainers as Bert Williams, Sophie Tucker, and Danish ballerina Adeline Genee. While appearing with her family at the Lotus Club in London, she was discovered by Lee Shubert, who promptly signed her to a long-term contract. At the age of fifteen, she made her Broadway debut at the Winter Garden Theatre in the Shuberts' *The Passing Show of 1914.* Her youthful joie de vivre and obvious talent did not go unnoticed by the critics. The reviewer for the *New York Sun* described her as "calcium sunshine" and further raved that "she is to *The Passing Show* what (Teddy) Roosevelt is to the Bull Moose."[29] After appearances in two more editions of the *Passing Show,* she was spotted in another Shubert revue, *The Show of Wonders,* by Billie Burke, who suggested to her husband Flo Ziegfeld that

In Ziegfeld's *Follies of 1921,* Fanny Brice surprised the audience by singing the doleful "My Man" ("Mon Homme").

National Museum of American History, Smithsonian Institution, Washington, D.C.

Marilyn Miller starred in Ziegfeld's production of *Sally* from 1920 to 1923.

Harry Ransom Humanities Research Center, The University of Texas at Austin.

Ziegfeld star Marilyn Miller appeared on the cover of the April 15, 1929, Ziegfeld Theatre program.

Dwight Blocker Bowers.

Marilyn Miller. By Nickolas Muray, c. 1925.

National Portrait Gallery, Smithsonian Institution, Washington, D.C.

Miller was a suitable candidate for the *Follies*. "She has a sweet voice, but not much of it," Burke reported, "and I've seen better dancing . . . but a delightful thing happens when she comes on the stage."[30] Through a lucky technicality, Ziegfeld was able to spirit her away from the Shuberts, further fueling their smoldering hatred of him.

If Miller revealed budding talents while entrenched in the Shuberts' Winter Garden, she blossomed beautifully with Ziegfeld's expert pruning. He pared the final "n" off her first name, carefully honed her material and costuming, and transformed the precocious teenager into a Broadway star of the highest magnitude. Ziegfeld, a notorious womanizer, may well have been guided by less-than-pure motives. But by all accounts Miller kept things strictly professional, rewarding her mentor with glowing onstage performances rather than secluded backstage assignations. In the *Follies of 1918*, her first Ziegfeld assignment, she more than held her own in an illustrious cast that included Will Rogers, W. C. Fields, and Eddie Cantor. In the legendary 1919 edition, she appeared with her idol Bert Williams and danced merrily in white satin and silver sequins to the pseudominstrel show strains of Irving Berlin's "Mandy." Her biographical sketch in the program for the *Follies of 1919* announced, "It is no secret that the impresario plans to star Miss Miller next season in a musical especially written for her."[31] Ziegfeld stood by his promotional hype, hiring Jerome Kern and Guy Bolton to convert their unproduced musical comedy *The Little Thing* into a showy vehicle for her show-worthy skills. Retitled *Sally*, after its dauntless dancing heroine, this effort, more than any previous endeavor, solidified her claim to theatrical immortality. Miller played Sally Rhinelander, an orphan who undergoes a Cinderella transformation from kitchen slavey to Ziegfeld star. Backed by shimmering Joseph Urban settings and clad in stylish creations by Lucile, she had, over the course of the evening, countless golden opportunities to clown, cry, cavort, and, on occasion, capably croon an ethereal ballad by Kern and lyricist B. G. DeSylva:

"Look for the Silver Lining," from *Sally* (1920). Sheet music.

Alice Becker Levin.

> Look for the silver lining
> Whene'er a cloud appears in the blue.
> Remember somewhere the sun is shining
> And so the right thing to do
> Is make it shine for you.
>
> B. G. DE SYLVA AND JEROME KERN,
> "LOOK FOR THE SILVER LINING," 1920

Ziegfeld beamed. Critics spewed superlatives. And audiences fairly rioted at the box office just for the chance to sit in a darkened theater and bask in the reflected glory of an undisputed musical comedy goddess. For the remainder of her all-too-brief career, Marilyn Miller essentially played the same role, whether the character's name was *Sally* or *Sunny* or *Rosalie* or *Smiles*—that of a spunky, peaches-and-cream ingenue who triumphs

Eddie Cantor was star of his own radio show when this caricature by Frederick J. Garner was made in 1933.

National Portrait Gallery, Smithsonian Institution, Washington, D.C.

over adversity and wins both love and success. Although she would work for other managements, she would remain the grand apotheosis of the Ziegfeld Girl.

A diminutive cyclone of clapping hands, skipping feet, and rolling eyes, Eddie Cantor was among Ziegfeld's most endearing discoveries, ranking in the upper echelons of the American musical theater's great clowns. Known as the "Apostle of Pep," his persona of a

Flo Ziegfeld and
Eddie Cantor in
Ziegfeld's office,
1930.

Harry Ransom Humanities
Research Center, The
University of Texas at
Austin.

milquetoast given to manic outbursts blended the raffish innocence of the street urchin
with the polish of the purebred Broadway professional. Like his friend and colleague
Fanny Brice, he infused his performances with strong, affectionate references to his own
ethnic heritage, which made him an instant favorite not only with the Jewish theater-going
population but also with general audiences. His philosophy was simple: "Every performer
should play to an audience as if it were the last performance of his life, as if this is what
he'll be remembered for."[32]

Cantor, born Isidore Itzkowitz, credited his abilities as an entertainer to his paternal
grandmother. A feisty, self-sufficient woman blessed with the gift of humor, she assumed
responsibility for the boy's care following the premature deaths of his parents, Russian Jewish immigrants. Raised in the melting-pot milieu of a tenement on Henry Street in Manhattan's Lower East Side, he escaped the desolation of his impoverished surroundings by
performing in amateur shows at local theaters and music halls. Soon, he was appearing in
vaudeville in producer Gus Edwards's touring kiddie show "Kid Kabaret," and at nineteen

he went solo, devising an act around his abilities as a blackface comedian. On the strength of his work in the Los Angeles musical comedy *Canary Cottage,* he was summoned by Ziegfeld to join the cast of his nightclub revue *Ziegfeld's Midnight Frolic.* He then starred in three successive editions of the *Follies* in 1917, 1918, and 1919. In these revues, Cantor seized every opportunity to capitalize on his appealingly nasal, high tenor voice and high-octane performance style in sketches like the ribald "The Osteopath's Office" (as a timid, victimized patient) and songs such as Berlin's "You'd Be Surprised" (revealing his penchant for accentuating saucy lyrics with wide-eyed leers).

Cantor sided with his fellow performers in the 1919 Actors' Equity strike, which demanded standardized contracts between artists and producers and parameters for unpaid rehearsals. His pro-union stance brought about a serious rift with Ziegfeld and impelled him to join up (albeit briefly) with the Shuberts. He starred in their productions of *The Midnight Rounders* (1920) and *Make It Snappy* (1922), but he soon judged their management techniques inferior in every way to the meticulous care he received from his former employer. Settling their differences in mid-1922, Cantor and Ziegfeld reteamed for three more Broadway productions: the 1927 edition of the *Follies* and the musical comedies *Kid Boots* (1923) and *Whoopee* (1928). Of these, *Whoopee* was classic Cantor, doing for his career what *Sally* had done for Marilyn Miller's. The show, adapted by Ziegfeld staffer William Anthony McGuire from a play by Owen Davis, recounted the story of a hysterical hypochondriac who heads west for his health and gets involved in numerous comic scrapes. Although the show had many other attributes, including brilliant Urban decor and the singing of costar Ruth Etting, it was clearly conceived as a Cantor vehicle, with few opportunities for him to leave the stage throughout the evening. The hit-filled score by Walter Donaldson and Gus Kahn yielded an enduring signature tune for the comedian in "Makin' Whoopee!" which provided an ironic view of matrimony:

"Makin' Whoopee!"
from Ziegfeld's production *Whoopee*
(1928). Sheet music.

William L. Simon.

He's washing dishes, and baby clothes
He's so ambitious he even sews.
But don't forget, folks
That's what you get, folks
For makin' whoopee.

GUS KAHN AND WALTER DONALDSON, "MAKIN' WHOOPEE!" 1928

Cantor and Ziegfeld maintained, for most of their long association, a near father-son relationship. For Cantor, life after Ziegfeld involved highly successful appearances on film and radio; however, he carried with him fond memories of his mentor, calling him "a man whose daring and finesse changed the picture of Broadway."[33]

If Ziegfeld bested the Shuberts in nearly every level of theatrical competition, the brothers from Syracuse held one wild card for which even Ziegfeld could not find a worthy substitute. And that was the electrifying Al Jolson, who was billed accurately, if immodestly, as "the greatest entertainer in the world." His performance style, like his ego, was gargantuan. His booming baritone voice and melodramatic pyrotechnics were perfect for cavernous Broadway houses. When he confidently strode onto a stage, the theater became a tabernacle, he its evangelist, and his songs were thrilling sermons that elevated the emotions of his audience to a frenzied fever pitch. To him, a spotlight was a lifeline; indeed, throughout his up-and-down existence, he never seemed as comfortable offstage as he did in front of cheering patrons. Jolson's relationship with the Shuberts, which lasted for over two decades, was often stormy; however, more often than not he emerged as the victor in his battles with them.

Jolson's earliest years were rooted in the vast migration of Eastern European Jews to America at the end of the nineteenth century. With his parents and three elder siblings, young Asa Yoelson fled his homeland of Lithuania and boarded a steamer for the United States, eventually settling in Washington, D.C., in 1894. The son of an aspiring opera singer–turned–cantor, he was educated largely by his father, who taught him to enunciate clearly when singing by propping his mouth open with matchsticks.[34] If Asa rejected the ways of the old world, he was nonetheless profoundly influenced by the sound of his father's cantillation in Jewish religious ceremonies, adapting its emotional musicality for his own style of singing. Following his mother's sudden death in 1895, he experienced a profound sense of loneliness, a specter that would haunt him periodically for the rest of his life.

Jolson found solace in the make-believe of the entertainment world: first as an observer, witnessing the variety acts at area theaters, and then as a performer himself, singing and dancing for pennies with his brother Harry on Washington street corners. At eleven, he ran away from home to join a down-at-the-heels carnival troupe called Riche and Hoppe's Big Company of Funmakers. Teaming with his brother Harry and a Yiddish dialect comedian named Joe Palmer, he toured with several burlesque companies. It was during this period that he adopted the guise of burnt cork makeup, finding an exhilarating sense of freedom onstage behind the mask of blackface.

Striking out on his own, he was signed by impresario Lew Dockstader for a featured spot in his minstrel company, one of the most prestigious troupes of its kind in the country. Immediate success followed and he was summoned by Lee Shubert, who hired him for *La Belle Paree* (1911), a new musical comedy that was set to open at the Winter Garden Theatre. Subtitled *A Cook's Tour through Vaudeville with a Parisian Landscape*, the show was an assemblage of variety acts linked by a plot about Americans vacationing in the City of Lights. Jolson performed in blackface as a character named Erastus Sparkler. Almost immediately, audiences warmed to his brand of theatrical energy, and his debut was proclaimed a sensation. For the next decade, he made millions for the Shuberts and for himself as a result of his appearances in the musical comedies *Vera Violetta* (1911), *The Whirl of Society* (1912), *The Honeymoon Express* (1913), *Dancing Around* (1914), *Robinson Crusoe, Jr.* (1916), *Sinbad* (1918), *Bombo* (1922), and *Big Boy* (1925). Aside from a change in locales, the shows were largely the same: gaudily mounted extravaganzas with large casts, serviceable scores, and loosely plotted libretti with countless opportunities for Jolson to cavort as a black domestic, singing an array of interpolated songs culled from his latest hit

recordings. And every show allowed Jolson the chance to balance on one knee, with his white gloved hands splayed and fluttering like uncaged doves, rattling the rafters with his overtly emotional rendition of a sentimental song:

> Rockabye your baby
> With a Dixie melody
> When you croon
> Croon a tune
> From the heart of Dixie
> Just rock that cradle, Mammy mine,
> Right on that Mason-Dixon line
> And swing it from Virginia
> To Tennessee with all the love that's in ya.

JEAN SCHWARTZ, SAM M. LEWIS, AND JOE YOUNG,
"ROCKABYE YOUR BABY WITH A DIXIE MELODY," 1918

Jolson would have other triumphs in early sound motion pictures, but no subsequent effort really surpassed his golden years as the Shuberts' star attraction.

While Jolson was bantering in burnt cork at the Winter Garden, a small group of African Americans struggled to carry forth the traditions of black American musical theater that had been established a generation earlier by such exemplars as Bert Williams, George Walker, Will Marion Cook, and Paul Laurence Dunbar. Williams's crossover into the mainstream of white show business as a star of the *Ziegfeld Follies* remained an isolated precedent; Jim Crowism was as much a part of the theater as it was of the nation at large. Broadway audiences continued to remain predominantly white. James Weldon Johnson pronounced the period between 1910 and 1917 a "term of exile" for African American theater professionals.[35] During this era, the black theater reconstituted itself uptown in Harlem on stages and in nightclubs. For more or less the first time in New York, black entertainers performed for principally black audiences.[36] When a movement in African American theater resurfaced again on Broadway in the 1920s, it introduced several brilliant new African American voices.

Of all the black performers of the 1920s, Florence Mills ranks as both one of the most extraordinarily gifted and the least remembered. The latter is due, in part, to the paucity of documentation that exists as evidence of prodigious talent. The greatest loss is perhaps her two recordings, made in 1924 for the Victor Company, which were never issued and are presumably lost forever. What does remain is a handful of images that preserve the legend of her great beauty.

Florence Mills, a native of Washington, D.C., made her pro-

Singer Florence Mills. By James VanDerZee, 1923.

Donna Mussenden VanDerZee.

Bert Williams was a regular in the _Ziegfeld Follies_ from 1910 to 1919. Sheet music.

National Museum of American History, Smithsonian Institution, Washington, D.C.

fessional bow as a child performer in vaudeville. As an adolescent, she teamed with her sister Olivia for appearances at Harlem nightclubs. Lew Leslie, a young white producer who specialized in presenting black artists in annual series of revues, discovered her and immediately set about grooming her for stardom. The first musical in which she originated a role was in Leslie's _Plantation Revue_, a Harlem nightclub floor show that transplanted itself to Broadway. Her "bell-like" soprano and graceful dancing were greeted rapturously by critics and led to an offer from Florenz Ziegfeld to appear in the next edition of his _Follies_.[37] However, she turned down the great showman's invitation, vowing to remain with Leslie in the hope that he would create a vehicle "for the glorification of the American High-Browns."[38] Leslie created expressly for her a new revue called _From Dover to Dixie_ and took the show for an extended European tour. When the show premiered in London, Mills became the city's darling. Critic St. John Ervine pronounced her "by far the most artistic person London has had the good fortune to see."[39] Leslie revised the show, retitled it *Dixie to Broadway*, and brought it to New York in the fall of 1924, billing his young star as "the sensation of two continents."[40] Although critic Theophilus Lewis found the show itself "extremely shoddy, garish, and vulgar," he had nothing but praise for Mills, "the most consummate artist I have ever seen on the musical stage."[41]

Blackbirds, Leslie's next creation for her, repeated the pattern set by the *Plantation Revue*, starting out far from Manhattan with engagements in Paris and London. Upon her return to New York, before the Broadway opening of *Blackbirds*, Mills died suddenly from a burst appendix. When her funeral procession traced its way through the streets of Harlem, an airplane hovered and emitted a flock of blackbirds, recalling the song most associated with her.[42] Her premature death halted what was potentially one of the great performing careers of the era.

Florence Mills first won notice on Broadway as a cast replacement in the long-running musical comedy *Shuffle Along*, which introduced, among others, a promising songwriting team in Eubie Blake and Noble Sissle.[43] Eubie (né James Hubert) Blake

Noble Sissle and Eubie Blake at the piano, c. 1921.

Eubie Blake Collection, Maryland Historical Society, Baltimore.

studied music from the age of six. Despite the misgivings of his highly religious mother, he began to play the piano professionally at the age of fifteen in bordellos and clubs in his native Baltimore. Born in Indianapolis, Noble Sissle credited his love for music to the influence of his father, a Methodist minister. Although his parents hoped that he would follow in his father's footsteps, he chose a path as a performer, appearing as a soloist with Edward Thomas's Male Quartett [*sic*] and Hann's Jubilee Singers. Briefly abandoning show business for a whirl at college, he attended DePauw University for one semester. There he polished his ability to write clever lyrics for football games and other campus activities.

Sissle and Blake met in 1915 when both were members of a Baltimore band. Later that year, they joined James Reese Europe's Society Orchestra, and during World War I Sissle toured with Europe's regimental band. After the war Sissle and Blake reteamed and formed a vaudeville act called "The Dixie Duo," for which they wrote most of the mater-

The Selwyn Theatre
marquee in New York
City, featuring
Shuffle Along (1921).

Eubie Blake Collection,
Maryland Historical
Society, Baltimore.

Sissle and Blake's
"I'm Just Wild about
Harry," from *Shuffle
Along* (1921). Sheet
music.

Eubie Blake Collection,
Maryland Historical
Society, Baltimore.

ial. One of the first African American acts to eschew the use of burnt cork, they appeared suavely dressed in tuxedos.[44]

Shuffle Along was born at a Philadelphia benefit held by the National Association for the Advancement of Colored People when Sissle and Blake shared the stage with the team of Flournoy Miller and Aubrey Lyles. Miller wanted to turn his vaudeville sketch about small-town politics into a full-scale musical comedy and, impressed by their original, rhythmic songs, invited Blake and Sissle to be his collaborators. The show was assembled quickly and financed largely out of their weekly vaudeville salaries. The sets and costumes were salvaged from several shows that had foundered earlier in the season, and Blake and Sissle wrote several of the score's songs to match the available decor and then shoehorned them into the plot. After a lengthy tryout tour, *Shuffle Along* arrived on Broadway on May 23, 1921, with an $18,000 deficit and no advance fanfare. Critical response was mixed to favorable; however, business boomed when the show instituted a policy of Wednesday midnight performances, which became the rage among Manhattan's cognoscenti.

Miller's plot, about the candidates for a mayoral race in the mythical hamlet of Jimtown, was funny but unexceptional and revealed little progress from the promise of the Williams and Walker shows decades earlier.[45] The show's chief attributes were its wonderfully varied music and lyrics, from the tender ballad "Love Will Find a Way," to the syncopated rhythms of "Baltimore Buzz," the latter a tour de force for its coauthor Sissle, who played the show's comic bon vivant, Tom Sharper. But the undisputed hit of the score and the one number to attain immortality is "I'm Just Wild about Harry." Blake originally wrote the melody in waltz time, in the style of his idol, British composer Leslie Stuart.[46] Leading lady Lottie Gee suggested its meter be altered to that of a one-step.[47] Although almost discarded during the tryout in Philadelphia, the song became an immediate hit following the New York opening. Sissle's lyric mates perfectly with the felicitous lilt of Blake's melody:

I'm just wild about Harry
And Harry's wild about me
The heavenly blisses
Of his kisses
Fill me with ecstasy.

NOBLE SISSLE AND EUBIE BLAKE, "I'M JUST WILD ABOUT HARRY," 1921

Shuffle Along had a Broadway run of 504 performances and a subsequent tour by three different companies to key cities across the country. It was also instrumental in facilitating the start of a breakdown in the strictly enforced segregated seating in Manhattan's legitimate theaters, allowing blacks to sit in the orchestra section (albeit those seats in the rear third of the auditorium).[48] Before the decade ended, Blake and Sissle had written the scores for two more musicals, *Elsie* (1923) and *The Chocolate Dandies* (1925). Neither approached the critical and commercial success of their first effort.

The era also produced two composers who were integral to the development of the modern American musical: Irving Berlin and Jerome Kern. No two men could have had more dissimilar cultural backgrounds, yet they generated song literature that set lofty standards for their colleagues and descendants, converting the traditional rhythms and structures of Tin Pan Alley into the seminal ingredients of an American folk opera.

Irving Berlin with
"The Eight Notes" of
the first *Music Box
Revue* in 1921.

American Society of
Composers, Authors and
Publishers, New York City.

Irving Berlin. By the
Pach Brothers, 1907.

National Portrait Gallery,
Smithsonian Institution,
Washington, D.C.

The rags-to-riches saga of Irving Berlin is as exciting and colorful as any Horatio Alger narrative. A Russian Jewish peasant by birth, he and his family fled religious persecution and journeyed to America in 1892. Unfortunately, the extreme poverty they encountered upon settling in a Lower East Side tenement was little better than the impoverished shtetl they had left behind in the Old Country. At fourteen, Berlin abandoned school, home, and childhood, striking out on his own in the world. He held a number of hardscrabble jobs, eventually securing the position of singing waiter at various Bowery saloons. His raw, uncultivated talent for making music became a battle cry of freedom from the despair of his surroundings. Joining the staff of the Von Tilzer Music Publishing Company, he became a song plugger or "boomer."[49] His principal duty was to sit incognito in theaters among the paying customers and wildly encourage the performers to sing multiple encores of the company's songs, thereby giving audiences full opportunities to become enthralled with the appeal of the music and lyrics. One of his earliest assignments took him to Tony Pastor's Music Hall, where he was introduced to the pleasures of the vaudeville stage.

Returning to the post of singing waiter at a rowdy Chinatown café, he scavenged the time to write the lyrics for his first published song, "Marie from Sunny Italy," with a melody by the restaurant's house pianist, Mike "Nick" Nicholson. As the song sheet attested, its lyricist had officially changed his name from Israel Baline to Irving Berlin, carefully selecting a new, more euphonious name to go with his new profession. Berlin continued to slave away at mastering the craft of songwriting, teaching himself to play the piano after hours at the café.[50] Assimilating the sensibilities (if not the true ragtime rhythms) of early African American jazz, he wrote both the words and music for "Alexander's Ragtime Band," which established him as a leading voice in Tin Pan Alley.

Berlin's earliest compositions for the musical stage were various interpolations into shows with scores written principally by other songwriters.[51] Teaming with Ziegfeld's occasional coproducer Charles Dillingham and Ziegfeld's former librettist Harry B. Smith, he wrote his first full theater score for the 1914 musical comedy *Watch Your Step*. Revealing Berlin's ability to capitalize on current trends, the show centered on the then-current national mania for ballroom dance and starred two of its finest practitioners, Vernon and Irene Castle.[52] The script, based on an old, forgotten French farce called *Round the Clock*, was wafer thin and humorously credited in the printed program as "Book (if any) by Harry B. Smith."[53] Interspersed throughout Smith's story, which concerned an inheritance and its potential claimants, was Berlin's masterful flow of colloquial words and rhythmic music. The anonymous critic for the *New York Times* heralded the twenty-six-year-old composer's accomplishment, trumpeting that "*Watch Your Step* belongs to Irving Berlin. He is the young master of syncopation."[54] The score contained many delights, but one number stood out from all the rest for its innovative framework. "Play a Simple Melody," introduced in the production by Charles King and Sallie Fisher, was the first example of Berlin's characteristic "partner songs." This consisted of a flowing, legato melody with a suitably sentimental lyric: "Won't you play a simple melody / Like my mother sang to me?" which was designed to be sung simultaneously in duet with a second song that reflected the up-to-the-minute syncopations and sentiments of ragtime:

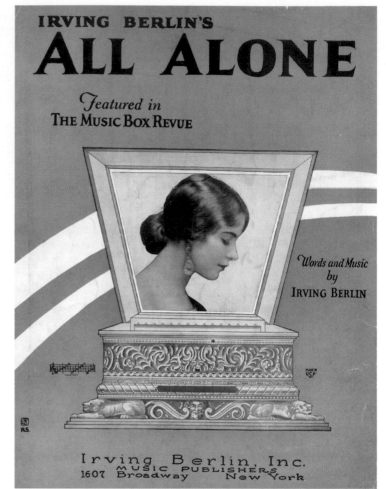

Irving Berlin's "All Alone," from the 1923 *Music Box Revue*. Sheet music.

Eric and Constance Kulberg.

> Musical demon
> Sets your honey a-dreamin'
> Won't you play me some rag?
>
> IRVING BERLIN, "PLAY A SIMPLE MELODY," 1914

Both the song and the show revealed a refreshing, all-American sound and sensibility that challenged the floridity of European operetta. Berlin's score for the 1917 all-soldier revue *Yip! Yip! Yaphank!* proudly trumpeted an appealingly forthright endorsement of patriotic fireworks that proved him a worthy successor to his spiritual mentor, George M. Cohan.

Berlin also produced a flurry of theatrical activity that included songs for several seasons of the *Ziegfeld Follies*. The legendary 1919 edition contained a Berlin ballad that

Program from the 1924 *Music Box Revue*.

Dwight Blocker Bowers.

would become known as the quintessential revue song:

A pretty girl is like a melody
That haunts you night and day
Just like the strain
Of a haunting refrain
It starts upon
A marathon
That flies around your brain.

IRVING BERLIN, "A PRETTY GIRL IS LIKE A MELODY," 1919

Berlin also showed himself an entrepreneur worthy of the company of a Flo Ziegfeld or Lee and J. J. Shubert, first, by setting up his own music publishing company, and then joining with producer Sam Harris to build the Music Box Theatre as a home for his own musical productions. *The Music Box Revues*, which he and Harris produced annually between 1921 and 1924, were exceptionally stylish shows that substituted wit and intimate chic for the more overblown splendor of Ziegfeld's *Follies*.

Over the next three decades Berlin would maintain an exalted position in the continuing evolution of the musical—a stance that would earn him show business immortality. Driven and fiercely ambitious in pursuit of continued success, he also revealed a refreshing pragmatism in his own assessment of his art and craft, asserting that "writing songs is a matter of having to pay bills and sitting down to make the money to pay them with."[55] But to his audiences and colleagues his work meant considerably more. His music and lyrics reflect both the eras in which they were written and a remarkable timelessness. To cite an often quoted assessment by Jerome Kern, "Irving Berlin has no *place* in American music. He *is* American music."

If Irving Berlin "*is* American music," Jerome Kern is remembered as "the father of the modern American musical theater." Certainly no other composer of his era was as adventurous in exploring, and breaking down, the boundaries of the form. In defining his own approach to writing for the musical theater, he explained, "It is my opinion that the musical numbers should carry the action of the play and should be representative of the personalities of the characters who sing them."[56] Furthermore, he asserted, a good musical must convey an aura of charm, or as he put it, "the odor of sachet."[57] His body of work, which encompasses the full scores for more than thirty stage musicals, represents the vital link between the European operetta and its eventual transformation into the distinctly indigenous form known simply as the "musical play."[58]

Jerome Kern was born into the genteel surroundings of a middle-class Jewish family on Manhattan's East Fifty-sixth Street, far uptown and a world away from the Lower East Side origins of so many of his contemporaries in the entertainment world of the early twentieth century.[59] His love for music was cultivated at an early age by his doting mother, who taught him the folk songs of her Bohemian heritage. Although his earliest musical training was in the realm of European classical traditions, he had, as an adolescent, already forfeited his heart to the lilting strains of Franz Lehár and Victor Herbert and fallen hopelessly victim to the charms of the musical stage. He studied theory and orchestration at the New York College of Music while moonlighting as an office clerk and occasional songwriter at Lyceum Publishing Company. In mid-1903, he moved to the T. B. Harms Co., which would remain his publisher for the rest of his long career.

Jerome Kern. By George Gershwin.

Rita Arlen.

Kern's first professional compositions for the theater were two songs ("Wine, Wine" and "To the End of the World Together") interpolated by Weber and Fields into their 1904 New York production of the British musical *An English Daisy*.[60] Shortly thereafter, Kern sailed to England and soon became an ardent, lifelong Anglophile. At that time London was in the thrall of producer George Edwardes, whose entertainments at his Gaiety Theatre were the first to identify themselves with the term "musical comedy."[61] Edwardes and American impresario Charles Frohman were but two of several producers who purchased Kern's melodies for interpolation into their West End entertainments. Returning to the States in 1904, Kern became the rehearsal pianist for the new musicals published by T. B. Harms, grasping every chance to audition his own tunes for the shows' producers. His ballad "They Didn't Believe Me," a collaboration with lyricist Herbert Reynolds (né M. E.

Rourke), was one of five songs he contributed to the American production of the English musical *The Girl from Utah*. At first, its lyricist wanted to sell it to Al Jolson, but it was decided that his bravura style possessed too much baritone brawn for the song's delicacy.[62] As sung in the original production by star Julia Sanderson, the number became an immediate commercial success and confirmed Kern's status as a bright rising star among American theater composers.

An even greater milestone in Kern's early career was his association with a revolutionary series of World War I–era musicals known as the Princess Theatre Shows. So named because they were, for the most part, staged at the Shubert-owned 299-seat Princess Theatre in New York City, these works were the idea of literary agent Bessie Marbury, who envisioned the tiny theater as the home for a new, intimate approach to musical comedy. It was Marbury who brought Kern together with her client, playwright Guy Bolton, to write the first two works in the series, the promising *Nobody Home* (1915) and the acclaimed *Very Good Eddie* (1915). Both of these works (and their successors) heralded a spirited breakaway from the stately opulence of European operetta and the lively vapidity of the American extravaganza.[63] They had modern, farce-oriented plots set in recognizably American locales, songs that grew out of plot and character elements rather than star specialties, small ensemble casts, one set for each act, and an eleven-piece orchestra wedged into the theater's tiny pit. In 1917 British author P. G. Wodehouse joined Kern and Bolton. The first, and perhaps greatest, success achieved by this triumvirate is *Oh, Boy!* (1917), which is generally considered to be the zenith of all the Princess Theatre Shows. Bolton's script is a masterful exercise in comic farce that is worthy of a Feydeau, and its delectable Kern Wodehouse score contains the musical weather forecast "Till the Clouds Roll By":

Jerome Kern (right) collaborated with P. G. Wodehouse (center) and Guy Bolton (left) in writing musicals for the Princess Theatre between 1915 and 1918.

Museum of the City of New York.

It is vain to remain and chatter
And to wait for a bluer sky
Helter-skelter
I must run for shelter
Till the clouds roll by.

P. G. WODEHOUSE AND JEROME KERN, "TILL THE CLOUDS ROLL BY," 1917

Even if he had only written one score, that for the 1927 musical *Show Boat*, Kern would still be assured prominent status in the vanguard of American theater composers. Easily the most influential musical of its generation, *Show Boat* endures as an epic synthesis of the old and the new, combining the arioso romanticism of the operetta, the native vigor of the musical comedy, and the infinite variety of performance styles in the revue. By the

Exterior of the Princess Theatre with Jerome Kern's *Oh, Boy!* featured on the marquee, 1917.

Museum of the City of New York.

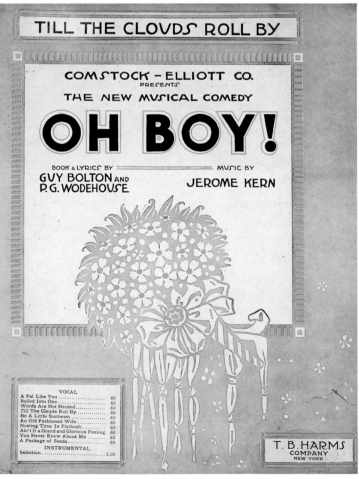

"Till the Clouds Roll By," from *Oh, Boy!* (1917). Sheet music.

National Museum of American History, Smithsonian Institution, Washington, D.C.

Oscar Hammerstein II, Flo Ziegfeld, and Jerome Kern outside of the National Theatre in Washington, D.C., for the premiere of *Show Boat*, 1927.

Rodgers and Hammerstein Organization, New York City.

very nature of its subject matter and the requirements of its sprawling cast of characters, it also blurred the distinctions between the white musical and the black musical. It is not surprising that a project so ambitious in vision and size should come to fruition under the aegis of the era's greatest impresario, Florenz Ziegfeld.

Kern immediately saw musical stage potential in Edna Ferber's 1926 novel *Show Boat*, which recounted a sprawling saga of late nineteenth- and early twentieth-century social history as viewed from the perspective of a show business family. The novel offered an unconventional source for adaptation, treating such controversial issues as racial bigotry, miscegenation, failed marriages, and compulsive gambling. Kern found an immediate ally in a young lyricist-librettist named Oscar Hammerstein II. Born to the theatrical purple, Hammerstein counted among his relatives grandfather Oscar Hammerstein, the founder and managing director of the Manhattan Opera House, his uncle Arthur, a Broadway producer, and his father William, manager of a Manhattan vaudeville theater. Kern and Hammerstein spent a full fourteen months on the show's creation, a period of development that was virtually unheard of in a time when shows were routinely assembled and put into rehearsal in just a few weeks. As Hammerstein recalled, "We had fallen hopelessly in love with it. We couldn't keep our hands off it. We acted out the scenes together and planned the actual direction. We sang to each other. We had ourselves swooning."[64] The lengthy period of development resulted in a richly textured work. Although Kern and Hammerstein retained the novel's panoramic sweep and many of its characters, they succeeded in giving Ferber's narrative a dramatic dimension that truly improved upon its source. Perhaps the authors' finest achievements were in their treatment of two of the leading characters, Magnolia and Joe. Magnolia, the heroine of *Show Boat*, reveals a level of dramatic development heretofore unseen in a typical commercial American musical of the era. Over the course of the play, she evolves from a love-struck ingenue

The James Adams Floating Theatre served as the model for Edna Ferber's *Show Boat* (1927).

Wisconsin Center for Film and Theater Research, Madison.

"Ol' Man River,"
from *Show Boat*
(1927). Sheet music.

National Museum of
American History,
Smithsonian Institution,
Washington, D.C.

to a strong and resourceful woman, as strong and dependable as the coursing of the waterways upon which she spends much of her life. Similarly, the character of Joe, an African American dockhand, becomes a choric figure uniting the various plot elements, locales, and characters with a song that reaffirms the show's principal theme, which equates the perpetual flow of the Mississippi with the need for constancy in human existence:

> Ah gits weary an' sick of tryin'
> Ah'm tired of livin' and skeered of dyin'
> But Ol' Man River
> He jus' keeps rollin' along.

OSCAR HAMMERSTEIN II AND JEROME KERN, "OL' MAN RIVER," 1927

Kern and Hammerstein were mutually convinced that the only American capable of producing such an epic work was Florenz Ziegfeld. Contrary to other reports, the great showman heartily concurred, proclaiming it "the opportunity of my life."[65] And with Ziegfeld came members of his illustrious production team, which included designers Joseph Urban and John Harkrider, who captured the breadth and intimacy of the story in their settings and costumes. For the vocal arrangements, Ziegfeld selected Will Vodery, the famed African American composer and musician who had been active in the musical theater since the first years of the century. And topping the production was its flawless cast headed by Charles Winninger, Norma Terris, Howard Marsh, Helen Morgan, and Jules Bledsoe, the latter a fine replacement for Paul Robeson, who had originally been cast in

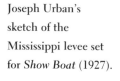

Joseph Urban's sketch of the Mississippi levee set for *Show Boat* (1927).

Joseph Urban Collection, Rare Book and Manuscripts Library, Columbia University, New York City.

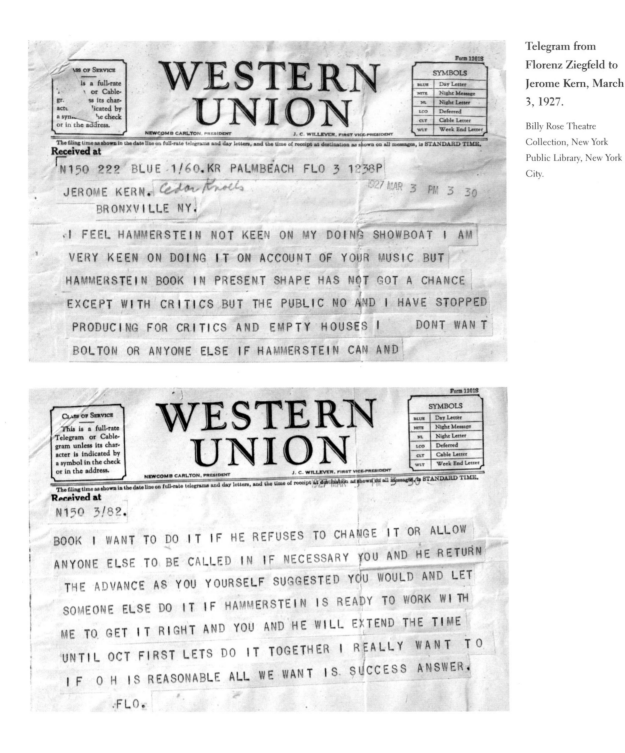

the role of Joe.[66] In assessing the merits of the 1927 Broadway production, *Variety* called
it "a Leviathan of a show," and in his *New York Times* review Brooks Atkinson proclaimed,
"*Show Boat* is one of those epochal works about which garrulous old men gabble for
twenty-five years after the scenery has rattled off to the storehouse."

   Representing the brilliant culmination of all that preceded it in the history of the American musical theater, *Show Boat* also took the chance to look toward the future, tantalizing one and all with the new possibilities it augured in writing, producing, designing for,
and performing on, the American musical stage. It was infused with a bracing voice of
Americanism—not the generic, jingoistic flag-waving of a Cohan, but instead consisting

The finale of the first act of *Show Boat*. By White Studios.

White Studios Collection, New York Public Library for the Performing Arts, New York City.

of a complexity of elements that captured "American sentiments in an American idiom."[67] While *Show Boat* was recognized instantly as a landmark in American theatrical achievement, it did not immediately spark a succession of descendants.[68] The frivolous nature of the musical comedy and the revue prevailed through most of the 1930s, perceived as they were, no doubt, as antidotes to the woes of the Depression. But through the efforts of key figures such as Kern, Hammerstein, George Gershwin and Ira Gershwin, and Richard Rodgers and Lorenz Hart, the innovations of *Show Boat* were carried forth in various experimental ways in various shows, finding their brightest manifestations a decade later in the musicals of Rodgers and Hammerstein.

WARNER BROS. SUPREME TRIUMPH
AL JOLSON
IN
"THE JAZZ SINGER"
WITH
MAY McAVOY
WARNER OLAND
Cantor Rosenblatt
Based upon the play by Samson Raphaelson as produced on the spoken stage by Lewis & Gordon and Sam H. Harris
Scenario by Al Cohn
DIRECTED BY ALAN CROSLAND
A WARNER BROS. PRODUCTION
ACME

BROADWAY AND HOLLYWOOD, 1927–1942

There may be trouble ahead,
But while there's music, and moonlight, and love, and romance,
Let's face the music and dance.

IRVING BERLIN, "LET'S FACE THE MUSIC AND DANCE," 1936

Light the Lights

Only weeks before *Show Boat* opened at the Ziegfeld Theatre, an event of equally seismic proportions took place a few blocks away at the Warners' Theatre—the opening on October 6, 1927, of *The Jazz Singer*, the mostly silent film based on Samson Raphaelson's Broadway play. Al Jolson was cast as Jakie Rabinowitz, a cantor's son who abandons his Jewish faith to become a "jazz singer." What electrified the glittering opening-night audience was Jolson's voice, first singing "Dirty Hands, Dirty Face," and then ad-libbing the immortal lines, "Wait a minute, wait a minute, you ain't heard nothin' yet!" before launching into "Toot, Toot, Tootsie!" By the end of the film, Jolson was performing "Mammy!" on one knee, and the audience—including Jolson himself and Irving Berlin—was practically sobbing. Financier Otto Kahn told his wife, "You and I will never see a moment like this again."[1]

The marriage of "talkies" with musicals became the rage, and by 1929 almost every director, set designer, composer, and performer who had ever worked on a musical—or even hummed a few bars—headed for Hollywood, including Florenz Ziegfeld himself; designer Joseph Urban; choreographer Busby Berkeley; songwriters Rodgers and Hart, Jerome Kern, Irving Berlin, and the Gershwins; and performers such as Fanny Brice and Fred Astaire. The Hollywood studios cranked out all-star musical revues, operettas, and—especially the vogue in these early years—backstage musicals of the "Let's do a show!" variety.

RIGHT: The premiere of *The Jazz Singer* at the Warners' Theatre, October 6, 1927.

Courtesy The Kobal Collection, New York City.

LEFT: Poster for *The Jazz Singer* (1927).

Michael Kaplan Collection.

81

Full chorus from *The Broadway Melody* (1929).

Photofest.

The first full-length "movie musical" was *The Broadway Melody*, released by Metro-Goldwyn-Mayer on February 1, 1929, and touted for its "all talking, all singing, all dancing." Although it was a decade away from the era in which Metro would come to define the big-budget Hollywood musical, *The Broadway Melody* won the Academy Award for best picture that year and recouped its production costs ten times over. MGM was so delighted that it immediately cast most of its biggest stars in *The Hollywood Revue of 1929*—a film now remembered largely for its score by Arthur Freed and Nacio Herb Brown. With an unlikely cast juxtaposing Buster Keaton, Marion Davies, Stan Laurel and Oliver Hardy, Lionel Barrymore, and Jack Benny, it featured a new song by Freed and Brown called "Singin' in the Rain."[2]

The intense interest in musicals waned in mid-1930, as audiences grew bored with the lack of variety in the films produced by the studios; by 1931 theater owners were advertising that their current offering was in fact *not* a musical. This slump continued until 1933, when, at the insistence of Warner Bros. production head Darryl F. Zanuck, that studio embarked on a new cycle of musicals—although this was unbeknownst to any of the Warner brothers themselves. The Depression had begun to make inroads not only on Broadway but on Hollywood by 1933, and Zanuck firmly believed that a rejuvenated kind of musical would offer American audiences an escape into fantasy.

To direct this new musical, Zanuck turned to dance director—these were the days before they were called "choreographers"—Busby Berkeley. Berkeley had established himself as one of the best dance directors on Broadway in the 1920s, notably with *The Earl Carroll Vanities of 1928*. A *New York Times* critic wrote that year that what Berkeley had done was to elevate the role of dance in musicals: "Of the various elements of the popular musical theatre, the music itself was the first to become the subject of evaluation by connoisseurs." No one yet had proclaimed the importance of the musical "book" (libretto), and until Berkeley came along, dancing was considered to be "on too low a level" for critical attention: "Now, however, the cognoscenti are beginning to be aware of 'qualities' in stage dancing, and this not because of any lowering of the critical eyeline, but rather because of the prodigious raising of the level of the dancing."[3]

Berkeley was not a musician, nor did he have any technical knowledge of dancing. He first began to stage dances when he was a director of drama in stock theater; occasionally, when the company performed a musical, it was up to Berkeley to stage those dances. He found he had a facility for incorporating jazz syncopation into the rhythms of his dance sequences, creating *ballets mécaniques* in which the dancers became virtual cogs in some vast Jazz Age machine.[4]

Busby Berkeley, c. 1933.

Photofest.

When the William Morris Agency approached him in 1930 about going to Hollywood to stage the musical numbers for the film version of *Whoopee*—which had been a triumph on Broadway in the Ziegfeld production starring Eddie Cantor—he leaped at the chance. The show had been bought by Samuel Goldwyn, and Cantor and Ziegfeld had already been engaged to work on the film. Goldwyn's advice to the Hollywood newcomer was to spend several weeks simply wandering around the studios, observing how filmmaking happened. Berkeley took his advice and realized how different were the techniques of Broadway and Hollywood: "In pictures you see everything through the eye of the camera. Unlike the theater, where your eyes can roam at will, the director and his cameramen decide where the viewer will look. It was obvious to me that film musicals so far had been disappointing because no one thought of imaginative things to do with the camera."[5]

The first thing he had to do was to learn something about photography, of which he professed "total ignorance." The art director of *Whoopee* told him to remember that "the camera has only one eye, not two," and Berkeley said that made all the difference to his entire approach. He won Goldwyn's approval early on to direct his own dance sequences, rather than to allow the film's director to handle them. And he also decided to film with only one camera; common practice had been to shoot from four

angles and then later to edit the sequences. Berkeley decided to shoot and edit entirely within the single camera. In *Whoopee* Berkeley used his famous overhead shots for the first time and also relied on close-ups of the chorus girls.

Whoopee did well, but Berkeley languished in the Hollywood musical doldrums of the early 1930s, when producers—and the general public—virtually abandoned movie musicals. Yet Berkeley would play a crucial role in their revival after Darryl Zanuck quietly brought him to Warners to direct the musical sequences of *42nd Street* in 1933.

The *42nd Street* production set the tone for the next several years, when Warner Bros. and RKO would revitalize the popularity of movie musicals. Starring Ruby Keeler—a "great little trouper," as she's called in the film—*42nd Street* is the quintessential backstage musical, in which Keeler steps in and plays the lead for Bebe Daniels, the ill star: and yes, the fictional producer—played by Warner Baxter—actually makes The Speech, exhorting the unknown ingenue, "You've got to go on and you've got to give, and give and give! . . . you're going out a youngster, but you've got to come back a star!"

The film was an enormous success. Louella Parsons wrote in her column, "Busby Berkeley has revolutionized musical comedies, and made it possible for the screen to feature girl revues comparable with the *Ziegfeld Follies*. It was Berkeley who saw the possibilities in photographical dance ensembles." A critic for the *New York Herald Express* went even further: "*42nd Street* is a cinematic effort by which Busby Berkeley, and he alone, is responsible for the current return of celluloid musicals."[6]

That same year, Berkeley staged the musical numbers for two more Warners' films, *Gold Diggers of 1933*, whose opening scene featured a young Ginger Rogers dressed in a coin costume and singing "We're in the Money"; and *Footlight Parade*, another backstage musical, this time starring James Cagney, Joan Blondell, Dick Powell, and Ruby Keeler. *Footlight Parade* was highlighted by an astonishing Art Deco number called "By a Waterfall," in which cascades of chorines were elevated by a hydraulic fountain to form a starburst on the surface. Nearly fifteen minutes long, the number came to Berkeley in a moment of divine inspiration: leaving the premiere of *Gold Diggers of 1933* with Jack Warner at Grauman's Chinese Theater, he suddenly turned to Warner and said, "I can see a big waterfall coming down through the rocks, with girls sliding down the rapids into a huge

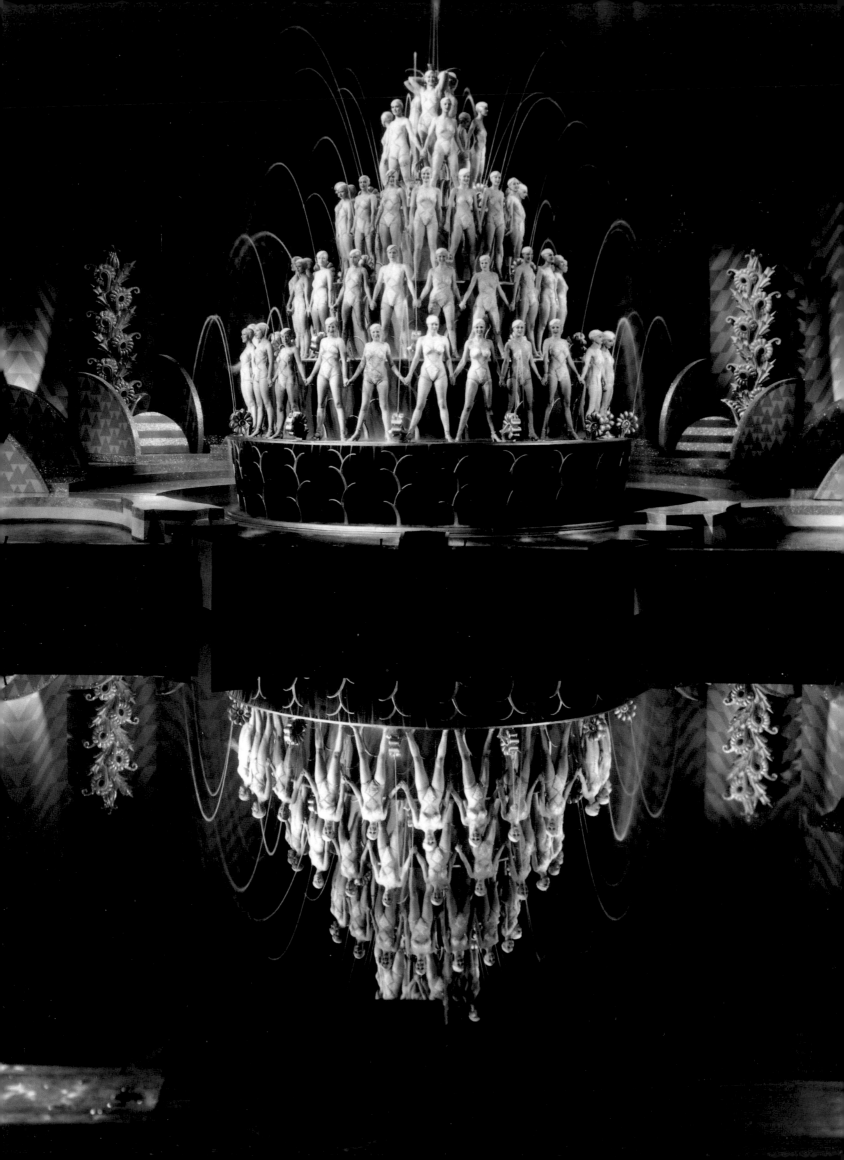

**The human fountain
from *Footlight Parade*
(1933).**

**James Cagney
rehearsing for
Footlight Parade
(1933).**

Ziegfeldian pool with twenty-four gold springboards and a gold fountain telescoping into the air." Warner thought that Berkeley had "just blown his top."[7]

Another classic Berkeley musical number, "The Lullaby of Broadway," was set in *Gold Diggers of 1935*, the film that marked his debut as a full-fledged director. Almost a self-contained film-within-a-film, "Lullaby" focuses on Broadway and a young girl who sleeps by day and lives by night. Berkeley's camera features a montage of New York scenes, and follows a young couple—Dick Powell and Wini Shaw—in a night on the town. They are first seen alone in a gigantic nightclub; then, they are joined by a pair of Latin dancers, and gradually, by a veritable battalion of tap-dancers, until over one hundred dancers are performing "The Lullaby of Broadway." The camera then winds the scene down, although now a darker side intrudes. Wini stumbles and falls to her death from a skyscraper. In the closing sequence, Berkeley returns to a New York montage—showing that life in the city goes on.

In the late 1930s, Busby Berkeley went on to MGM, where he directed such Judy Garland–Mickey Rooney films as *Babes in Arms* (1939), *Strike Up the Band* (1940), and *Babes*

on *Broadway* (1941), as well as *For Me and My Gal* (1942) with Gene Kelly and Judy Garland, and Twentieth Century Fox's *The Gang's All Here* (1943), featuring Carmen Miranda as "The Lady in the Tutti-Frutti Hat." Yet his real contribution to musicals remained with the work he had accomplished for Warners—the machine-age ballet constructions he created out of a silvery Art Deco fantasy. "In an era of breadlines, Depression and wars," he once said, "I tried to help people get away from all the misery . . . to turn their minds to something else. I wanted to make people happy, if only for an hour."[8]

If Warner Bros. musicals were immersed in stories of "the underdog" overcoming (usually) those breadlines, RKO focused instead on its two incandescent stars, Fred Astaire and Ginger Rogers. And Astaire and Rogers somehow superseded Depression-rooted vernacular concerns of the "let's-do-a-show" backstage variety so favored by Warners. Fred and Ginger were not always removed from Depression themes, but the overlay was emphatically that of glamour and stylized elegance. Perhaps the musical number that best illustrates this combination of Depression and glamour is "Let's Face the Music and Dance," from *Follow the Fleet* (1936). Astaire, dressed in white tie and tails, has just lost all of his money gambling in Monte Carlo. Despondent, he walks alone along a casino terrace, but just as he takes out a small pistol, he sees Rogers—impeccably dressed in a beaded gown—about to jump off a parapet. He dances over to her, shows her his empty wallet; she tries to grab the gun. He then throws the wallet and gun into the darkness, and they begin to dance while he sings, "There may be trouble ahead / But while there's music, and moonlight, and love, and romance / Let's face the music, and dance."

The two first appeared together in the 1933 RKO film *Flying Down to Rio*, the same year that Busby Berkeley was setting the tone at Warners with *42nd Street, Gold Diggers of 1933*, and *Footlight Parade*. Rogers's career had soared since she first began in "show business" by winning the Texas state Charleston Championship in 1925; only fourteen, she embarked on the vaudeville circuit with her mother. By 1928 she was playing the Paramount Theater in New York and made her Broadway debut a year later, in *Top Speed*. She made several short

Fred Astaire. By Martin Munkacsi, 1936.

National Portrait Gallery, Smithsonian Institution, Washington, D.C.

Fred Astaire in his
dressing room during
the filming of *Flying
Down to Rio* (1933).

Wisconsin Center for Film
and Theater Research,
Madison.

Fred Astaire and
Ginger Rogers danc-
ing in *Top Hat*
(1935).

Natural History Museum of
Los Angeles County, Los
Angeles, California.
© 1935 RKO Pictures, Inc.
Used by permission of
Turner Entertainment Co.
All rights reserved.

Adele and Fred Astaire. By Edward Steichen, 1925.

Courtesy *Vanity Fair.*
© 1925 (renewed 1953)
by the Condé Nast
Publications, Inc.

Fred Astaire and choreographer Hermes Pan at a 1936 rehearsal. By Robert W. Coburn.

Photofest.

films, but her first appearance in a full-length motion picture came in 1930, in Paramount's *Young Man of Manhattan.* Here, she played a wisecracking flapper whose line, "Cigarette me, big boy," became a favorite piece of national slang. The same year, she returned to Broadway to star in the Gershwins' hit show, *Girl Crazy,* in which she sang "Embraceable You" and a song written especially for her by George Gershwin, "But Not for Me."

Hollywood soon beckoned, and 1933 proved a milestone year for her: she played "Anytime Annie" in *42nd Street* and sang her unforgettable pig-latin version of "We're in the Money" for *Gold Diggers of 1933.* But it was *Flying Down to Rio* that catapulted her to stardom and established her and Fred Astaire as the screen's most popular dancing partners.

Fred Astaire had been teamed with his sister Adele since the age of seven, when they appeared in vaudeville. Adele was apparently the "star" of the act, with one agent pointedly reporting in 1908 that "the girl seems to have talent." They appeared on Broadway from 1917 to 1931 in such landmark shows as *Lady, Be Good!* (1924), written for them by George and Ira Gershwin, *Funny Face* (1927), and *The Band Wagon* (1931). After his sister married, Fred appeared in one more show, *The Gay Divorce* (1932), before turning to Hollywood. His first film was *Dancing Lady,* with Joan Crawford, but his real break would be *Flying Down to Rio.*

Although they hardly received top billing for *Flying Down to Rio*—Fred was billed fifth, after Ginger   Astaire and Rogers stole the show. Playing a song and dance team in Gene Raymond's traveling band, they appear sporadically as the picture wanders down to Rio to allow Raymond to pursue Dolores Del Rio (pun intended, given the level of writing in this film). In the film's big production number, however, it is clear that something very special is happening on screen. In "The Carioca" (music by Vincent Youmans, lyrics by Edward Eliscu and Gus Kahn), Astaire and Rogers tango across the classically Art Deco set designed by Van Nest Polglase—the first of what dance critic Arlene Croce has labeled the "B.W.S.," the "Big White Set" found in every Astaire-Rogers film thereafter.[9]

The nine Astaire-Rogers films that followed transformed movie musicals. In place of what one critic referred to as "the thundering herd" populating Busby Berkeley's films at Warner, the Astaire-Rogers films had a lightness of spirit and a commitment to coherence in their dance sequences. "In the old days," Astaire once said, "they used to cut up all the dances on the screen. In the middle of a sequence, they would show you a close-up of the actor's face, or of his feet, insert trick angles taken from the floor, the ceiling, through lattice work or a maze of fancy shadows." Instead, he "always tried to run a dance straight in the movies, keeping the full figure of the dancer, or dancers, in view and retaining the flow of the movement intact." He also disliked chorus numbers, unless they were used "when you have a definite idea of something for the chorus to do which will heighten the whole dance number."[10]

Normally, the dance sequences were created after the musical book was written, so that the story, the character, or a piece of music inspired a dance routine. "Each dance ought to spring somehow out of character or situation, otherwise it is simply a vaudeville act," Astaire argued—although sometimes "you get an idea that it would be swell to do a dance on roller skates, or to your own shadow. When this happens, you have to fit your idea into the book, or, perhaps, even build the book around the idea." Next, the music would be written, a pattern would be devised for the dance, and then the actual dance steps would be worked out. "If the dance is right, there shouldn't be a single superfluous movement. It should build to a climax and stop!"[11]

This creative process could be exhausting: the roller skating sequence in *Shall We Dance,* for example, was shot thirty times, and the "Never Gonna Dance" number from *Swing Time* was done in forty-eight takes. Because the studio floors were so highly waxed, Astaire and Rogers had to dance for the camera in plain-soled shoes without metal taps. Days later, they would go into a soundproof room with a small screen and projection equipment and per-

"Top Hat, White Tie, and Tails," from *Top Hat* (1935). Sheet music.

National Museum of American History, Smithsonian Institution, Washington, D.C.

form the dances again, this time recorded with taps.[12] It was a highly collaborative process. Hermes Pan was choreographer for the Astaire-Rogers films, but the input from both of the principals was enormous. Astaire has long been credited with playing a major role in creating the dance routines, but Rogers also made her creative views known, as in the "Isn't This a Lovely Day (To Be Caught in the Rain)?" sequence from *Top Hat.* Set in a park gazebo, the number lacked a "finish," until Rogers suggested that they both "go to the edge of the gazebo, reach out to feel the rain, sit down, and shake hands." Both Astaire and Pan liked the idea, and, as Rogers often said, "I had plenty of input in our routines and got to be known as the 'button finder'. . . . the one who puts the last word or finishing touch on a scene."[13]

Astaire and Rogers worked with the finest composers of their day, many of whom had had—and continued to have—successful careers on Broadway before venturing to Hollywood in the early 1930s. Of their ten films together, one featured music by Cole Porter (*The Gay Divorcée,* 1934), two by Jerome Kern (*Roberta,* 1935; and *Swing Time,* 1936), one by the Gershwins (*Shall We Dance,* 1937), and three by Irving Berlin (*Top Hat,* 1935; *Follow the Fleet,* 1936; and *Carefree,* 1938). With the exception of some of the early Kern-Bolton-Wodehouse Princess Theatre shows, and the epic *Show Boat,* Broadway musicals were still basically little more than revues in format. The Astaire-Rogers films for RKO, however, depended on a story line fully integrated into song and dance. As became evident from *The Gay Divorcée* on, when Astaire and Rogers danced "Night and Day" in an empty ballroom, the music and dance in these films would be used to express character and style to advance the story; indeed, the dance sequences were so strong—and the "stories" generally so frivolous—that the films were virtually carried by the music and dance, with little interference from the plot lines themselves.

The best and brightest of Broadway went west after 1929, both because of an increasingly depressed Broadway economy and because of the enormous craze in 1929–30 for

Ginger Rogers. Self-portrait, c. 1937.

Robertson E. Collins.

movie musicals. From its peak year of theatrical activity in 1927–28, when 264 shows opened, Broadway after the Crash began an economic downslide—and an eventual transformation to movie and burlesque houses. During the 1929 holiday season, *Variety* reported, one out of every five Broadway theaters was not in use; moreover, no new theaters would be built in the district after 1929.[14] Tin Pan Alley forged a new alliance with Hollywood as its songs became vital to the new movie musicals; the major studios bought out the music publishing firms—Warners, for example, acquired T. B. Harms—and brought songwriters to Hollywood in droves.

When George and Ira Gershwin went to Hollywood in 1930, they had just produced a smash Broadway hit, *Girl Crazy*, and were among Broadway's hottest teams. Two years earlier, they had had three shows running concurrently on the Great White Way: the 1927 *Funny Face*, starring Fred and Adele Astaire; *Rosalie*, a combination musical comedy-operetta-extravaganza they had written for Florenz Ziegfeld and Marilyn Miller; and their long-running 1926 hit, *Oh, Kay!* Born to Russian émigrés and raised in New York, Ira and George found their early mentors in the Princess Theatre group during the 'teens; with Ira being most influenced by P. G. Wodehouse and George by Jerome Kern.

A new temperament marked Broadway in the twenties—one that suited the Brothers Gershwin perfectly. As one chronicler of the decade wrote, "The country felt that it ought to be enjoying itself more than it was . . . [and ought to] take up the new toys that were amusing the crowd, go in for the new fads, savor the amusing scandals."[15] The subjects of

the Gershwin cycle in the mid-twenties reflected this sense of amusement, whether spoof-
ing society parties in the Hamptons in *Lady, Be Good!* or bootleggers in both *Oh, Kay!*
(1926) and *Funny Face*. In 1930 their lighthearted romp, *Girl Crazy*, proved to be one of
their greatest Broadway hits: not only did it make a star of nineteen-year-old Ginger
Rogers, it launched the career of Ethel Merman. Merman wrote that "the audience
yelped" when, as she sang "I Got Rhythm,"

RED, HOT & BLUE

I got rhythm,

I got music,

I got my man—Who could ask for anything more?

she held the high note for sixteen bars.[16] Irving Berlin once told Alan Jay Lerner, "If you ever write lyrics for Ethel Merman they had better be good, because *everybody* is going to hear them."[17]

In Hollywood, the Gershwins worked on a 1931 Fox picture called *Delicious*; most of the songs were taken from the Gershwin "trunk" rather than created for this pastiche of a movie, although one that stood out—and that probably expressed the Gershwins' attitude toward Hollywood—was the witty "Blah, Blah, Blah":

Blah, blah, blah, your hair,

Blah, blah, blah, your eyes,

Blah, blah, blah, blah, care,

Blah, blah, blah, blah, skies.[18]

With Hollywood facing an economic slump in the early 1930s, the Gershwins turned their energies back to Broadway.

As great as their success had been with *Girl Crazy*, George told a reporter that they actually hoped to create "a new style of musical comedy."[19] They were particularly interested in bringing political satire to the musical stage and in establishing an American strain in the tradition of Gilbert and Sullivan. They embarked on such an effort when they joined with playwrights George S. Kaufman and Morrie Ryskind in the political trilogy that was to mark a radical departure in musical theater history—*Strike Up the Band* (1927/1930), *Of Thee I Sing* (1931), and *Let 'Em Eat Cake* (1933). With *Of Thee I Sing*, the Gershwins made a conscious attempt to integrate the music with the action. "In this show," wrote Ira, "you develop ideas, condensing pages of possible dialogue into a few lines of song."[20] The show satirized contemporary American politics and was a great success. The vitriolic score touted "Wintergreen for President" with such lyrics as "He's the man the people choose / Loves the Irish and the Jews" and proudly pronounced a potential First Lady "the illegitimate daughter of the illegitimate son of an illegitimate nephew of Napoleon." Critic George Jean Nathan called it a "landmark in American satirical musical comedy," while his colleague Brooks Atkinson found that it "nearly succeeded in liberating the musical comedy stage from the mawkish and feeble-minded formula that has long been considered inevitable. It is funnier than the government and not nearly so dangerous."[21] The production played for 441 performances and was awarded the Pulitzer Prize—although, in some bit of whimsy comprehensible only to the awarding committee, the prize was given for book and

lyrics, but not for music. The $1,000 prize was split three ways—among George S. Kaufman, Morrie Ryskind, and Ira Gershwin—with Kaufman receiving $333.34: "I got the extra penny because I was the eldest."[22]

The bitter sequel *Let 'Em Eat Cake* did not prove as popular as *Of Thee I Sing,* and George decided that they needed to take a different direction entirely. Years before, he had written a one-act mini-opera called *Blue Monday*—about a tragic incident in a Harlem saloon—for the *George White Scandals of 1922;* in the years that followed the idea of writing a serious piece of music based on a totally American theme continued to intrigue him. "I'd like to write an opera of the melting pot in New York City itself, with its blend of native and immigrant strains. This would allow for many kinds of music, black and white, Eastern and Western, and would call for a style that should achieve out of this diversity, an artistic unity." New York seemed the perfect setting, "a meeting-place, a rendezvous of the nations. I'd like to catch the rhythms of these interfusing peoples, to show them clashing and blending. I'd especially like to blend the humor of it with the tragedy of it."[23]

He grew even more determined after reading Du Bose Heyward's novel *Porgy* in 1926 and wrote Heyward to suggest a musical adaptation. It would not be until 1934 that the project actually got under way, when George and Heyward met in Charleston, South Car-

LEFT: Fred Astaire, George Gershwin, and Ira Gershwin, 1937.

Museum of the City of New York.

ABOVE: Ethel Merman with chorus in *Girl Crazy* (1930). By White Studios.

White Studios Collection, New York Public Library for the Performing Arts, New York City.

olina; Ira would soon join the collaboration. Heyward wrote that they evolved a system "which, between my visits North, or George's dash to Charleston, I could set scenes and lyrics. Then the Brothers Gershwin, after their extraordinary fashion, would get at the piano, pound, wrangle, swear, burst into weird snatches of song and eventually emerge with polished lyrics."[24] Along the way, the locale of the opera shifted from New York's "melting pot" to Charleston's Catfish Row, but Gershwin retained the feel of the clash and blend of "the rhythms" that he felt made the music so distinctively American.

Porgy and Bess opened in Boston on September 30, 1935, and in New York on October 10. The critics found what Gershwin called a "folk opera" to be neither fish nor fowl; in particular, Olin Downes of the *New York Times* complained that the style "is at one moment of

**George Gershwin. By
Will Cotton, 1935.**

Metropolitan Opera
Archives, New York City.

opera and another of operetta or sheer Broadway entertainment." Gershwin was also criticized for attempting to write about a slice of African American life. To this he responded: "I have adapted my method to utilize the drama, the humor, the superstition, the religious fervor, the dancing and the irrepressible high spirits of the race." Duke Ellington was not swayed, saying, "The times are here to debunk Gershwin's lampblack Negroisms." It was clearly a different era from that of *Show Boat* in 1927, which had earned success with a racially mixed cast and characters etched with a dramatic universality. Composer Virgil Thomson suggested that *Porgy and Bess* was an example of a "libretto that should never have been chosen [by] a man who should never have attempted it. . . . Folk-lore subjects recounted by an outsider are only valid as long as the folk in question is unable to speak for itself, which is certainly not true of the American Negro in 1935."[25] After 124 performances, *Porgy and Bess* went on the road; the tour ended only two months later in Washington, D.C., a commercial failure.

Once their absorption with *Porgy and Bess* had abated, the Gershwins turned back to Hollywood in 1936. Broadway's attraction had paled considerably for them, both artistically and financially. Ira wrote that they had turned down nearly a dozen serious offers in favor of the lure of the film colony: "But revues we no want and libretti offered are, at best, fair. Boy, what pix have done to the legit! True, given a cast, there's still a good chance to make plenty monyeh in musical comedy, but for the time being, let others test."[26] Most of the leading Broadway songwriters had been drawn to Hollywood by this time, including Jerome Kern, Rodgers and Hart, Cole Porter, and Irving Berlin. There was a real camaraderie among the Broadway-Hollywood crowd, and the Gershwins seem to have been at the very hub, with a social circle including Moss Hart, Lillian Hellman, Edward G. Robinson, Rouben Mamoulian, Oscar Levant, Harold Arlen, and E. Y. "Yip" Harburg. Ginger Rogers recalled sitting on the floor in George Gershwin's apartment one afternoon, doing a charcoal sketch of Irving Berlin; and Mrs. Vincente Minnelli said that her husband had lived with the Gershwins when he first came to Hollywood from New York.[27]

The Gershwins signed to work on the new Astaire-Rogers film, *Shall We Dance*—although there was some discussion, in the wake of *Porgy and Bess* as well as some of his concert pieces, as to whether George had grown too "serious" a writer for movie musicals. Hearing these concerns from his agent, he wired instantly, "Rumors about highbrow mu-

"Summertime," from
Porgy and Bess
(1935). Sheet music.

sic ridiculous. Am out to write hits." If there were any doubts about Gershwin's ability to appeal to a popular audience, *Shall We Dance* dispelled them handily, with such numbers as "They All Laughed," "Let's Call the Whole Thing Off," and "They Can't Take That Away from Me."

After the release of *Shall We Dance* in May 1937, it would be fifteen months before Fred Astaire and Ginger Rogers appeared in another film together, so the Gershwins signed on to work with Astaire in *Damsel in Distress*. Here, Fred was teamed with Joan Fontaine rather than Ginger, and with George Burns and Gracie Allen. The Gershwin score was highly sophisticated, crafted to spotlight the debonair Astaire in such numbers as "Things Are Looking Up," "A Foggy Day," "Nice Work If You Can Get It," and "I Can't Be Bothered Now." As soon as their work for this film was completed, the Gershwins charged right into the production of *The Goldwyn Follies*, their third film within a year. Ira reported that they had "managed to finish five songs the first six weeks of our contract," but those weeks would turn out to be the last of George's life. "Love Is Here to Stay" would be the last song he wrote before succumbing to a brain tumor shortly before his thirty-ninth birthday in July 1937.

In the next several years, Ira would become part of other successful collaborations, working with Moss Hart and Kurt Weill in 1941 on the Broadway musical *Lady in the Dark*, starring Gertrude Lawrence, and with Jerome Kern in 1944 on the film score for *Cover Girl*, starring Rita Hayworth and Gene Kelly. But the death of George Gershwin really marked the end of an era—of a collaboration that integrated song and dance with character and story line and drove it all with enormous energy and sophistication.[28]

Irving Berlin was another of the great Tin Pan Alley and Broadway songwriters who came to Hollywood in the thirties. His career had just gone through a fallow period but

George Gershwin and Irving Berlin, 1937.

American Society of Composers, Authors and Publishers, New York City.

"Tour Guide and Spectators" set design by Jo Mielziner for *Of Thee I Sing* (1931).

Robert L. B. Tobin Collection, courtesy Marion Koogler McNay Art Museum, San Antonio, Texas.

Ethel Waters in *As Thousands Cheer* (1933). By Alfredo Valente, 1933.

National Portrait Gallery, Smithsonian Institution, Washington, D.C.

revived with the Broadway shows *Face the Music* (1932) and *As Thousands Cheer* (1933)—both collaborations with the witty young dramatist Moss Hart, and both inspired by the Gershwins' great success with *Of Thee I Sing*, which was having a very long and lucrative run at Berlin's own Music Box Theatre. *As Thousands Cheer* was a striking novelty: the show was to be a "topical revue" using a format straight out of the newspapers, including headlines, gossip, comics, and Sunday supplements, all organized around loosely connected sketches. Hart, who had been hovering on the margins of the theater by acting, writing plays, and working on revues, made his Broadway debut collaborating with George S. Kaufman in the hit comedy *Once in a Lifetime* (1930); Kaufman called Hart "'Forked lightning'. . . . I think his head plays around the lightning, deliberately. . . . Ideas pour forth, and the simplest things of life are highlighted and made interesting."[29] To *As Thousands Cheer* he brought a strong satiric edge, as he had earlier to *Face the Music*.

As Thousands Cheer boasted the classic Berlin number "Easter Parade" and three memorable songs delivered by Ethel Waters: "Heat Wave," an animated weather report; "Harlem on My Mind," an affectionate send-up of American expatriate entertainer Josephine Baker; and the haunting ballad "Supper Time," which Waters sang as a rising backdrop proclaimed "UNKNOWN NE-GRO LYNCHED BY FRENZIED MOB." While the musical's theoretical star was Marilyn Miller, formerly of Ziegfeld fame, Waters practically stole the show.[30]

One reviewer put *As Thousands Cheer* in context of the battle being waged between Broadway and Hollywood: the Berlin-Hart revue "provides the stage with a formula to combat the inroads of Hollywood's musical comedy films." Another "modern direction" the show took was in its dance sequences, directed by Charles Weidman: "And so dancing, once an interlude of feminine exhibition, is becoming a highly specialized part of these modern revues, with a definite yearning toward the impressionistic."[31]

Reinvigorated by his recent success, but wary of Broadway's financial fickleness, Berlin flew to Hollywood in late 1934 to begin work on *Top Hat.* He had had some connections with films before—Al Jolson had sung Berlin's "Blue Skies" in *The Jazz Singer,* and Berlin added three new songs (although by long distance, from New York) to the Marx Brothers' film version of his 1925 comedy, *The Cocoanuts.* But early Hollywood had not proved welcoming, and a bad experience working on a film called *Reaching for the Moon* had seriously affected Berlin's confidence. "Musicals were the rage out there, and then they weren't," he later said. "Out went the songs. I developed the damnedest feelings of inferiority. I got so I called anybody in to listen to my songs. . . . I had two, 'Say It Isn't So' and 'How Deep Is the Ocean?' They're as good ballads as any I've written, but I didn't think they were good enough then."[32]

Top Hat would change all that, for this 1935 Astaire-Rogers film fielded a Berlin score containing what would become some of the most popular songs of the era, including "Cheek to Cheek," "No Strings," "Isn't This a Lovely Day (To Be Caught in the Rain)?" and the Astaire anthem, "Top Hat, White Tie and Tails." Berlin worked well with Astaire and even considered some of the performer's suggestions, such as singing "Cheek to Cheek" almost as if he were talking. Berlin told dance director Hermes Pan, "I'd rather have Fred Astaire introduce one of my songs than any other singer I know—not because he has a great voice, but because his delivery and diction are so good that he can put over a song like nobody else."[33]

Irving Berlin. By Ginger Rogers, c. 1937.

Roberta Olden.

Berlin immediately began work on the next Astaire-Rogers film, the 1936 *Follow the Fleet,* and the resulting score—while not the great success that *Top Hat* had been—included "We Saw the Sea," "I'm Putting All My Eggs in One Basket," and his haunting paean to the Depression, "Let's Face the Music and Dance." Two years later, Berlin contributed his last score to the Astaire-Rogers RKO cycle, *Carefree,* with numbers including "Change Partners," "I Used to Be Color Blind," and "The Yam." Now fifty, the songwriter was getting impatient with the Southern California way of life: "I feel slow in Hollywood," he reported. "The tempo there is slow."[34] He returned to New York in 1938—but it was to a changed Broadway, one depleted by the exodus of so many of his colleagues to Hollywood.

Like Irving Berlin, Cole Porter shuttled back and forth between Broadway and Hollywood in the thirties. Unlike Berlin, who had grown up on New York's Lower East Side and never lost an appreciation for its staccato rhythm, Porter eased comfortably into the "slowness"—and high living—of Hollywood. He had grown up in wealth in Peru, Indiana, before moving on to Yale (where he wrote the school's fight song, "Bingo, Eli Yale"). After marrying the rich and social Linda Lee Thomas, he caromed between the Art Deco fantasy

of well-heeled Manhattan and the white sands of Cap d'Antibes. Porter's life was guided by the philosophy that "anything goes"—in his shows even gangsters were swathed in a kind of sleekness and spoke in witty internal rhyme. As one Porter historian has put it, "his was a message of civilized cheer."[35] Style, elegance, sophistication—these were the renowned Porter characteristics that became virtually synonymous with the decade's glamour. Fellow songwriter Johnny Mercer said that Porter was "definitive" of that era: "He is the style of all those shows, all that period. He represents it better than anybody else. . . . Porter's so . . . thirties!"[36] It is hardly surprising that Fred Astaire's first starring film role was in a Porter vehi-

cle, *The Gay Divorcée* (1934). Astaire had starred in the 1932 Porter Broadway production, *The Gay Divorce*; on the silver screen, the combination of Astaire and Rogers dancing to "Night and Day"—the only original Porter song left in the script—was pure elegance.

The urbane Porter was best known for witty lyrics that were both colloquial and literate. This was evident most often in his "list songs," which were virtual catalogs of the contemporary culture. An amused chronicler more than a social critic, Porter scored his first genuine hit with the song "Let's Do It," from the 1928 Broadway show *Paris*, in which he delighted in juxtaposing "sedate barn-yard fowls" with "high-browed old owls." In his 1934 success *Anything Goes*, "You're the Top" combined Shakespeare's sonnets with Bendel's bonnets, Waldorf salads with Berlin's ballads, and Mahatma Gandhi with Napoleon brandy. *Anything Goes* has been called the "best 1920s musical of the 1930s" but recalls even more the buoyant musicals of the Princess Theatre days—not surprisingly, since two of his collaborators here were Princess Theatre veterans P. G. Wodehouse and Guy Bolton.[37]

Set on a transatlantic liner, this show featured Ethel Merman, for whom Porter relished writing such songs as "I Get a Kick out of You" (with its hedonistic references to champagne and cocaine) and "Blow, Gabriel, Blow." Born in Astoria to encouraging parents, Merman had begun her career at the local Republican Club at the age of five, billed as "Little Ethel Zimmerman"; she worked in vaudeville and nightclubs in her teens before making her sensational Broadway debut in the Gershwins' 1930 *Girl Crazy*.[38] Taken up next by composer Porter—as she would be a decade later by Irving Berlin—Merman solidified her showstopping reputation with *Anything Goes*, a romp whose emphasis was on pure, rich fun—and this in some of the darkest days of the Depression. Rather than a strong plot punctuated by song and dance, the show offered a loose arrangement of jokes, comic sketches, and a lot of bright, brassy music: the quintessential Merman mix.[39] Porter gave Depression audiences three hours of total escape, creating a shipboard atmosphere

Ethel Merman in
Anything Goes
(1934). By Van
Damm Studio.

Van Damm Studio
Collection, New York
Public Library for the
Performing Arts, New York
City.

that was scrupulously carefree; indeed, the ship existed as a world unto itself, disconnected from reality, happily floating somewhere out in the middle of the Atlantic. If the Gershwins and Irving Berlin had begun to take account of the current political and cultural scene in some of their shows—notably *Of Thee I Sing* and *As Thousands Cheer*—Porter pointedly did not. He would much rather write

Lyricist Lorenz Hart.

Rodgers and Hammerstein Organization, New York City.

> You're a rose,
> You're Inferno's Dante,
> You're the nose
> On the great Durante

COLE PORTER, "YOU'RE THE TOP," 1934

Another of the great lyricists of the thirties was Lorenz Hart, who, teamed with Richard Rodgers from 1919 to 1942, brought a cutting edge and wit to musical theater rivaled only by Ira Gershwin and Cole Porter. Like Porter, Hart indulged freely in the slang and colloquialisms so rampant in these years. "If it hadn't been for Larry Hart," Oscar Hammerstein later said, "none of us would have felt free to write colloquial lyrics. He took the way people talked and put them into lyrics."[40] Both Rodgers and Hart had grown up in middle-class Jewish families on New York's Upper West Side. When they first met in 1918, Rodgers was sixteen and Hart twenty-three. Even at sixteen, Rodgers was determined to become a composer. He had seen the Kern, Bolton, and Wodehouse Princess Theatre show *Very Good Eddie* a dozen times, later writing in his autobiography, "I was watching and listening to the beginning of a new form of musical theater in this country. Somehow I knew it and wanted desperately to be a part of it."[41] A friend recommended that he meet lyricist Hart, who was then looking for a composer to form a partnership with. Meeting at Hart's brownstone one Sunday afternoon, they listened to the songs of Jerome Kern and P. G. Wodehouse on the Victrola, and when Rodgers left, he said he had acquired "a career, a partner, a best friend, and a source of permanent irritation."[42] Hart—barely five feet tall and so tormented by his ambivalent sexuality that he was already an alcoholic—would prove a difficult partner indeed during the next twenty-five years, but his cynicism would be tempered by Rodgers's less-jaundiced worldview.

Their professional collaboration started auspiciously when the great Lew Fields bought their song "Any Old Place with You" (sample lines: "I'd go to hell for ya / Or Philadelphia") for his 1919 production *A Lonely Romeo*. After this initial good fortune, years of struggle followed. Just as they were about to end their partnership, they achieved critical and popular acclaim for their songs for the 1925 revue *Garrick Gaieties*, which included the memorable ditty "Manhattan," a jaunty paean to their hometown:

> We'll take Manhattan,
> The Bronx and Staten Island too.
> It's lovely strolling through
> The Zoo.

LORENZ HART AND RICHARD RODGERS, "MANHATTAN," 1925

Lorenz Hart, Richard Rodgers, and Margot Hopkins at rehearsal of *Pal Joey* (1940).

Rodgers and Hammerstein Organization, New York City.

"The Lady Is a Tramp," from *Babes in Arms* (1937). Sheet music.

National Museum of American History, Smithsonian Institution, Washington, D.C. © 1937 Chappell & Co. (renewed). Rights for the Extended Renewal Term in the United States Controlled by the Estate of Lorenz Hart and Williamson Music. Rights on behalf of the Estate of Lorenz Hart Administered by WB Music Corp. All Rights Reserved. Used by Permission.

Rodgers later wrote that "if one song can be said to have 'made' Rodgers and Hart, it surely was 'Manhattan.'"[43] This was followed by such moderate successes as 1927's *A Connecticut Yankee* and *Simple Simon* (1930). *A Connecticut Yankee*, a lively adaptation of the Mark Twain classic boasting such songs as "Thou Swell" and "My Heart Stood Still," reteamed them with impresario-director Lew Fields and his son, librettist Herbert Fields. *Simple Simon*, a romp for comedian Ed Wynn, featured Ruth Etting performing "Ten Cents a Dance," one of the most haunting songs of the Depression era.

In 1931 Rodgers and Hart joined their colleagues in Hollywood, where they spent the next four years. Their best work was heard in the 1932 Paramount film *Love Me Tonight*, a sophisticated Gallic fairy tale starring Maurice Chevalier and Jeanette MacDonald. The score contained the soaring ballad "Lover" (sung by MacDonald as she roamed the French countryside in a horse-drawn cart), and the lovely "Isn't It Romantic," which is used early in the film to establish the distinct personalities of the two leads. The set of lyrics for Chevalier's character, a bon vivant Parisian tailor, are cleverly sardonic—"Isn't it romantic? / While I sit around / My love can scrub the floor"—while those for MacDonald, a lonely chateau-bound princess are innocently optimistic: "Isn't it romantic? / He'll be strong and tall / And yet a slave to me."

Back on Broadway, they joined forces with George Abbott, first on the extravaganza *Jumbo* (1935) and, more important, on the landmark 1936 musical *On Your Toes*, which Rodgers and Hart had originally envisioned as a film for Fred Astaire. While Hollywood had begun to fuse song, dance, and action, Broadway in the mid-thirties still largely favored the revue format. However, choreographer George Balanchine—formerly of Diaghilev's Ballet Russe de Monte Carlo—demonstrated in *On Your Toes* how dance could become integral to the story, especially in the final scene, which featured stars Ray Bolger and Tamara Geva in a mini-ballet called "Slaughter on Tenth Avenue." Hart told an interviewer that he and Rodgers were seeking "a new form of musical show for Broadway and it will not be operetta. The songs are going to be part of the progress of the piece, not extraneous interludes without rhyme or reason." Rodgers concurred, saying, "I should like to free myself for broader motifs, more extended designs—but within the framework of the theater, for that is where I belong."[44] Their search would evolve over the next several years. *Babes in Arms* (1937) was not a major advance in form, although the score was bejeweled with such enduring songs as "The Lady Is a Tramp," "My Funny Valentine," and "I Wish I Were in Love Again"—the last containing the oft-quoted Hart lines,

> When love congeals
> It soon reveals
> The faint aroma of performing seals,
> The double-crossing of a pair of heels.

LORENZ HART AND RICHARD RODGERS, "I WISH I WERE IN LOVE AGAIN," 1937

George Abbott (1889-1995)

George Abbott.

Courtesy Mrs. George Abbott.

"His is the theater of snappy curtain lines, wise-cracking dialogue," critic George Jean Nathan once wrote of George Abbott, "all staged as if the author had used a pepper shaker in lieu of an inkwell." From the 1920s through the 1960s, "Mr. Abbott," as everyone called him, reigned as the dean of Broadway showmen. As play-wright, director, actor, producer, and play doctor, his career cataloged some of theater's greatest shows: *Jumbo* (1935), *On Your Toes* (1936), *The Boys from Syracuse* (1938), *Pal Joey* (1940), *On the Town* (1944), *Where's Charley?* (1948), *Call Me Madam* (1950), *A Tree Grows in Brooklyn* (1951), *Wonderful Town* (1953), *Pajama Game* (1954), *Damn Yankees* (1955), *Once upon a Mattress* (1959), *Fiorello!* (1950), and *A Funny Thing Happened on the Way to the Forum* (1962). And this is just a partial list of the more than 120 productions he was associated with on and off Broadway and on the road.

Six feet two inches tall and always standing ramrod straight, Mr. Abbott made an auspicious Broadway debut in *The Misleading Lady* (1913). He played twelve roles on Broadway during the next two decades, earning a reputation as the kind of actor who, according to journalist Heywood Broun, "could put over a kindly and sympathetic quality before he as much as spoke a line." At the same time he established himself as a successful playwright and director with the 1926 hit *Broadway*, which he directed and cowrote with Jed Harris; *Broadway* inaugurated a series of Abbott farces and musicals that would revolutionize the American theater. In a 1982 interview at the National Portrait Gallery, he said that the change he had effected had to do with fixing the "books" of these farces and musicals: previously "terrible," they would evolve in the hands of Abbott and his collaborators as narratives brimming with character and common

sense, and featuring songs that were integrated into the play's pattern.

By the late 1920s Abbott had also proved his talent as a "play doctor," often being brought in at the last moment to resuscitate plays that suffered various ailments during their pre-Broadway

George Abbott.

Courtesy Mrs. George Abbott.

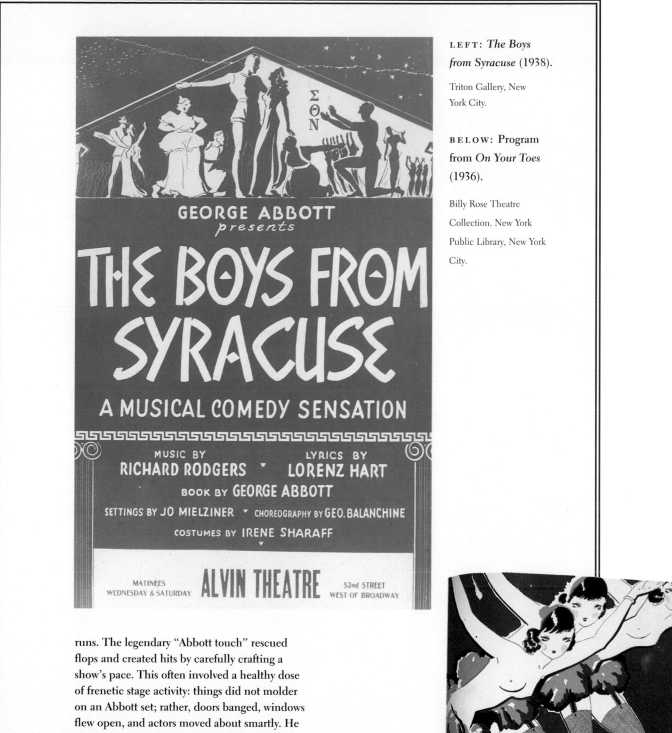

LEFT: *The Boys from Syracuse* (1938).

Triton Gallery, New York City.

BELOW: Program from *On Your Toes* (1936).

Billy Rose Theatre Collection. New York Public Library, New York City.

runs. The legendary "Abbott touch" rescued flops and created hits by carefully crafting a show's pace. This often involved a healthy dose of frenetic stage activity: things did not molder on an Abbott set; rather, doors banged, windows flew open, and actors moved about smartly. He also confessed to having a starmaking "Pygmalion complex" about actors, and over the years nurtured such careers as those of Ray Bolger, Shirley Booth, José Ferrer, Butterfly McQueen, Tom Bosley, Van Johnson, Carol Burnett, Shirley MacLaine, and Liza Minnelli. And, at the beginning of their careers, he took chances on such virtual unknowns as Leonard Bernstein, Jerome Robbins, Betty Comden and Adolph Green, Harold Prince, and Bob Fosse.

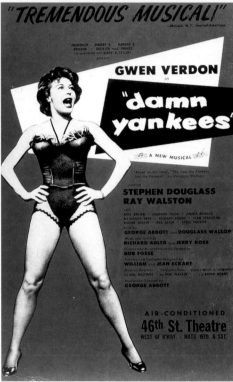

Abbott's hits included *The Pajama Game* (1954), *Damn Yankees* (1955), and *Fiorello!* (1959).

Triton Gallery, New York City.

Mr. Abbott did not like to be bored and never had much patience for plays that failed to amuse him or that carried some tendentious "message." He likewise dismissed the mumblings of "Method" actors, once saying that the magical "Abbott touch" consisted of forcing actors to "say their final syllables." To one unfortunate such actor, who deigned to ask Mr. Abbott what his "motivation" was for the play, the response was surgical: "Your job."

More in line with their ambitious theatrical goals was the political fantasy *I'd Rather Be Right* (1937), with George M. Cohan brought out of retirement to portray President Franklin D. Roosevelt, and *The Boys from Syracuse*, Broadway's first musical comedy to officially cite a Shakespearean work (*The Comedy of Errors*) as its source. But it was *Pal Joey* in 1940 that became the true capstone of Rodgers and Hart's contribution to the evolution of the American musical.

Pal Joey was derived from a series of thirteen short stories John O'Hara had written for the *New Yorker*. As O'Hara wrote Richard Rodgers in 1939, the stories were about "a guy who is master of ceremonies in cheap nightclubs, and the pieces are in the form of letters from him to a successful bandleader." O'Hara thought they might be made into a successful book musical and wondered if Rodgers and Hart would be interested in working on it.[45] They were, and the resulting 1940 show would be a major step in the progress of Broadway "book musicals"—that is, those that closely integrate music and story. The score included

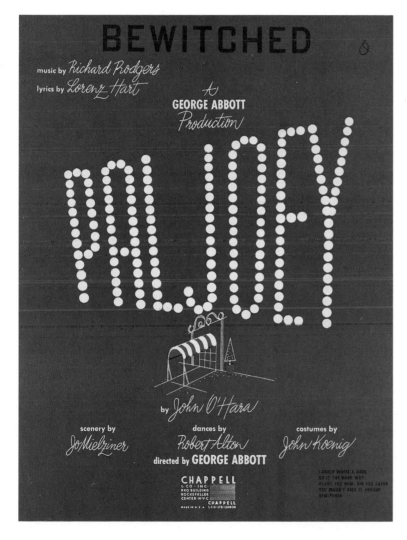

"Bewitched," from *Pal Joey* (1940). Sheet music.

"Bewitched, Bothered, and Bewildered," a lusty, matter-of-fact confession delivered in the original production by Hart's friend Vivienne Segal in the role of a libidinous society matron,

> I'm dumb again,
> Numb again,
> A rich, ready, ripe little plum again,
> Bewitched, bothered, and bewildered, am I.
>
> LORENZ HART AND RICHARD RODGERS,
> "BEWITCHED, BOTHERED, AND BEWILDERED," 1940

as well as "Zip," a striptease parody that lightened up the harsh realism of the show,

> Zip!
> That Stokowski leads the greatest of bands.
> Zip!
> Jergens Lotion does the trick for his hands.
> Zip!
> Rip Van Winkle on the screen would be smart.
> Zip!
> Tyrone Power will be cast in the part.
>
> LORENZ HART AND RICHARD RODGERS, "ZIP," 1940

There was one romantic ballad, "I Could Write a Book," sung by a young Gene Kelly in the title role. But even it was used cynically as Joey's pick-up line aimed at the show's gullible ingenue. The show made no attempt at a traditional happy ending.

With *Pal Joey*, Rodgers and Hart advanced musical theater to the next step in what had been a slow Broadway progression from *Show Boat* to *Of Thee I Sing* and *Porgy and Bess*. But the way *Pal Joey* dwelled on the dark side of human nature was still not something easily accepted by Broadway audiences: although the production had a successful run, many still wondered, along with *New York Times* critic Brooks Atkinson, "Can one draw sweet water from a foul well?" What were musicals for, anyway?

To that, Marc Blitzstein provided an ideological answer. In 1937 the Federal Theatre Project produced—and Orson Welles directed—*The Cradle Will Rock*, Blitzstein's blistering socialist attack on "The Rich." The year before, when asked if he composed for a specific audience, he responded, "Since my orientation is toward a proletarian society and a revolutionary art, the answer . . . is yes. . . . Music is intended for somebody, not nobody."[46] *The Cradle Will Rock* takes place in Steeltown, U.S.A., and features the anti-union "Liberty Committee," the town boss Mr. Mister, Reverend Salvation, and the union-organizing hero, Larry Foreman. Blitzstein takes colloquial dialogue into new realms of idiomatic authenticity, writing and setting to music the vernacular speech of immigrants, blue-collar workers, and what he considered the "petty bourgeoisie." The searing title song sounded a cry for action that demanded to be heard:

> Well, you can't climb down
> And you can't say no.
> You can't stop the weather
> Not with all your dough.
> And when the wind blows
> And when the wind blows
> The cradle will rock!
>
> MARC BLITZSTEIN, "THE CRADLE WILL ROCK," 1937

Richard Rodgers and Lorenz Hart (far left) **in a production meeting for** *By Jupiter* **(1942). By Mary Morris.**

Richard Rodgers Collection, New York Public Library, New York City.

Orson Welles, director of Project 891, one of the Works Progress Administration's Federal Theatre Project outlets, was to direct *The Cradle Will Rock* for the Actors' Repertory Company, with John Houseman as producer. Will Geer was chosen to play Mr. Mister, and Howard da Silva was Larry Foreman; there was also a mixed black and white chorus numbering forty-four.

Although it had a strong ideological bent, the play was intended not so much as a truly "agitprop"—agitational propaganda theater—piece as it was a warning and challenge to the middle class: in the historic struggle for industrial unionism, it asked, which side are you on? As word of the play's leftist slant seeped down to Washington, Martin Dies and his House Committee on Un-American Activities became increasingly worried. On June 10, six days before the play was to open, Federal Theatre personnel in New York were notified that they were to be cut by 30 percent; furthermore, no new openings could take place before July 1. Publicity people for the Federal Theatre announced that the show had been canceled, and armed guards were posted at the doors of the Maxine Elliott Theater, where the play was to have opened, to ensure that no one removed any Federal Theatre property, including sets, props, costumes, and scores. Meanwhile, Actors' Equity informed Welles that none of the performers, while employed by the Federal Theatre, could appear *on stage* in this production in any other location. So Welles and Houseman suggested that the actors perform from the *interior* of whatever house they could find, acting out the play from the audience.

As it happened, they found a site at the Venice Theater, a run-down building that currently served as home to a weekly Italian variety show. An overflow crowd of 1,742 saw the

Marc Blitzstein at the Moviola composing the score to *Valley Town*.

Wisconsin Center for Film and Theater Research, Madison.

The Cradle Will Rock, left to right: Howard da Silva, Bert Weston, Olive Stanton, Marc Blitzstein (at piano), and Blanche Collins. By Al Hirschfeld, 1938.

National Portrait Gallery, Smithsonian Institution, Washington, D.C.

show go on—not with an orchestra, but with a piano; not with full staging, but with a single working spotlight; and with the performers acting out their parts from seats in the house. And when it was all over, the audience exploded; as John Houseman wrote in his memoir of the event, they were "not sure what they were applauding—the girl, the song, Marc or the occasion."[47] Although it ran only until July 1, the play would be revived by popular acclamation in December: the whole thing had become a cause célèbre, to the point that critics now embraced it. Walter Winchell, for one, who had somehow missed the June production, now called it one of the town's "better diversions," while *New York Times* critic Brooks Atkinson praised it as "the best thing militant labor has put into a theatre yet."[48]

From Berlin to Blitzstein, songwriters of the thirties were preoccupied by the reinvention of American culture and helped to define the changing national experience through their words and music. The America of a "genteel," rural, and largely local tradition had disappeared, transformed by vast immigration, urban industrialism, and the centrifugal forces of the Depression. Into that vacuum, a nationally based popular culture arose to web the country together. Films, radio, recordings, and high-circulation newspapers and magazines—all were part of a media-generated entertainment culture that forged a national audience in the thirties. And musicals, because of their central role in American entertainment, helped to create the unifying new myths and social ideals.

Such cultural mythmaking was aided considerably by the fact that the thirties were, as John Updike has written in an essay on Cole Porter, a "heyday of light verse: there were book reviews in verse, and sports stories; there were droll ballades and rondeaux and triolets."[49] Magazines such as the *Saturday Evening Post* and *Collier's* flooded the newsstands with verse and short stories laced with vernacular language; Hollywood films and national network radio carried the word to neighborhoods and households. This milieu itself nurtured a golden age of popular song, and lyricists such as Porter, Gershwin, and Hart were some of the decade's greatest cultural troubadors.

Marc Blitzstein and Leonard Bernstein at Tanglewood in Massachusetts, July 1946.

Wisconsin Center for Film and Theater Research, Madison.

The theater audience in the late days of the Depression had come to accept (if not embrace) not only Blitzstein's "proletarian" musicals, but the seamy fatalism of *Pal Joey* in 1940. The next year they were mesmerized by playwright Moss Hart's adventurous collaboration with Kurt Weill (music) and Ira Gershwin (lyrics) in *Lady in the Dark*, starring Gertrude Lawrence. Hart here drew from his own experiences with Freudian psychoanalysis—considered wildly avant-garde in New York in these years—to create a play that he saw as "completely experimental." It featured "Four revolving stages, fifty-one stagehands, a full orchestra, company of over a hundred."[50] The play introduced Danny Kaye in a rollicking tongue-twister of a song called "Tchaikovsky," but the show belonged to Gertrude Lawrence, whose rendition of "Jenny" became a musical milestone. *New York Times* critic Brooks Atkinson wrote, "All things considered, the American musical stage may take a bow this morning. . . . Moss Hart's musical play uses the resources of the theatre triumphantly and tells a compassionate story magnificently . . . the music and the splendors of the production rise spontaneously out of the heart of the drama. . . . [A]s for Gertrude Lawrence she's a goddess; that's all."[51]

In addition to such soul-searching musicals as *Pal Joey* and *Lady in the Dark*, at the end of the Depression audiences flocked to the sugary escapism of Hollywood operettas. The operetta strain had been present from the earliest "all talking, all singing, all dancing" days, beginning with Warners' 1929 film version of *The Desert Song*, starring John Boles. In the early thirties, Paramount invested its reputation in an

Eleanor Powell (1912-1982)

"I would rather dance than eat! Dancing to me is some sort of a God," Eleanor Powell once declared. "It encompasses you. . . . Very possessive. I really didn't know what the outside world was all about when I was making pictures." Appearing in vaudeville as a teenager, she became a Broadway star at seventeen in *Follow Through* because of a sensational tap routine: she had learned the routine by having her feet weighed down by sandbags, so the resulting lightness in performance gave her dancing a true aerial quality.

"Once I was identified as a tap dancer, that was it!" she later explained. "Because nobody had ever seen that kind of thing before." She was soon appearing in *George White's Music Hall Varieties* (1932), and most notably in the 1935 Broadway production *At Home Abroad*,

ABOVE: Eleanor
Powell in *Born to
Dance* (1936).

RIGHT: "I've Got
You Under My Skin,"
from *Born to Dance*
(1936). Sheet music.

Alice Becker Levin.

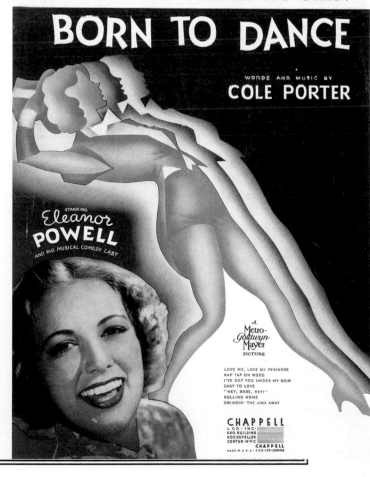

staged and designed by Vincente Minnelli.
Discovered by Hollywood, she appeared in the
1935 film of *The George White Scandals*. For
the next fifteen years, Eleanor Powell would star
in movie musicals for MGM, where her quintessential technical tap ability made her one of
America's iconic musical performers.

Her two best-remembered dance sequences
were the ritual drum dance in *Rosalie* (1936), in
which she pique-tap-turned down a series of
drum heads, and the unforgettable "Begin the
Beguine" number she danced with Fred Astaire
across a black glass floor in *Broadway Melody of
1940*. But Ellie Powell always retained a
nonchalant view of the magic she had brought
to the silver screen: "A tap dancer is nothing
but a frustrated drummer! You're a percussion
instrument with your feet! You're a musician!"

operetta cycle that featured Jeanette MacDonald and Maurice Chevalier, notably in the 1932 *Love Me Tonight*, directed by Rouben Mamoulian, and in Ernst Lubitsch's 1934 *The Merry Widow*. But this drift into pseudo-European settings and lush romanticism was derailed by the turn toward musicals set in the harsher reality of Depression-era America, led by the loud burst of dancing feet along "naughty, gaudy, bawdy" *42nd Street*.

It would be left to MGM to pick up the gauntlet, and the studio dedicated to "More Stars Than There Are in Heaven" would do so in its own inimitable way. This was the studio, after all, whose head—Louis B. Mayer—made it his credo that "My unchanging policy will be great star, great director, great play, great cast. Spare nothing, neither expense, time, nor effort. Results only are what I am after."[52] Mayer soon had all the major non-heavenly stars hoofing, starting with Joan Crawford and Clark Gable in *Dancing Lady* (1933)—which has been aptly described as lacking the "vitality and the brazen, amusing vulgarity of the Warners spectacles."[53] MGM's reach for a higher elegance was no fluke, but it was at once obvious that Crawford's destination lay elsewhere. The studio then enlisted Eleanor Powell, arguably the best female tap-dancer to appear on film. MGM constructed a series of *Broadway Melody* musicals around Powell, beginning with *Broadway Melody of 1936*, starring Powell, Robert Taylor, and Jack Benny. The production numbers tended to be splashy enough, though without Berkeley's touch; the music, by Arthur Freed and Nacio Herb Brown, included some good numbers—"I've Got a Feelin' You're Foolin'" and "My Lucky Star"; but the high point centered on Powell's tap-dance, "Sing before Breakfast," which she performed on a New York rooftop.

In the *Broadway Melody of 1938*, Powell was teamed again with Taylor, and the music again was that of Freed and Brown. The last of the *Melody* films was the best, when Powell was paired with Fred Astaire for the *Broadway Melody of 1940*. Performing here for the first time in an MGM film since a cameo appearance in *Dancing Lady*, Astaire danced companionably with Powell—their mutual admiration was clear. As Astaire wrote in his memoir, *Steps in Time*, Ellie Powell "really knocked out a tap dance in a class by herself."[54] Their circular tap performance to Cole Porter's "Begin the Beguine" was sheer magic and formed an elegant conclusion to the whole *Melody* cycle.

Another MGM musical foray began in 1939, when the studio teamed Mickey Rooney with Judy Garland, who had just completed filming *The Wizard of Oz*. They had already appeared in two films together, including *Love Finds Andy Hardy*, but their new partnering would prove most lucrative for Metro. Their first bona fide musical was to be *Babes in Arms*, based on the 1937 Broadway hit by Rodgers and Hart; it would be directed by Busby Berkeley, hired away from Warners by MGM production chief Arthur Freed.[55] The plot involved a group of old-time vaudevillians who go on tour, while a group of "youngsters"— that is, Garland and Rooney and company—decide, "Let's put on a show!" The interpolated musical numbers include "I Cried for You," "I'm Just Wild about Harry," and the ultrapatriotic "God's Country," written by E. Y. "Yip" Harburg and Harold Arlen: there was no mistaking the country's mood in this 1937 song, especially in the line, "We've got no Duce—we've got no Fuhrer / But we've got Garbo and Norma Shearer."[56] The only Rodgers and Hart songs left were the title song, "Where or When," and a quick orchestral excerpt from "The Lady is a Tramp." *Babes in Arms* was a huge success—a New York showing caused such a stampede of filmgoers that the police had to be called out—and the "Mickey-and-Judy" musicals were launched.

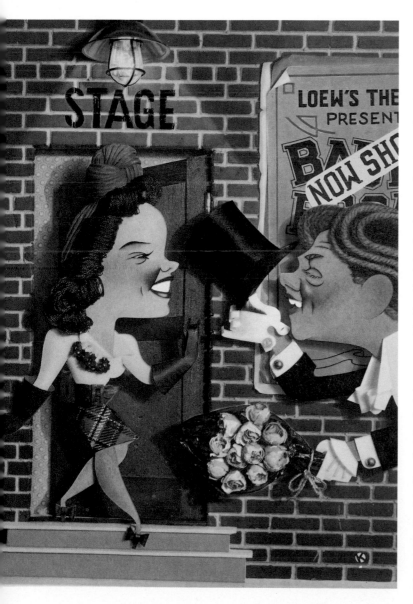

Judy Garland and Mickey Rooney in *Babes on Broadway* (1942). By Joseph Kapralik.

Michael Kaplan Collection.

The next film for the popular box office duo was *Strike Up the Band* (1940), with the title being the only remnant of the earlier Gershwin Broadway show. Laden with the heavy-handed sentimentality favored by Louis B. Mayer, the story follows Mickey's travails as he attempts to win a dance contest sponsored by Paul Whiteman. Judy plays the band singer who falls for Mickey, and, after several missteps, the two get together and all ends well. Berkeley's involvement is especially evident in a big production number called "Do the Conga," as well as in the flag-waving finale to the title song.[57]

In 1941 *Babes on Broadway* again combined Mickey and Judy, with Busby Berkeley as director. This was basically a reprise of the "let's put on a show" variety, with the great saving grace that Garland and Rooney were allowed to display their talents. The musical numbers include "How about You?" "Hoe Down," and a boffo finale—albeit in blackface—in which Garland belts out "Franklin D. Roosevelt Jones" and "Waiting for the Robert E. Lee."

Although they would sing "I Wish I Were in Love Again" for the 1948 Rodgers and Hart "bio-pic" *Words and Music*, Mickey and Judy's final full-length musical pairing came in *Girl Crazy* (1943), which was only vaguely related to the smash 1930 Gershwin show. Here, Mickey goes west, where he discovers Judy in Cody, Wyoming; they put on . . . a rodeo! The Gershwin music remains superb and includes "Bidin' My Time," "Could You Use Me?" "But Not for Me," "Embraceable You," and Berkeley's show-stopping finale, "I Got Rhythm." Although the Mickey-and-Judy films were box office favorites, they were not MGM's most extravagant musical outlay. It was simply unnecessary to spend more, from Louis B. Mayer's perspective, as these films could project the fresh-faced,

Mickey Rooney and
Judy Garland. By
Harold Edgerton,
1985 from 1940 nega-
tive.

National Portrait Gallery,
Smithsonian Institution,
Washington, D.C.
© The Harold E. Edgerton
1992 Trust, courtesy of
Palm Press, Inc.

middle-class family values for which they were intended without enormous expenditures on spectacle. Extravagance was left for a special indulgence, the series of operettas that would star Mayer's adored Jeanette MacDonald and a newcomer named Nelson Eddy.

Jeanette MacDonald had begun her career as a chorus girl at New York's Capitol Theatre in 1917. During the twenties, she appeared in several Broadway shows and starred in the successful 1927 run of *Yes, Yes Yvette*, in which she was billed as "the girl with gold-red hair and sea-green eyes." In 1929 Ernst Lubitsch saw her screen test and signed the co-quettish MacDonald to appear in his first sound film, *The Love Parade*, with Maurice Chevalier. She and Chevalier would appear together in *One Hour with You* (1932), *Love Me Tonight* (1922), and *The Merry Widow* (1934); *The Merry Widow*'s failure at the box office ironically led to MacDonald's best-known work, her pairing with Nelson Eddy in a greatly popular cycle of film operettas. Because she was such a favorite of Mayer's, he decided to showcase her in a 1935 production of *Naughty Marietta*. Very loosely based on the 1910 Victor Herbert–Rida Johnson Young operetta, the film would be the first to team MacDonald with Nelson Eddy, a young baritone with a background in opera and radio. There is a persistent rumor in Hollywood lore that MacDonald at first did not want to play the "tiresome" role of Princess Marie de la Bonfain, and that Mayer had to get down on his knees and sing to her to convince her; overcoming that challenge, she nevertheless accepted the role.

Set mostly in colonial America, the story is a spun-sugar concoction about a disguised French princess (Jeanette) and a captain of a mercenary troop (Nelson). It was the music rather than the plot that counted in this film, with such renowned Herbert songs as "Tramp, Tramp, Tramp," "'Neath the Southern Moon," "The Italian Street Song," "I'm Falling in Love with Someone," and the unforgettable "Ah, Sweet Mystery of Life."

The release of *Naughty Marietta* launched a popular vogue for MacDonald-Eddy films, and it was quickly followed up by the 1936 *Rose Marie*. The plot involves Marie (MacDonald), a popular opera singer, trying to protect her fugitive brother (a young James Stewart) after he has killed a Mountie while escaping from prison. The intrepid Mountie trailing the brother is the typecast, stoic Nelson Eddy—and, inevitably, Marie and the Mountie fall in love. The score by Rudolf Friml, Herbert Stothart, Oscar Hammerstein II, and Otto Harbach is well known and often parodied, particularly "Indian Love Call," which Jeanette and Nelson sing as they paddle a canoe across a moonlit lake.

The next year, MGM produced *Maytime*, remotely adapted from Sigmund Romberg's 1917 operetta. Considered perhaps the best of the MacDonald-Eddy films, it was set at a 1906 May festival in which an older woman recalls life in the court of Louis Napoleon, when she was young and in love. There are opera sequences and a lavish court ball; the featured Jeanette-Nelson duet is one of their best known, Romberg's "Will You Remember (Sweetheart)." *May-*

Jeanette MacDonald on the cover of *Modern Screen* magazine, October 1937.

Alice Becker Levin.

SEND YOUR SNAPSHOT—WIN TRIP TO EUROPE! See Page 24

Modern Screen

OCTOBER 10 CENTS

THE LARGEST CIRCULATION OF ANY SCREEN MAGAZINE

Hepburn, HOLLYWOOD'S SHOW-OFF!

Jeanette MacDonald

Jeanette MacDonald and Nelson Eddy in *Rose Marie* (1936).

time was a great success, and although they appeared in several more films—including *The New Moon* (1940)—it also proved to be the high point of their work together. Through their series of films, MGM had succeeded in bringing high-gloss operetta to the screen, conveying—through the style of acting, sets, costumes, and European-rooted music—the sense of "culture" with which Mayer longed to be associated.

If MGM had been established as the most glamorous and elitist of the studios, Mayer had also insisted on its "moral" leadership, whether by demanding that its stars lead unblemished (public) lives or by imparting middle-class moral values to the films that bore

the Mayer imprimatur. But MGM was not alone in its moral quest, for over at newly merged Twentieth Century-Fox, Darryl F. Zanuck—who had left Warners after securing Busby Berkeley for them—was intent on purveying a studio style that featured such family entertainment as homespun comedies, fictionalized histories, and light musicals. As head of production, he attempted to provide Depression America with comfortable patriotic fare that would reinforce traditional values, at least as defined by Darryl F. Zanuck. And the centerpiece of his campaign was a five-year-old bedimpled moppet named Shirley Temple.

Before she had signed to do the Fox feature film *Stand Up and Cheer* in 1934, Shirley was already a veteran of a series of "Baby Burlesque" shorts—one-reel takeoffs on famous films and glamorous stars, with toddlers in diapers playing the parts. She graduated easily into full-length films and instantly tapped into something deeply responsive in the American spirit, cheering it on during the Depression. The nation's top box office attraction for four years, from 1935 to 1938, she would make more than forty films—including *Curly Top, The Littlest Rebel, Wee Willie Winkie*, and *Heidi*—and become America's darling; newsreels captured her charming everyone from the Roosevelts to Amelia Earhart.

The Shirley Temple–Fox films themselves often offered few redeeming story lines: in *Stand Up and Cheer,* a new cabinet post is created for the government—the secretary of amusement. His job is to banish all negative thoughts; when he ultimately succeeds, he declares, "The Depression's over!" But kitschiness did not matter. The "basic ingredient of the child alone," film historian Jeanine Basinger has argued, "was mixed together with crusts of old codgers, heaps of adoring adults, pinches of heartbreak, and generous helpings of cheerful poverty (which quickly melted into lavish living)—all stirred up with the subtlety of a McCormick reaper and garnished with a few songs and dances."[58] The songs and dances

Dear Friend,
    Will you please come to my birthday party on April 23, 1938
    Shirley Temple.

did matter, because of the way young Shirley put them across—singing "On the Good Ship Lollipop," in *Bright Eyes* (1934), dancing the stair dance with Bill Robinson in *The Little Colonel* (1935), or tapping merrily through a large-scale production number with George Murphy in *Little Miss Broadway* (1938).[59]

The Little Colonel was the first of four films to team Shirley with Bill "Bojangles" Robinson—followed by *The Littlest Rebel* (1935), *Rebecca of Sunnybrook Farm* (1938), and *Just around the Corner* (1938). He also did the choreography for *Dimples* (1936). Robinson had toured on the black TOBA circuit and was one of the few African American dancers to star on the Keith vaudeville circuit before venturing to Hollywood. He would make fourteen films for major studios between 1930 and 1939, most popularly those with Shirley Temple, where he performed such of his best-known routines as the stair dance. Called the greatest tap-dancer of his time—it was once said that he "had castanets for feet"—Robinson was one of the few African Americans to appear in mainstream studio musicals in these years: he starred in the first all-black talking film, *Harlem in Heaven* (1932), and would later have a leading role in MGM's 1943 film, *Stormy Weather*.[60]

In general, the major studios offered little to African Americans until the 1950s, when Harry Belafonte and Dorothy Dandridge broke through the color barrier as major stars in Twentieth Century-Fox's 1954 *Carmen Jones*. In addition to Robinson, and excluding the studios' very few all-black films such as *Cabin in the Sky* and *Stormy Weather*, among those who appeared in mainstream Hollywood during the thirties were Academy Award winner (for *Gone With the Wind*) Hattie McDaniel, the Nicholas Brothers, Buck and Bubbles, Ethel Waters, and Lena Horne.[61]

Lena Horne, arguably the most successful African American to create a career in Hollywood in this era, began her career as a sixteen-year-old singer at Harlem's Cotton Club, where she worked with such top names as Duke Ellington, Count Basie, Cab Calloway, Ethel Waters, and Billie Holiday. She toured with several bands, including that of Noble Sissle, and appeared in Lew Leslie's 1939 edition of his perennial *Blackbirds* revue on Broadway. She went to Hollywood in 1942 and made a sensation at the Little Troc Club; columnist Elsa Maxwell wrote that Lena Horne "has Hollywood agog. She has put poise into seduction, dignity into daring; she has given glamour manners."[62] MGM composer and arranger Roger Edens heard her at the Troc and orchestrated an audition with producer Arthur Freed, who put her under contract—only the second African American woman to sign with a major Hollywood studio.[63] Her first appearance was a specialty spot in the 1942 film version of Cole Porter's 1940 Broadway hit, *Panama Hattie*. This led to her costarring role as the temptress Georgia Brown in MGM's

Bill Robinson. By George Hurrell, 1935.

National Portrait Gallery, Smithsonian Institution, Washington, D.C.
© 1935 by the Condé Nast Publications, Inc.

**Lena Horne. By
Edward Biberman,
1947.**

National Portrait Gallery,
Smithsonian Institution,
Washington, D.C.

all-black 1943 film version of *Cabin in the Sky.* The 1940 Broadway show of *Cabin in the Sky* had enjoyed modest success, with a score by Vernon Duke and John Latouche and choreography by Katherine Dunham and George Balanchine; the Broadway cast was headed by Ethel Waters and included Dunham, Todd Duncan, Dooley Wilson, and Rex Ingram.

The MGM decision to film an all-black musical was considered risky; only three other such films had been produced previously by major studios—King Vidor's 1929 *Hallelujah*, Fox's *Hearts in Dixie* the same year, and Warners' 1936 music drama, *The Green Pastures*.[64] Ethel Waters would repeat her starring role in *Cabin in the Sky*, with Horne replacing Dunham and Eddie "Rochester" Anderson taking on the Dooley Wilson part; E. Y. "Yip" Harburg and Harold Arlen were commissioned to add to the original Duke-Latouche score. Upon its release in April 1943, *Cabin in the Sky* proved an enormous success. Yet, astonishingly enough, this, and a loan-out to Twentieth Century-Fox for the 1943 all-black musical *Stormy Weather*, would be the only acting assignments Lena Horne would garner in her seven years at Metro: she appeared in several more films, including *As Thousands Cheer* (1943), *Ziegfeld Follies* (1946), and *Till the Clouds Roll By* (1946) but henceforth always as an elegantly gowned chanteuse limited to guest shots that could easily be edited out for Southern theaters.[65]

Inescapably linked to the wider culture and clearly dependent on its acceptance, musicals during the Depression rarely wandered far from what was perceived to be—at least by the major studios and Broadway investors—a common cultural ground. And one theme most commonly expressed in nearly all thirties musicals, stage and screen, was that if people rolled up their sleeves and worked hard enough, good would triumph over evil and the show would go on—whether it was Ruby Keeler "going out a youngster, coming back a star" or Fred and Ginger picking themselves up, dusting themselves off, and starting "all over again." At some point, literally or metaphorically, the inevitable announcement would be made that "the Depression's over!"

If Broadway ended the era with the less sanguine message of *Pal Joey*, Hollywood wafted along in unwavering faith. Two film musicals in the late thirties especially encapsulated this optimism, although in very different ways: Walt Disney's first animated feature, *Snow White and the Seven Dwarfs* (1937), and MGM's *The Wizard of Oz* (1939).

Katherine Dunham (b. 1912)

Katherine Dunham was the first to bring African American dance to the concert stage in the early 1930s. One of the founders of the anthropological dance movement, she distilled elements of Caribbean and African ritual into modern American choreography. Attending the University of Chicago, she studied anthropology and founded a dance company alternately called the Ballet Nègre and the Negro Dance Group; the Ballet Nègre performed Dunham's first notable piece of choreography—"Negro Rhapsody"—at the 1931 Chicago Beaux Arts Ball.

Researching her master's thesis, she absorbed the cultures of Jamaica, Martinique, Trinidad, and Haiti in the mid-1930s. When she returned to Chicago, she incorporated some of the cultures she had seen in her fieldwork into her choreography, explaining that from the first she "aimed at sociological as well as artistic targets." In 1940 the vibrant dancer appeared in and helped to choreograph (with George Balanchine) the all-black Broadway production, *Cabin in the Sky*, where her performance was described as "torrid."

When the national tour of *Cabin* ended in San Francisco, Dunham and her company remained in California. Her sinuous, colorful choreography can be seen in the 1941 film version of *Cabin in the Sky*, as well as in a Technicolor short film for Warner Bros. called *Carnival of Rhythm*, which depicts a dawn-to-dusk slice of everyday Caribbean life. Two years later, she and her company appeared in one of their most successful films, *Stormy Weather*, starring Lena Horne and Bill Robinson. Her legs now insured by Lloyd's of London, Katherine Dunham continued her film career in such films as *Casbah* (1948) and *Mambo* (1950), but concentrated on concert works such as "Carib Song" (1945), "Bal Nègre" (1946), and "Brazilian Suite" (1950).

A pioneer of dance performance, Dunham has been described by fellow choreographer Agnes de Mille as having "given us a panorama of black dancing in the West which is historically important and aesthetically beautiful and moving."

Katherine Dunham.
By Paul Colin,
c. 1962.

National Portrait Gallery,
Smithsonian Institution,
Washington, D.C.

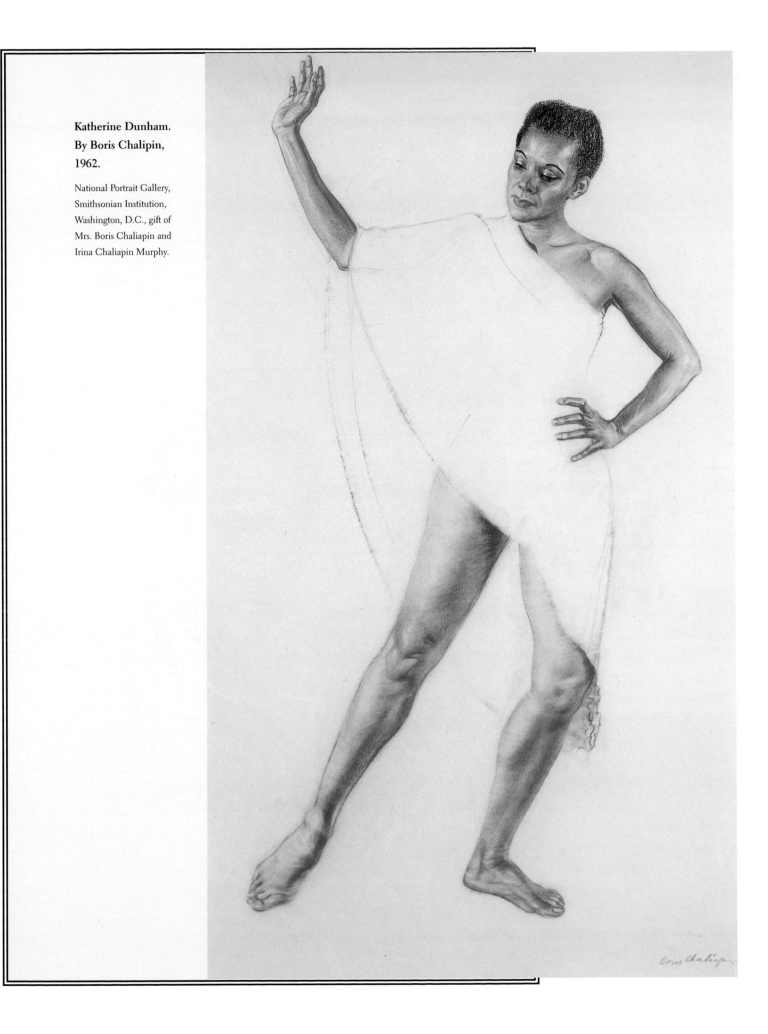

Katherine Dunham. By Boris Chalipin, 1962.

National Portrait Gallery, Smithsonian Institution, Washington, D.C., gift of Mrs. Boris Chaliapin and Irina Chaliapin Murphy.

The Brothers Grimm version of *Snow White* was too violent for Disney, who made the story less menacing by toning down the still-frighteningly wicked stepmother-crone. In addition, the score (by Frank Churchill and Larry Morey) had a softening effect, with such songs as "Some Day My Prince Will Come," "Whistle While You Work," and "Heigh-Ho." Scenes depicting everyday life contributed to a homespun sensibility as well, such as the dwarfs washing up for dinner, or dancing to welcome Snow White. For Disney, the movie represented a nostalgic look at a simpler and happier past—one distant from the daily media reports about unemployment, labor unrest, and rising poverty. His cartoon short, *The Three Little Pigs*, had carried a similar moral message: released in May 1933 in the midst of the New Deal's "hundred days" campaign of legislation to turn the Depression around, the cartoon's cheerily defiant song, "Who's Afraid of the Big, Bad Wolf," became a national hit. What Disney harkened back to were the pastoral days of pre-urban America, when the rules of the "genteel tradition" still held fast. The resolution to *Snow White* is never really in question: Snow White will ride off with her Prince Charming, and the Queen will die at the hand of her own wickedness.[66]

Snow White opened at Radio City Music Hall on December 21, 1937, with few aside from Walt Disney himself believing that a cartoon based on a Brothers Grimm fairy tale could capture the public imagination. But the film was received with an outpouring of popular and critical approval—so much so that other Hollywood studios quickly looked around for a comparable project. *The Wizard of Oz* emerged as the favorite; at one time, according to the *New York Times*, five major studios were bidding for rights, then owned by Samuel Goldwyn.[67] *The Wonderful Wizard of Oz* had first appeared in 1900 as a book written by L. Frank Baum. Two years later Baum had rewritten it for Broadway, where Ziegfeldian Julian Mitchell helped to turn it into a "musical extravaganza" featuring vaudevillians Fred Stone as the Scarecrow, and David Montgomery as the Tin Woodman. There had been a one-reel film version in 1910 and a silent in 1925 in which Oliver Hardy played the Tin Man. In 1933 Goldwyn negotiated to get film rights, planning to make *Oz* with Eddie Cantor as the Scarecrow. When Cantor refused to renew his contract, Goldwyn lost interest, and MGM later decided to acquire it as a star vehicle for the young Judy Garland.

Judy Garland had spent her early childhood on the vaudeville circuit as part of an act known as the "Gumm Sisters"—a name that changed to the "Garland Sisters" after Frances Gumm changed her name to Judy Garland when she was twelve. Touring in

Walt Disney. By Samuel Johnson Woolf, 1938.

National Portrait Gallery, Smithsonian Institution, Washington, D.C.

ABOVE: Publicity
cel for *Snow White
and the Seven Dwarfs*
(1937).

Stephen H. Ison.

BELOW: Cel for
Snow White singing
"I'm Wishing" at the
wishing well, 1937.

Stephen H. Ison.

This original release poster for the animated film *Snow White and the Seven Dwarfs* (1937) was designed by Gustaf Tenggren.

Stephen H. Ison.

"Some Day My Prince Will Come," from *Snow White and the Seven Dwarfs* (1937). Sheet music.

Alice Becker Levin.

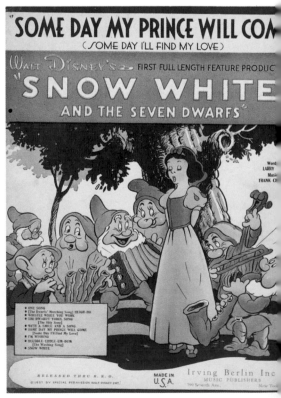

Hollywood in the fall of 1934, the sisters appeared as a "prologue" at Grauman's Chinese Theater. *Variety* reviewed them and singled Judy out as turning the trio into "class entertainment." She had a voice that could be heard throughout the large Grauman: "She handles ballads like a veteran, and gets every note and word over with a personality that hits audiences. . . . Nothing slow about her on hot stuff and to top it, she hoofs. Other two sisters merely form a background."[68]

It was arranged for twelve-year-old Judy to sing at one of MGM producer Joseph L. Mankiewicz's parties. Mankiewicz later recalled that her voice was "something incredible

Judy Garland (center), when she was Frances Gumm, performing with the "Gumm Sisters," c. 1933.

Photofest.

even then and you knew, as you sat there, that you were in the presence of something that wasn't going to come around again in a long time."[69] He promised to approach Louis B. Mayer about signing her, although Mayer's taste ran more to waltz-filled operettas. A screen test was subsequently arranged, with Garland performing a version of "Casey at the Bat." Mayer was not overwhelmed but told Ida Koverman, the head of his personal staff, "If you want her, sign her." She signed a seven-year contract with MGM in September 1935, at $100 per week. The studio then spent some time trying to figure out what to do with the now teenage Garland; in 1936 they paired her with another young singer, Deanna Durbin, for a one-reel short called *Every Sunday*, in which Durbin sang in her style—"classical"—while Garland sang in hers—"hot." Judy next appeared in a minor role in *Pigskin Parade* (1936), but she got her break in the *Broadway Melody of 1938* for singing "Dear Mr. Gable (You Made Me Love You)." She was also in *Thoroughbreds Don't Cry* (1937) and, in 1938, *Everybody Sing*, *Love Finds Andy Hardy*, and *Listen, Darling*.

In February 1938 MGM announced that it had acquired the screen rights to *The Wizard of Oz* and that Garland had been cast as Dorothy. Billie Burke, Margaret Hamilton, Bert Lahr, Ray Bolger, Jack Haley, and Frank Morgan would eventually round out the cast, while E. Y. "Yip" Harburg and Harold Arlen were signed to write the score. Harburg wrote "Over the Rainbow" for the early part of the film, in scenes depicting Kansas in a sepia monochrome. He later said that he was "writing for a situation of a little girl who was desperate, had never seen anything beyond an arid Kansas where there was no color in her life. . . . It was all brown and sepia . . . she wanted to escape in a song of escape—where could she go? The only thing colorful that she's ever seen in her life was the rainbow": "Somewhere, over

the rainbow, / Skies are blue, / And the dreams that you dare to dream, / Really do come true" (E. Y. Harburg and Harold Arlen, "Somewhere over the Rainbow," 1939). In the film, Dorothy would leave drab Kansas behind by climbing over the rainbow to the colorful world of Munchkinland.[70] Arlen at first thought it too weighty a song for "a little girl in Kansas," but changed his mind as he came to know Garland. Later, he recalled that "Judy was an unusual child. . . . Just like a great cantor, she combined the superb voice with an understanding of the music and lyrics. . . . Judy Garland was to singing what Gershwin's music was to music. They brought a quality and vitality that was typically and uniquely American."[71]

Shooting finished in March 1939, and press previews that August were enthusiastic. Many agreed with the *Los Angeles Examiner* that it was "just as much a screen classic as was *Snow White*," while the *New York Times* called Garland's Dorothy "a pert and fresh-faced miss with the wonder-lit eyes of a believer in fairy tales."[72] *Oz* was an accessible Depression-era parable—proposing, as *Snow White* had in its own way, a nostalgic view of the American past.

The Wizard of Oz forecast an era of musicals that not only fully integrated story, music, and dance but boasted a deep fascination with Americana. Like *Oz*, Rodgers and Hammerstein's 1943 Broadway sensation *Oklahoma!* would be set in the country's rural heartland. When Curly sings of "The bright, golden haze on the meadow," it is as much an affirmation of the pastoral American tradition as when Dorothy, having been returned to her Kansas farm after seeing the wonders of Oz, proclaims, "There's no place like home." Both clearly marked the end of Depression-based musicals: if Broadway and Hollywood had helped to forge a national popular culture in the thirties, they now began a self-conscious campaign to refashion that culture along more traditional, homespun lines. Instead of glamorous production numbers on enormous, Bakelite stages, the setting was more likely to be Kansas in August. It was a long way from Forty-second Street.

"Over the Rainbow," from *The Wizard of Oz* (1939). Sheet music.

Alice Becker Levin.

There's a bright golden haze
on the meadow
There's a bright golden haze
on the meadow
The corn is as high
As a elephant's eye
And it looks like it's climbin'
Clear up to the sky.

OSCAR HAMMERSTEIN II AND
RICHARD RODGERS, "OH, WHAT A
BEAUTIFUL MORNING," 1943

New York, New York, a helluva town
The Bronx is up and the
Battery's down
The people ride in a hole in
the ground
New York, New York
It's a helluva town!

BETTY COMDEN, ADOLPH GREEN,
AND LEONARD BERNSTEIN, "NEW
YORK, NEW YORK," 1944

The Heights

In the early 1940s, when the harsh effects of the Depression were abruptly superseded by World War II, the American musical effervesced with a renewed spirit of patriotism and an embracing of all that sprouted from native soil. This nostalgia for America's regional cultural heritage had an immediate and enduring effect on the American stage and film musical, creating generations of works that transformed folk elements and aspects of local color into the stuff of the commercial entertainment industry.

Along with its concerted efforts to portray vibrant, idealized aspects of American life, the American musical assumed a new maturity and adventurousness in form and content. More than ever before, music, drama, dance, and decor combined into a glorious *Gesamtkunstwerk*. Ambitious, more substantive narrative topics became essential to the progress of the genre. And this bold experimentation was driven by a period of wild commercial success, both on stage and on screen. No longer was profit measured solely by

Mary Martin in costume for *South Pacific.* **By Philippe Halsman, 1949.**

© Halsman Estate.

RIGHT: Broadway during the war years: the marquee for *Meet Me in St. Louis* (1944) proclaimed "War Bonds on sale here."

Academy of Motion Picture Arts and Sciences, Los Angeles. Courtesy Turner Entertainment Co.

TOP, LEFT:
Richard Rodgers composing "Bali Ha'i" for *South Pacific* (1949) at Joshua Logan's apartment, c. 1948.

Rodgers and Hammerstein Organization, New York City.

BOTTOM, LEFT:
Oscar Hammerstein wrote his lyrics while standing at his specially built desk.

Rodgers and Hammerstein Organization, New York City.

ABOVE: Richard Rodgers and Oscar Hammerstein in front of *The King and I* marquee, 1951.

Rodgers and Hammerstein Organization, New York City.

ticket sales. A variety of subsidiary outlets, headed by the recording and broadcast industries, made musicals America's most financially prosperous entertainment genre.

Without question, Richard Rodgers and Oscar Hammerstein II stand in the forefront of those artists and craftsmen of the 1940s whose work ushered in what would be, in retrospect, perhaps the most expansive era in the evolution of the American musical. Throughout the decade and into the next, they devised a series of shows that have proved extraordinarily durable, with an optimistic, upbeat point of view that conveys, to quote one of their songs, "plenty of heart and plenty of hope."[1] Their landmark *Oklahoma!*, easily the most influential musical of its generation, brilliantly, if belatedly, fulfilled the promise of *Show Boat* nearly two decades earlier in reinterpreting distinctly American themes and traditions. For all its determinedly homespun facade, the show was, and is, amazingly sophisticated in its approach, presenting a laudable meshing of drama, dance, and song.

The creative impetus for *Oklahoma!* came from Theresa Helburn, codirector of the Theatre Guild, the prestigious organization that had been founded in 1918 to present classic and contemporary dramatic works on Broadway. With her colleagues Lawrence Langner and Armina Marshall, Helburn, a soft-spoken, diminutive dynamo, had established the Theatre Guild as a major force in the American theater. But by the early 1940s the Guild was nearly bankrupt. Helburn had the idea that a musical version of Lynn Riggs's play *Green Grow the Lilacs*, which the Guild had produced in New York a decade earlier, might refill the organization's all-but-empty coffers. As Helburn recalled in her autobiography, she envisioned the work as "a new type of play with music, not musical comedy, not operetta in the old sense, but a form in which the dramatic action, music, and possibly ballet could be welded together into a compounded whole, each helping to tell the story in its own way."[2] She first approached Rodgers and Hart to make the adaptation. But Hart was too engulfed in willful self-destruction to muster any enthusiasm for the project and walked out on Rodgers, ending the team's twenty-two-year partnership. Rodgers turned immediately to Oscar Hammerstein II, whose career was in the doldrums.[3] Curiously, Hammerstein had recently tried, and failed, to interest his frequent partner Jerome Kern in a musical version of the Riggs play. Shortly thereafter, Rodgers and Hammerstein signed contracts with the Theatre Guild and embarked on their first collaboration.[4] One of the earliest results of their joint labors was the show's opening number, "Oh, What a Beautiful Morning," which exquisitely evoked the homespun optimism and romanticism that would be so integral to their adaptation of Riggs's play and their work in general:

Oh, what a beautiful mornin'
Oh, what a beautiful day
I got a beautiful feelin'
Everythin's goin' my way.

OSCAR HAMMERSTEIN II AND RICHARD RODGERS,
"OH, WHAT A BEAUTIFUL MORNING," 1943

Hammerstein's libretto borrowed freely from Riggs's original play in recounting the story of early twentieth-century Oklahoma territory farm folk and cowboys. With its sunlit perspective and evocative uses of regional dialect and folkways, Hammerstein's script affirmed all that was good about being an American. Rodgers's melodies were beguilingly

Agnes de Mille (far right) and dancers rehearsing for the film version of *Oklahoma!* By Burt Glinn, 1955.

© Magnum Photos.

Agnes de Mille in the ballet *Rodeo* (1943). By Maurice Seymour.

Courtesy Ronald Seymour.

appropriate to the locale and period, capturing the naive energy of hoedowns and folk ballads while revealing his remarkable gifts as a theater composer.

For the other key figures in the production team, Helburn hired Rouben Mamoulian as director, Agnes de Mille as choreographer, and Lemuel Ayers as scenic designer. Russian-born Mamoulian had already attained legendary status as a director in both the musical theater and the musical film. High among his Broadway accomplishments was his direction of the original 1935 Broadway production of *Porgy and Bess.* For the screen, he directed two milestones in the early film musical: *Applause* (1929), a tender-tough look at the world of burlesque starring Helen Morgan, and the Jeanette MacDonald–Maurice Chevalier vehicle, *Love Me Tonight* (1932).[5] On the other hand, de Mille was essentially a neophyte at staging a Broadway musical, with a reputation solely built upon her involvement in the world of ballet.

The daughter of playwright William C. de Mille and niece of film epic director Cecil B. De Mille, Agnes de Mille was born of show business royalty. She received her training in her native California and choreographed dances for several films, including her uncle Cecil's 1934 version of *Cleopatra.* Her work for the commercial musical theater was limited to the dances for the 1933 London production of Cole Porter's musical *Nymph Errant* and those for the Broadway productions *Flying Colors* (1933) and *Hooray for What?* (1937), although she was fired from the last two shows during their pre-Broadway tryouts. After further study in Europe, she was commissioned by the American Ballet Theatre in 1942 to stage *Rodeo*, a new ballet with a score by Aaron Copland. Her choreographic patterns and captivating performance of the leading role, that of a tomboyish cowgirl, won immediate acclaim for the striking synthesis of classical ballet and a variety of popular dance styles, the latter including square dances and tap routines. Helburn, recognizing the vigorous Southwestern spirit captured in the ballet, dispatched a telegram to de Mille the day after *Rodeo*'s opening, inviting her to join with Rodgers, Hammerstein, and Mamoulian on the *Green Grow the Lilacs* project. Although de Mille would not always agree with her collaborators, she shared their desire to make the dances an integral part of the narrative.

The coup de grace of de Mille's contribution to the show was the justly famous ballet "Laurey Makes Her Mind Up," which closes the first act. The sequence created dramatic suspense in the narrative, conveying solely through dance the triangle of conflicting emotions among the characters of farm girl Laurey Williams, cowpoke Curly McLain, and sinister farmhand Jud Fry. In Hammerstein's original outline, the number was planned as a razzle-dazzle circus ballet, incorporating the trendy pop Freudianisms that had infiltrated the American musical two seasons earlier in the fabulously successful *Lady in the Dark*, which had a circus dream sequence of its own. De Mille argued that razzle-dazzle under the Big Top was all wrong in illustrating Laurey and her romantic predicament. "We've got to get inside that girl's mind," she insisted, and then she fashioned a strikingly original ballet that did just that.[6] Using classically trained ballerinas and ballerinos as dance counterparts for Laurey, Curly, and Jud, she staged the entire number as if viewed from Laurey's naively romantic perspective, merging the naive innocence of the dream with the unstoppable horror of the nightmare. Music, story, and dance were combined with levels of artistry and narrative pertinence that had never been quite achieved previously on Broadway.

Helburn recruited her design staff from alumni of previous Theatre Guild productions. Her decision was artistic as well as pragmatic, for these designers were already used to working within the organization's tiny budgets. Miles White credited the inspiration for his costumes to the illustrations he found in a 1904–5 Montgomery Ward catalog.[7] Lemuel Ayers studied the paintings of Grandma Moses as background in preparing his scenic decor, which consisted primarily of stylized painted drops depicting broad expanses of farmlands fronted by spare uses of wing pieces and props. Of Ayers's work, Helburn recalled fondly, "He captured at once the clear blue blaze of sky we wanted, the hot yellow sunshine of Oklahoma, the shades of wheat and tall corn."[8]

In its development and rehearsal stages, the show, known then as *Away We Go!* was cattily deemed "Helburn's Folly" by the theatrical cognoscenti. Impresario Mike Todd, upon viewing the New Haven tryout, delivered the now-famous riposte, "no gags, no girls, no chance." Undaunted, Rodgers, Hammerstein, Mamoulian, and de Mille continued to refine their work under Helburn's sage guidance. It was Helburn who suggested the title switch to *Oklahoma!* after a number in the show, which Rodgers and Hammerstein had written in response to her request for a "song about the earth." On March 31, 1943, *Oklahoma!* opened at the St. James Theatre in New York to rapturous praise. "The most thoroughly and attractively American musical comedy since Edna Ferber's *Show Boat* was done by this same Hammerstein and Jerome Kern," raved Burns Mantle in his review in the *New York Daily News*.[9] Immediately, *Oklahoma!* fever overtook Broadway, creating an

Scene design for the dream ballet in Act 1 of *Oklahoma!* (1943).

Rodgers and Hammerstein Organization, New York City.

Singer Alfred Drake rose to fame as Curly in *Oklahoma!* Here he is shown in costume for *Kismet.* By Everett Raymond Kinstler, 1978.

Players Club Collection, New York City.

unprecedented demand for tickets that led to a run of 2,212 performances and a residency that endured for over five years. Of the original company, the all-but-unknown Alfred Drake parlayed his success in the role of Curly into a career that made him the preeminent male musical theater star of his era.

Alfred Drake (né Alfredo Capurro), a native New Yorker, had his first professional experience singing in stock productions of Gilbert and Sullivan. He made his Broadway debut in 1936 in the operetta *White Horse Inn* as a member of the chorus and as understudy to its star, William Gaxton. Featured roles in such shows as *Babes in Arms* (1937) and *One for the Money* (1939) brought him to the attention of Rodgers and Hammerstein, who elevated him to leading man status in *Oklahoma!* In the 1940s, he appeared frequently in the American musical theater, in such varied fare as the folk anthology *Sing Out Sweet Land!* (1944) and as Macheath in *Beggar's Holiday* (1946), John Latouche and Duke Ellington's adaptation of the John Gay ballad opera, *The Beggar's Opera.* Drake found his finest role in Cole Porter's *Kiss Me, Kate* (1948), as the volatile, Orson Welles–inspired impresario Fred Graham. In 1953 he won his only Tony Award as the wily beggar Hajj in *Kismet*, a gaudy but popular show strongly rooted in Viennese operetta traditions. In addition to his onstage baritone bravura, Drake also distinguished himself as a librettist and as a director.

Soon, the *Oklahoma!* mania spread like wildfire across the nation and around the world through various efforts and sources. Of course, as with many previous musicals, the sheet music of songs from the show was widely promoted. In October of 1943, a national tour embarked on a route that would endure, with cast replacements, until May 1954. A London production (with a largely American cast) opened in 1947 to great acclaim at the historic Royal Drury Lane Theatre and paved the way for innumerable productions in other European cities. But what made the initial production of *Oklahoma!* such a household word across the country and around the world was the set of recordings produced by Decca executive Jack Kapp that exclusively featured members of the original Broadway company performing the songs as they did in the theater.[10] These were not, contrary to legend, the first American recordings of a theater score made by its original New York cast.[11] However, no previous effort had captured quite so vividly on disc the sheer exhilaration of the Broadway musical experience from overture to finale, from the out-and-out hits to the less familiar character songs. More than anything, these recordings solidly confirmed that the music and lyrics for *Oklahoma!* are essential ingredients in the narrative structure of the show and not just a series of traditionally catchy, easily isolated popular songs.[12]

Curly (Alfred Drake) and Laurey (Joan Roberts) in *Oklahoma!*

Rodgers and Hammerstein Organization, New York City.

Carousel, the second association of Rodgers, Hammerstein, Helburn, de Mille, and Mamoulian, proved that the team's triumph with *Oklahoma!* was by no means a fluke. Dark and mystical where its predecessor is bright and forthright, *Carousel* is yet another excursion into romanticized American regionalism, transplanting the Budapest locale of Hungarian playwright Ferenc Molnar's tragic fantasy *Liliom* to the sand- and sea-washed coast of Maine in the 1870s. But, even more than *Oklahoma!*, *Carousel* charged at the boundaries and expanded the artistic horizons of the commercial musical. Story, song, dance, and spectacle blend harmoniously to convey a narrative that is both intimate and epic in its emotions.

In retelling Molnar's drama of a brutish carnival barker and the quiet but strong-willed woman who loves him, Rodgers and Hammerstein created what endures as their most consistently adventurous and mature exercise in Americana. Innovations abound throughout the work. As in *Oklahoma!*, dance is integral to the narrative. In lieu of an overture, the first-act curtain rises on an atmospheric de Mille ballet that swiftly defines the mutual attraction between the two principal characters, Billy Bigelow and Julie Jordan. Later, in Act II, another ballet illustrates the troubled adolescence of Billy and Julie's coltish daughter Louise. Spoken dialogue is used sparingly throughout, and whole scenes are revealed principally through the elements of song. The most impressive of these song sequences is Billy Bigelow's "Soliloquy," the first number the authors composed for the score. In an ambitious eight-minute song-aria of operatic proportions, Billy contemplates his impending fatherhood and considers the prospects of being a father to a son or a daughter. As in much of the rest of the score, Hammerstein's words for the piece are both universal and character-specific. It is the work of a seasoned dramatist who has learned to manipulate the traditions of the theater lyric for its maximum effect. The original Broadway production of *Carousel* was further distinguished by its remarkable cast, headed by John Raitt and Jan Clayton.

Rodgers favored *Carousel* among his own works. Hammerstein preferred the 1947 musical *Allegro*, the team's final association with the Theatre Guild. An ambitious and con-

ABOVE: Window card for *Carousel* (1945).

Courtesy Triton Gallery, New York City.

RIGHT: Jo Mielziner preparing scenery for *By Jupiter* (1942). By Mary Morris.

Richard Rodgers Collection, New York Public Library, New York City.

troversial theatrical experiment, *Allegro* was a Norman Rockwell-esque view of the joys and eccentricities of everyday American life, recalling the atmosphere of Thornton Wilder's 1939 drama *Our Town.* The libretto, an episodic account of a boy's passage from birth and childhood to maturity, strived, according to Hammerstein, to be a modern allegory "about a man not being allowed to do his own work because of worldly pressures."[13] Its characters, including its Everyman hero, were archetypal rather than three-dimensional, and a large onstage vocal ensemble, functioning like the chorus in ancient Greek drama, provided omniscient musical commentary throughout on the play's action.

Just as Theresa Helburn's vision had guided the formation of both *Oklahoma!* and *Carousel*, Rodgers and Hammerstein asserted complete control over every aspect of *Allegro*'s genesis. Early on in the development process, they brought in de Mille. Promoting her to the exalted post of director-choreographer, they charged her to create patterns of continuous movement that would seamlessly mesh the dialogue scenes and musical numbers. Seeking a physical production as adventurous as the script, the score, and the staging, they engaged Jo Mielziner, who had created the sets for *Carousel* two seasons earlier.

Jo Mielziner had begun his career in stage design in the late 1910s, working as an apprentice in the scenic studios of Joseph Urban.[14] Subsequently, he studied with theatrical-design titans Robert Edmond Jones and Lee Simonson. From the latter, he learned to appreciate and assert the integral importance of evocative lighting in the overall effect of scenic design.[15] In addition to his work for countless Broadway dramas and comedies, he contributed settings to such vintage musicals as *Of Thee I Sing* (1931), *Gay Divorce* (1932), *On Your Toes* (1936), *The Boys from Syracuse* (1938), *South Pacific* (1949), *The King and I* (1951), and *Gypsy* (1959).

Mielziner's design for *Allegro* completely discarded the stylized realism considered so de rigueur in musicals of the era. Instead, his scenery recalled the stark architecture found in playing areas of ancient Greek theater buildings. The central element in the design was an unadorned two-leveled platform that left most of the stage clear for de Mille's animated stage pictures. Locality and focus were established throughout by the use of evocative lighting, suggestive fragments of sets and props sliding in and out of the wings, and a series of abstract painted drops and images projected onto the upstage cyclorama. These elements allowed Mielziner to achieve a graceful fluidity throughout the production, keeping the action virtually continuous and making virtually unnecessary any stage waits for the shifting of scenery. His work for *Allegro* often brought striking visualization to Joseph Urban's dictum that "speed is the essential of the musical show."

For all its lofty aims and innovations, *Allegro* failed to win the critical acclaim and financial prosperity enjoyed by *Oklahoma!* and *Carousel*. Critics were sharply divided on its merits. Louis Kronenberger found it "a very grave disappointment," while his colleague Richard Watts Jr. proclaimed it "another landmark in pushing back the frontier of the American musical drama." Both the nine-month Broadway run and subsequent brief national tour proved to be commercial disappointments, and the RCA Victor cast recording captures precious little of the impressive score. Undeservedly far less familiar than the other 1940s Rodgers and Hammerstein classics, *Allegro* reveals Hammerstein's adventurous interpretation of Americana.

While its locale was an exotic and remote Polynesian island, *South Pacific* was perhaps Rodgers and Hammerstein's most complex view of American life and values. Based on *Tales of the South Pacific*, James Michener's Pulitzer Prize–winning collection of intertwined short stories, the show was remarkably adult and, for its era, remarkably realistic in its perspective on U.S. military life during World War II. Moreover, the script had as its principal leitmotif a controversial, benignly militant stance against the seeds of racial intolerance, a weighty and timely issue for the likes of a postwar Broadway musical.[16] This view was manifested in Hammerstein's lyrics for "(You've Got to Be) Carefully Taught," a bitter, ironic indictment of bigotry:

> You've got to be taught to be afraid
> Of people whose eyes are oddly made
> And people whose skin is a different shade
> You've got to be carefully taught.

OSCAR HAMMERSTEIN II AND RICHARD RODGERS,
"(YOU'VE GOT TO BE) CAREFULLY TAUGHT," 1949

The libretto, a collaboration between Hammerstein and the show's director, Joshua Logan, centered on two Michener stories: "Our Heroine," about the wartime romance between Navy nurse Nellie Forbush and French planter Emile de Becque; and "Fo' Dolla,'" which recounts the bittersweet and ultimately tragic affair between Marine lieutenant Joe Cable and island girl Liat. To leaven the plot with much-needed humor, Hammerstein and Logan interpolated two of Michener's most colorful characters: Liat's mother, a Rabelaisian Tonkinese named Bloody Mary, and her nemesis, the enterprising Luther Billis, who were rivetingly portrayed in the original production by Juanita Hall and Myron Mc-Cormick, respectively. Although lacking the expansive musico-dramatic brilliance of *Carousel* or the lyric audacity of *Allegro*, the score for *South Pacific* is notable for containing perhaps the highest quota of Rodgers and Hammerstein's most memorable songs, including such classics as "A Cock-Eyed Optimist," "Some Enchanted Evening," "There Is Nothing like a Dame," "Bali Ha'i," "I'm Gonna Wash That Man Right Outta My Hair," "A Wonderful Guy," "Younger than Springtime," and "This Nearly Was Mine."

Whatever it might have in common with its predecessors, *South Pacific* presented definite departures from the previously established Rodgers and Hammerstein formula for musical theater success. Primary of these was the absence of de Mille story ballets; in fact, the show had no formal choreography (or choreographer) at all. In place of the stylized pliés and tours jetés were naturalistic movements attuned to the realism inherent in the script. Jo Mielziner's physical production, a succession of exotic tableaux bathed in rays of hot orange, sunny yellow, and cool

Window card for *South Pacific* (1949).

Courtesy Triton Gallery, New York City.

Jo Mielziner's transformation backdrop for "Bali Ha'i," from *South Pacific* (1949).

Robert L. B. Tobin Collection, courtesy Marion Koogler McNay Art Museum, San Antonio, Texas.

aqua, elaborated on the seamless, near-cinematic scene-to-scene transitions that were introduced in *Allegro*. To imbue the production with near-operatic surges of emotion beyond the set musical numbers, orchestral underscoring was used extensively throughout in the spoken dialogue scenes. Much of the innovation revealed in *South Pacific* was deservedly credited to the show's director and coauthor, Joshua Logan.[17]

Joshua Logan conducted his theatrical studies at Princeton University, where he was one of the founding members of the University Players, and with Constantin Stanislavski at the Moscow Art Theatre. Although he had his first assignment on Broadway as director in 1935, he did not direct for the musical theater until 1938, when he guided the Rodgers and Hart musical *I Married an Angel* to success. Throughout the 1940s and 1950s, he was at the helm of such musicals as *By Jupiter* (1942), *Wish You Were Here* (1952), and *Fanny* (1954). Above all, Logan's direction for the musical theater was distinguished by a healthy earthiness and vibrant naturalism.

South Pacific offered one other major departure from Rodgers and Hammerstein's previous efforts. Unlike *Oklahoma!*, *Carousel*, and *Allegro*, which had casts of talented unknowns, *South Pacific* had bona fide luminaries in its two principal roles. Ezio Pinza, the noted Metropolitan basso, made an impressive Broadway debut as Emile de Becque, singing the ethereal "Some Enchanted Evening." But it was Mary Martin, in the role of all-American girl Nellie Forbush, whose incandescent performance confirmed her status as one of brightest stars of the American musical theater.[18]

Mary Martin started performing as a tot in her native Weatherford, Texas, regaling family and friends with her prodigious imitations of Fanny Brice and torch-singer Ruth Etting. As a young woman, she headed west to Hollywood, where she tried, with virtually no success, to establish a career in motion pictures.[19] In 1938 her agent Buddy Schwab sent her to New York for a chance at Broadway. There, she won immediate and lasting fame in the Cole Porter musical *Leave It to Me!* with her coy rendition of (and modest striptease to) "My Heart Belongs to Daddy."

Martin briefly returned to Hollywood, where she played leading roles in several undistinguished Paramount film musicals. Turning down the chance to play Laurey in the original company of *Oklahoma!* she made a triumphant return to Broadway in the Kurt Weill–Ogden Nash–S. J. Perelman musical *One Touch of Venus*. Her spirited performance in the national touring company of *Annie Get Your Gun* persuaded Rodgers and Hammerstein to cast her in *South Pacific*. During the 1950s and 1960s, Martin appeared fre-

quently in stage musicals, including the classics *Peter Pan* (which she subsequently presented on television) and *The Sound of Music* (1959), the latter reuniting her with Rodgers
and Hammerstein. Perhaps more than any other female performer of her generation, she
typified the musical theater heroine of the golden age of the American musical: virginal
yet spirited, boisterous but tender, and more cozily small-town than sophisticatedly urban.
For her effervescent charm and enduring commitment to the lyric stage, Martin earned
the sobriquet "the First Lady of the American Musical Theater."

Following *South Pacific*, Rodgers and Hammerstein wrote five more stage musicals: *The
King and I* (1951), *Me and Juliet* (1953), *Pipe Dream* (1955), *Flower Drum Song* (1958),
and *The Sound of Music* (1959). Although only three of these had American locales, they
all revealed lingering evidences of the simplicity and vigor of the American spirit, which
was such a central message in their first four theatrical efforts.[20] Moreover, Rodgers and
Hammerstein's stylistic approach and its subsequent artistic and commercial success
proved overwhelmingly influential on the musical theater of the 1940s and 1950s. Americana, in various colorful guises, abounded on Broadway in works by other authors as varied as *Bloomer Girl* (1944), *Finian's Rainbow* (1947), *The Golden Apple* (1954), and *The
Music Man* (1957).[21] Rodgers and Hammerstein themselves sponsored one of the finest
and most financially profitable works in this vein not to emerge from their own pens. Assuming the roles of Broadway producers, they were vital forces behind the rollicking 1946
musical comedy *Annie Get Your Gun*.

Most likely, there never would have been an *Annie Get Your Gun* without Dorothy
Fields. It was she who conjured up the idea of starring her good friend Ethel Merman as
sharpshooter Annie Oakley and persuaded her childhood cronies Rodgers and Hammerstein to serve as producers.[22] The daughter of knockabout comic and impresario Lew
Fields and sister of dramatists Joseph and Herbert Fields, her first ambition was to be an
actress; however, her efforts were continually thwarted by her father, who grew irate at the
mere mention of such an aspiration. Determined somehow to join the world of show

ABOVE,
OPPOSITE: Richard
Rodgers, Oscar
Hammerstein, Joshua
Logan, and Leland
Hayward taking a cur-
tain call with the cast
at Mary Martin's last
performance in *South
Pacific*, June 1, 1951.

Rodgers and Hammerstein
Organization, New York
City.

BELOW,
OPPOSITE: Mary
Martin in *Peter Pan*
(1954).

Photofest.

ABOVE, LEFT:
The Sound of Music
(1959).

Courtesy Triton Gallery,
New York City.

ABOVE, RIGHT:
The King and I
(1951).

Courtesy Triton Gallery,
New York City.

Dorothy and Lew Fields, c. 1928.

Harry Ransom Humanities Research Center, The University of Texas at Austin.

business, Dorothy chose an alternate route into the theatrical world, trading her dreams of an onstage career for a life offstage as a lyricist and librettist. Her earliest professional efforts, written with composer Jimmy McHugh, were created for several editions of the revues at Harlem's famed nightspot, the Cotton Club. Fields and McHugh moved onto Broadway with the songs for *Blackbirds of 1928*, which was designed to capitalize on the twenties mania for shows that were showcases for African American performers. In the 1930s Fields, like so many of her colleagues, moved to the West Coast and forged a successful career as a screen lyricist. In 1936 she and her frequent collaborator Jerome Kern won an Oscar for the song "The Way You Look Tonight," which was written for the Astaire-Rogers film *Swing Time*. The song's words bear glowing evidence of colloquiality, wit, and dramatic flavor, all of which are hallmarks of the Fields lyric. Beginning in 1941, she teamed with brother Herbert on the scripts for a number of successful, if formulaic stage musicals, including the wartime hit *Something for the Boys* (1943), which had songs by Cole Porter and starred her pal Merman.[23]

In addition to coauthoring (with her brother Herbert) the script for *Annie Get Your Gun*, Fields was also originally slated to write the show's lyrics to Jerome Kern's music. Kern's death threw the project into a tailspin. Rodgers suggested Irving Berlin as Kern's replacement, although Berlin's tradition of writing both the words and music meant that

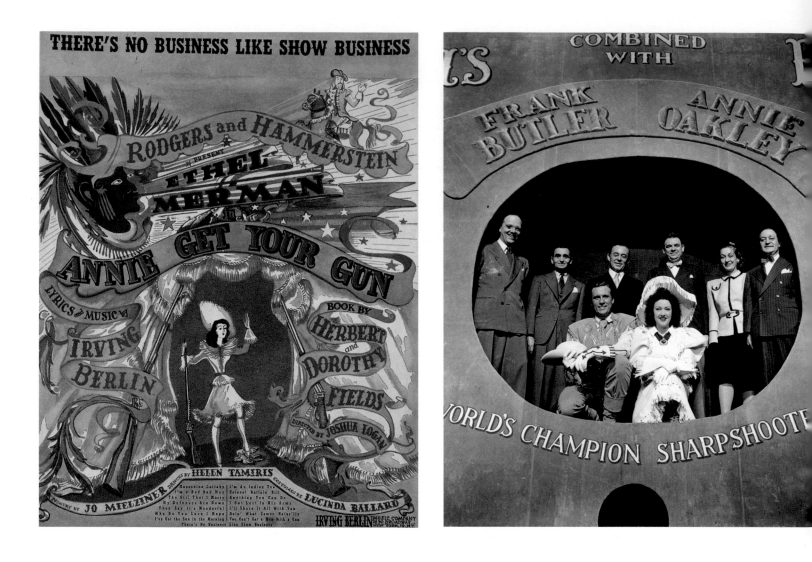

Dorothy would have to relinquish her job as the show's lyricist. When Berlin accepted the challenge, she happily turned over the job, encouraging him to transform whole portions of the script's dialogue into song. In doing so, she facilitated Berlin's transition from a Broadway tunesmith of another era into a full-fledged member of the modern musical theater. To be sure, the score had its share of hit parade winners, including the ballad "They Say It's Wonderful" and the anthem "There's No Business like Show Business"; however, it also contained songs rooted in situation and character, like Annie's comic-pathetic assessment of herself:

I'm quick on the trigger
With target not much bigger
Than a pin point, I'm number one
But my score with a feller
Is lower than a cellar
Oh, you can't get a man with a gun.

IRVING BERLIN, "YOU CAN'T GET A MAN WITH A GUN," 1946

The show also gave Ethel Merman a chance to alter and refine her stage persona from a flinty, jazzy self-caricature to a more complex and vulnerable, albeit spirited, woman.

LEFT: "There's No Business Like Show Business," from *Annie Get Your Gun* (1946). Sheet music.

National Museum of American History, Smithsonian Institution, Washington, D.C.

RIGHT: Ray Middleton, Ethel Merman, and the creative team for *Annie Get Your Gun*, 1946. By Eileen Darby.

Rodgers and Hammerstein Organization, New York City.

Lacking the artistic ambitions (some would say pretensions) of an *Oklahoma!* or a *Carousel*, *Annie* is, in itself, a fascinating hybrid. At its heart, it was a genuine star vehicle in the grand tradition of Cohan or Ziegfeld. However, the influence of Rodgers and Hammerstein's vision is apparent throughout the show, from its character-rooted songs and reliance on dance to propel the story (as in Helen Tamiris's ballet that illustrates Annie's initiation into the Sioux tribe) to its overall romantic evocation of a colorful era in America's more innocent past.

In terms of artistic and financial prosperity, the only other composer-lyricist/librettist team to rival Rodgers and Hammerstein's reign was Alan Jay Lerner and Frederick Loewe. In the years between 1942 and 1959, their partnership had yielded six stage works: two fast flops (*The Life of the Party*, 1942; *What's Up?* 1943), one promising but unprofitable

Sheet music for "You're Just in Love" from *Call Me Madam* (1950) featured Peter Arno's famous caricature of Ethel Merman.

National Museum of American History, Smithsonian Institution, Washington, D.C.

Frederick Loewe
(seated) and Alan Jay
Lerner, 1962.

Photofest.

Broadway venture (*The Day before Spring*, 1945), two works that had respectable critical receptions and lengthy Broadway stays (*Brigadoon*, 1947; *Paint Your Wagon*, 1951), and one that became a globe-engirdling hit of mammoth proportions (*My Fair Lady*, 1956). As with Rodgers and Hammerstein's oeuvre, the majority of their work reaches into the mythos of the past for its milieux; however, in Lerner and Loewe's best musicals, the taste for nostalgic local color is largely European in perspective. Aside from this, their shows are clearly proud descendants of the Rodgers and Hammerstein ideal of close integration between story, song, and spectacle.

The middle son of a wealthy Manhattan businessman, Alan Jay Lerner was raised on a satin-covered cushion of luxury. As a child, he often accompanied his father to the theater, where he fell in love with the shows of Porter, Kern and Hammerstein, and Rodgers and Hart. His education was conducted at the finest American and European schools, culminating in studies at Harvard, where he contributed sketches and lyrics to the university's annual Hasty Pudding revues. Following his graduation in 1939, he found employment as a radio writer, but continued to pursue a career writing for the theater. He found a staunch

Poster for *Brigadoon*
(1947)

Courtesy Triton Gallery,
New York City.

early supporter in Lorenz Hart. Then nearing an untidy, untimely end to an illustrious career, Hart, in a symbolic passing of the torch, encouraged Lerner to refine his promising skills as a lyricist. In 1942 he formed a partnership with Frederick Loewe, a German émigré seventeen years his senior.

Loewe was introduced to the pleasures of musical theater by his father, a Viennese operetta star who originated the role of Count Danilo in the Berlin premiere of Lehár's *The Merry Widow*. At fifteen, "Fritz" was an accomplished concert pianist and had to his credit the composition of a hit popular song called "Katrina." He journeyed to America in 1924, eager to pursue an international career in music. After a series of jobs that included stints as a cowpoke and a prizefighter, he won attention on Broadway in 1938 as the composer of the unsuccessful operetta *Great Lady*, written with lyricist Earle Crooker. Although his first three efforts with Lerner were more promising than prosperous, the team won favor with *Brigadoon*.

A gossamer fantasy about a Scottish village that protects itself from the evils of the world by coming to life for only one day in every century, *Brigadoon* was created very much in the *Oklahoma!–Carousel* mold. It was brightly wrapped in a tartan plaid of quaint customs, Broadway equivalents of regional dialects, a romantic rural setting, and grand folk ballets by Agnes de Mille. Even its principal ballad, "Almost Like Being in Love," recalled the indirect expressions of affection in *Oklahoma!*'s "People Will Say We're in Love" and *Carousel*'s "If I Loved You." *Paint Your Wagon*, the team's next effort, attempted to be (and often succeeded at being) a bracing portrait of the Gold Rush era. Many of its songs ("They Call the Wind Maria," "I Talk to the Trees," "Wandrin' Star") were redolent with the genuine flavor of the Old West, and de Mille was on hand again to muster up a progression of rumbustious folk ballets. But it was their work on *My Fair Lady* that put Lerner and Loewe on the map as two of the most successful authors of the American musical theater. Described by critic Walter Kerr as "a miraculous musical," the show's rampant success was credited by Lerner to the fact that "the right people at the right moment in their lives embarked on the right venture."[24]

The idea of a musical version of George Bernard Shaw's comedy *Pygmalion* had long intrigued a number of theater professionals, but none, including Rodgers and Hammerstein, could find a satisfactory point of departure for its conversion to the lyric stage. In 1954, after several failed attempts and a temporary rift in their partnership, Lerner and Loewe hit upon a solution by opening up the scope of Shaw's tight drawing room polemic, introducing onstage those incidents that occur offstage in Shaw's original. Lerner's script remained true to the wit and wisdom of its source, retelling a cynical Cinderella story of cockney flower girl Eliza Doolittle and her transformation from a "squashed cabbage leaf" to a blossoming cabbage rose who becomes a lady under the tutelage of Henry Higgins, a mysogynistic phonetics professor. As in *Pygmalion*'s 1938 film version, Lerner's script altered Shaw's ending by implying that Higgins and Eliza belonged together. Lerner's adroit lyrics, coupled with Loewe's dramatic and graceful melodies, resulted in one of the greatest American theater scores of the century. Nowhere was its brilliance more evident than in its opening number, "Why Can't the English?" which swiftly established both the characters of Higgins and Eliza and introduced the show's central theme:

> Why can't the English
> Teach their children how to speak?
> This verbal class distinction
> By now should be antique.
> If you spoke as she does, sir
> Instead of the way you do.
> Why, you might be selling flowers, too.

ALAN JAY LERNER AND FREDERICK LOEWE,
"WHY CAN'T THE ENGLISH?" 1956

LEFT: "I Could Have Danced All Night," from *My Fair Lady* (1956). Sheet music.

Alice Becker Levin.

ABOVE: Set designer Oliver Smith. By Martha Swope, c. 1956.

American Ballet Theatre, New York City.

In addition to Lerner and Loewe, the remainder of the show's production team was comprised of a group of theatrical novas. Oliver Smith designed a variety of elegant settings, ranging from the facade of Covent Garden Opera House to Higgins's cluttered study. The scenery was mounted on two revolving stages that made it possible for the action of the show to remain almost continuous throughout. English designer Cecil Beaton concocted an array of costumes that reached their summit in a dazzling study in black and white for the scene at Ascot. And standing firm at the helm of the proceedings (and contributing an uncredited assist on the script) was Moss Hart.

Lerner claimed that stage and film star Rex Harrison was his only choice for Higgins. In truth, the part was offered to many, including Noel Coward and Michael Redgrave, before Harrison accepted the assignment. Similarly, a number of actresses were considered for Eliza. Heading the list was Mary Martin, who rejected the project upon hearing a first draft of the score ("Those boys have lost their talent," she cried to her husband Richard Halliday). After much discussion of others, the plum role was handed to a twenty-year-old English soprano named Julie Andrews with a four-octave range.[25]

Although a relatively fresh face in the New York theater, Andrews had already amassed a lifetime of show business experience in her native England. Propelled by the ambitions of her mother and stepfather, both vaudevillians, she made her professional debut at the age of twelve in a revue at London's Hippodrome Theatre. Successful engagements followed in variety shows, provincial touring companies, and holiday pantomimes. She made her American debut in 1954 in the Broadway production of the English import, *The Boy Friend*. On the strength of her performance in that show, Andrews was approached by Lerner to audition for him and Loewe. At first, she experienced great difficulty in grasping the role; but with Higgins-like tutoring from director Hart, she revealed a dynamism that established her as a major star of the American lyric stage.

If *Oklahoma!* and *South Pacific* were commercial bonanzas, their financial success was a mere prelude to that enjoyed by *My Fair Lady*. Goddard Lieberson, a CBS recording executive and an ardent musical theater devotee, arranged for his company to finance the entire $400,000 production in exchange for the exclusive rights to the cast recording. Furthermore, the songs were recorded in the language of virtually every country in which the show was performed, resulting in more than sixty individual albums of the score alone. In the initial year of its release, the cast album became the best-selling LP in the history of Columbia Records and, along with the 1943 Decca cast album of *Oklahoma!*, one of the most internationally popular cast recordings of all time. Along with the take from cast album sales, *My Fair Lady*'s profits were significantly bolstered by countless spin-off recordings by pop vocalists and instrumentalists.

While Rodgers and Hammerstein and their disciples were spearheading a revolution in the form and content of the American musical theater, songwriter-turned-MGM-film-producer Arthur Freed was leading a similar transformation in the sensibilities of the motion picture musical. Although they had a style and look all their own, many of the musicals produced under Freed's aegis shared several qualities with Rodgers and Hammerstein's works, most notably their hearty endorsement of the values of home, community, and the power of romantic love. These films were also greatly influenced by Rodgers and Hammerstein's techniques for achieving a smooth synthesis of drama, song,

Julie Andrews as Eliza in *My Fair Lady* (1956).

Photofest.

dance, and decor. Freed's guidance was profound in creating a golden age for the Hollywood musical, displaying a Ziegfeldian ability "to know talent, to recognize talent, and to surround himself with it."[26] Although its principal members were director Vincente Minnelli, musical arranger Roger Edens, and stars Judy Garland and Gene Kelly, the Freed Unit at MGM Studios became at one time or another an artistic refuge for most of the major figures in the evolution of the modern American musical.

Director Stanley Donen, an esteemed alumnus of both the MGM musical and the Freed Unit, perhaps best defined the reasons why Freed was "singularly equipped" to stand at the helm of such an impressive assemblage of talent: "Nobody else had the musical background, the Broadway background, the film background, the appreciation for what was good in musicals, and the love of film, the love of people who created musicals."[27]

The eldest son of Hungarian Jewish immigrants, Arthur Freed was born in Charleston, South Carolina, and spent his formative years in Seattle, Washington. His father Max, an itinerant art dealer, was an enthusiastic amateur singer and created a home environment in which music was an integral presence.[28] Arthur began playing the piano at the age of six and, as a teenager, continued his musical studies at Philips Academy in Exeter, New Hampshire, where he discovered a complementary talent for writing song lyrics. At twenty, he landed a job as a song plugger at the Chicago branch of the Waterson, Berlin, and Snyder Publishing Company. His entry into the world of show business followed soon after. The legendary Minnie Marx hired him as a singer and pianist for a madcap vaudeville act that starred her young sons Leonard (Chico), Julius (Groucho), Adolph (Harpo), and Herbert (Zeppo). As a sergeant in the American Expeditionary Force during World War I, Freed parlayed his experiences in vaudeville into a series of variety shows that he produced for the troops stationed at Camp Lewis in Washington State.

After the war, Freed returned to the West Coast and formed a songwriting partnership with composer Nacio Herb Brown. In 1929 the team was hired by MGM executives Louis B. Mayer and Irving Thalberg to write the songs for the studio's first "100% All Talking! All Singing! All Dancing!" release, *The Broadway Melody*. The film turned out to be a huge success at the box office and garnered the 1929 Academy Award for best picture. Moreover, it established the formula for what would quickly become a Hollywood staple—the backstage musical, in which songs and dances were featured as onstage numbers in a narrative with a theatrical setting. For the next decade, Freed worked steadily at MGM, writing the lyrics for such well-loved film songs as "Singin' in the Rain," "Temptation," "You Are My Lucky Star," and "You Were Meant for Me." At the same time, he fostered an ambition to become a studio producer. Ever resourceful, he grabbed up every opportunity to become more involved in the production aspects of the films for which he served as lyricist. In 1938 Louis B. Mayer rewarded him for his efforts above and beyond the call of duty by hiring him as producer Mervyn LeRoy's assistant on *The Wizard of Oz*. One year later, Freed made his debut as a full-fledged producer on *Babes in Arms*, a movie version

ABOVE: Songwriter-turned-producer Arthur Freed (at piano) with director Vincente Minnelli, 1944.

Courtesy Turner Entertainment Co.

ABOVE, RIGHT: Poster for *Meet Me in St. Louis* (1944).

Alice Becker Levin.
© Turner Entertainment Co.

BELOW, RIGHT: Vincente Minnelli, c. 1936.

Liza Minnelli.

of the 1937 Rodgers and Hart stage musical that combined the talents of director Busby Berkeley and Metro's rising stars, Judy Garland and Mickey Rooney. To act as the film's musical supervisor and his right-hand man, Freed brought in Roger Edens, who had joined the MGM staff four years earlier.[29] Edens, a Virginian with considerable experience as a musical accompanist and arranger on Broadway, was eminently qualified to create the new sound and the new style for the film musical that Freed so eagerly sought.[30] Edens became a key figure in the collaborative artistic assembly line that became known as the Freed Unit. His influence was considerable in helping Freed to formulate the conceptual groundwork for some of the finest screen musicals ever created.

The first out-and-out masterpiece to emerge from the handiwork of the Freed Unit was 1944's *Meet Me in St. Louis*. A beautifully realized excursion into a romanticized American past, the film was, in many ways, a screen equivalent to the period atmosphere and musico-dramatic innovation evidenced in *Oklahoma!* Its source was Sally Benson's charming *New Yorker* short stories about the everyday vicissitudes and storms in the lives of an early twentieth-century St. Louis family. Short on narrative action but rich in affectionately drawn characters and atmosphere, Benson's stories were, as she described them, "like a Valentine in the palm of your hand."[31] Freed, a sentimentalist by nature, was immediately taken with Benson's work and steadily promoted its merits to Mayer and other top MGM executives. "What I wanted to make was a simple story," he explained, "a story that basically says, 'There's no place like home,'" recalling the central theme of his earlier *The Wizard of Oz*.[32] Initially, the studio brass responded with pessimism, arguing that the Benson property was virtually devoid of the action and conflict deemed essential for an effective motion picture. Freed countered by asserting, "I'll make a plot with song and dance and music. That's the way my characters will come to life—that'll be my plot!"[33]

Freed's first hurdle was convincing his former protégée Judy Garland to play the pivotal role of Esther Smith. After numerous appearances on screen as a perky adolescent, twenty-one-year-old Garland had her sights set on more sophisticated roles and swiftly rejected the idea of playing a teenage ingenue. For once in Garland's brilliant but troubled career at Metro, management agreed with her and insisted that the role would "set her career back twenty years."[34] While he was eliciting support from all corners of the studio, Freed found a strong ally in designer-director Vincente Minnelli. Minnelli, born in the year of the film's setting, found the property "magical" and eventually convinced Garland of its attributes, eliciting from her one of the finest performances of her career.[35]

If Freed created the environment that made *Meet Me in St. Louis* possible, it was director Minnelli who lovingly nurtured all of the creative seeds into full bloom. His meticulous artistry fused all elements of the production—story, songs, performances, decor—into a beautifully symmetrical whole. He

LEFT: Vincente
Minnelli on the set of
Meet Me in St. Louis
(1944).

Academy of Motion
Picture Arts and Sciences,
Los Angeles. Courtesy
Turner Entertainment Co.

ABOVE: Judy
Garland and
Vincente Minnelli on
the set of *Meet Me in
St. Louis* (1944).

Academy of Motion
Picture Arts and Sciences,
Los Angeles. Courtesy
Turner Entertainment Co.

RIGHT: *Lion's Roar*
magazine cover
depicting Judy
Garland and
Margaret O'Brien in
Meet Me in St. Louis
(1944).

Academy of Motion
Picture Arts and Sciences,
Los Angeles. Courtesy
Turner Entertainment Co.

worked tirelessly with designer Lemuel Ayers (late of *Oklahoma!*), art director Jack Martin Smith, and costumier Irene Sharaff to create a striking visual ambiance that recalled in its Technicolor splendor the composition in Thomas Eakins's paintings. To impose structure on an essentially plotless narrative, he divided the story into vignettes or acts that corresponded to the four seasons. Each seasonal segment was introduced with a sepia-toned view of the Smiths' American Gothic house framed in filigree, as if it were a greeting card of the era. In partnership with his cast and choreographer Charles Walters, Minnelli achieved a beguiling naturalness in the musical numbers, whether it was the aching tenderness of "The Boy Next Door" or the exuberance of "The Trolley Song." As a result of his work on *Meet Me in St. Louis*, Minnelli set a standard against which all subsequent musicals of the era were judged.[36]

As with many in his production team, Freed had recruited Vincente Minnelli from the New York theater. The only son of touring performers, Minnelli was, by his own admission, "born in a tent."[37] He first stepped on stage at the age of three-and-a-half, appearing with his mother in a production of the melodrama *East Lynne*. Largely self-taught as a sketch artist,

he designed window displays at the Marshall Field department store in Chicago. Soon, he talked his way into a post as costume designer for the stage shows produced for the Balaban and Katz chain of movie theaters. He immigrated to New York in 1931 and first attracted critical praise for his costume and set designs for the stage shows at Radio City Music Hall. In these, he established his gift as a superior colorist, achieving breathtaking visual effects through stylish juxtapositions of iridescent hues. In 1935 Lee Shubert hired him to supervise a series of Broadway revues, including *At Home Abroad*, a travelogue set to music starring Beatrice Lillie and Ethel Waters. Billed as "a Vincente Minnelli production," it prompted critic Brooks Atkinson to exclaim: "Under his direction the revue has such unity of appearance that it is more difficult than usual to pluck out the best numbers. The whole thing stirs with the life of superior stage entertainment."[38]

A brief fling in Hollywood at Paramount Studios proved unproductive, and he resisted the call to join the staff at MGM. "Come on out for five or six months," Freed offered, "take enough money for your expenses—no contract, no nothing. If you don't like it at any time, you can leave."[39] After serving an apprenticeship as a consultant for Freed-produced films *Strike Up the Band* (1940), *Babes On Broadway* (1941), *Lady, Be Good* (1941), and *Panama Hattie* (1942), he made his first mark as a director with *Cabin in the Sky*. A film adaptation of the 1940 Broadway musical *succès d'estime*, *Cabin* was praised by the *Daily Variety* critic as "a fantastic piece of American folklore."[40]

While Minnelli was putting the cast of *Cabin in the Sky* through its paces on one MGM soundstage, on another *For Me and My Gal* was in production under Busby Berkeley's supervision, starring Judy Garland and a new addition to the Freed Unit, Gene Kelly. Kelly had left his native Pittsburgh in 1937 to make a name for himself on Broadway as a dancer-choreographer. After a series of small roles in the musicals *Leave It to Me!* (1938) and *One for the Money* (1939) and in William Saroyan's drama *The Time of Your Life* (1939), he rocketed to fame as the titular antihero of Rodgers and Hart's *Pal Joey*. Although Freed had wooed him for his stable of talent at MGM, Kelly came to Hollywood in 1941 under the auspices of impresario David O. Selznick. When Selznick was unable to come up with a suitable vehicle for Kelly's screen debut, he sold his contract to MGM. In *For Me and My Gal* he more than held his own

LEFT: Vincente Minnelli (center) with Eddie Anderson and Lena Horne working on the movie version of *Cabin in the Sky* (1944).

Mrs. Vincenté (Lee) Minnelli and Liza Minnelli

Gene Kelly.

Academy of Motion Picture Arts and Sciences, Los Angeles. Courtesy Turner Entertainment Co.

opposite Garland, whom he credited publicly for helping him make the transition from stage to film player. In this initial celluloid appearance, he established an on-screen persona that exuded confident charm in his acting and an athleticism in his dancing that contrasted with the suave ballroom techniques of Fred Astaire, the reigning king of motion picture dance. As Kelly explained, "I have a lot of Cohan in me. It's an Irish quality, a jaw-jutting, up-on-your-toes cockiness—which is a good quality for a dancer to have."[41]

The 1944 movie *Cover Girl*, made on loan-out to Columbia Pictures, gave Kelly his first real opportunity to show off his gift for cinematic choreography. The film contained

ABOVE: Leslie Caron, Gene Kelly, and Vincente Minnelli on the set of *An American in Paris* (1951).

Mrs. Vincenté (Lee) Minnelli and Liza Minnelli.

RIGHT: Poster for *An American in Paris* (1951).

Alice Becker Levin. © Loew's Inc., 1951, National Screen Corp. Service. Courtesy Turner Entertainment Co.

a fantasy dance number entitled "Alter Ego," which used double exposure photography to allow Kelly to partner himself in depicting the emotional duality of his character's psyche. However, his most consistently stylish and enduring efforts for the screen were done in collaboration with the Freed Unit at MGM. *The Pirate* (1948) teamed him with Garland and Minnelli in an exotic comedy of manners set in a remote, rococo West Indies. As roving actor Sarafin, a role that combined John Barrymore's melodramatic pyrotechnics with the macho swashbuckling physicality of Douglas Fairbanks, he proved an able farceur and executed a highly erotic "Pirate Ballet" bathed in vivid technicolor hues of red and yellow. His own favorite was *On the Town* (1949), a film adaptation of the 1944 Bernstein-Comden-Green stage musical, which he codirected with Stanley Donen. It was notable chiefly for its innovative use of actual locations (as opposed to Metro soundstages) as the settings for musical numbers and for its stylized dream ballet, "A Day in New York."

But two films stand out as his crowning achievements—*An American in Paris* (1951) and *Singin' in the Rain* (1952)—both representative of the Freed Unit at its highly polished best. Freed conjured the idea for *An American in Paris* one evening in 1949 during a game of pool with Ira Gershwin. Without any concepts for story or cast, he proposed a lavish movie musical founded on the title of George Gershwin's famous 1928 tone poem and featuring an all-Gershwin score. Obtaining Ira Gershwin's permission and support, he immediately enlisted Minnelli as director and hired Alan Jay Lerner to write the screenplay with Gene Kelly in mind. With only the sketchiest outline, Lerner set out to write a story about an ex-G.I. émigré painter caught up in the splendor of postwar Paris. "I didn't want it to be just a cavalcade of songs," explained Lerner. "I wanted to write a story so the songs would appear because of the emotional and dramatic situations."[42]

Along with its delightful rediscovery of Gershwin songs, what distinguishes *An American in Paris* is the seventeen-minute ballet that functions as the film's finale. Audacious, arty, and immensely entertaining, the idea was initially judged as preposterous. With Kelly at its center, the ballet lifts the film out of the ordinary and assures it of a spot among cinematic greats. Kelly's choreography, which combines ballet, modern, and jazz dance styles, is an unquestioned tour de force for both him and his costar, seventeen-year-old Leslie Caron. Nowhere is Minnelli's skill as a colorist more brilliantly realized than in this imaginative sequence. Working with designers Cedric Gibbons and Irene Sharaff, he conceived on the MGM soundstages various highly stylized perspectives of Paris in the manner of some of its finest painters. Perhaps the most striking was the ballet's principal setting, a Dufy-inspired Place de la Concorde with a mammoth central fountain. At the 1952 Academy Awards ceremonies, *An American in Paris* won Oscars for best picture and best screenplay, and Kelly received an honorary award "in appreciation of his versatility as an actor, singer, director, and dancer, and specifically for his brilliant achievement in the art of choreography on film."

The Freed-Kelly chemistry reached its zenith in *Singin' in the Rain*, a funny, nostalgic backward glance at Hollywood in the 1920s during the silent screen's transition to sound. The film marked something of a full circle for Freed in that the score consisted of some of

ABOVE: Irene Sharaff working with costume for *Me and Juliet* (1953).

Museum of the City of New York; gift of Mary Martin.

RIGHT: Poster for *Singin' in the Rain* (1952).

Alice Becker Levin. Courtesy Turner Entertainment Co.

Fountain scene from
An American in Paris
(1951).

his most memorable collaborations with Nacio Herb Brown. Comden and Green's screenplay endures as a masterpiece, lampooning the foibles of the fledgling movie industry with affection and genuine wit. The musical numbers, staged by Kelly and codirector Stanley Donen, are a parade of showstoppers, from the joyous abandon of the title number, with Kelly hopping off curbs into puddles and wrapping himself around a lamppost, to the flashy, climactic "Broadway Ballet."

Freed's swan song was *Gigi*, which was released in 1958. A final teaming with Minnelli and Lerner, this adaptation of Colette's novella about a coltish Parisienne being groomed as a courtesan was a triumph for all. Like *St. Louis*, it is a thoughtful, visually stunning foray into a gentler, more gracious past; in this instance, the past is fin de siècle Paris in the springtime. The dialogue and score (by Lerner and Loewe) could not be wittier, the cast could not be more perfect, and Minnelli's skills as a director and designer were never given a finer display. It was rewarded with a record nine Oscars, including one for best picture and one to Minnelli for best direction.

For all its brilliance, *Gigi* was perhaps the last of its cinematic breed. Economic costs, the dissolution of the studio system, the fragmentation of audiences by age groups and mu-

Gene Kelly in "Broadway" ballet scene from *Singin' in the Rain* (1952).

© Turner Entertainment Co.

THE FIRST LERNER-LOEWE MUSICAL SINCE "MY FAIR LADY"

M-G-M Presents
AN ARTHUR FREED PRODUCTION
Starring
LESLIE CARON
MAURICE CHEVALIER · LOUIS JOURDAN
HERMIONE GINGOLD · EVA GABOR · JACQUES BERGERAC · ISABEL JEANS
Screen Play and Lyrics by **ALAN JAY LERNER** · Music by **FREDERICK LOEWE** · Based on the Novel by COLETTE
Costumes, Scenery & Production Design by CECIL BEATON · in CinemaScope And METROCOLOR · Directed by **VINCENTE MINNELLI**

Poster for *Gigi*
(1958).

Courtesy Cinemonde,
Nashville, Tennessee.

sical tastes, and, finally, the rise of television brought an end to the Freed Unit and the virtual demise of the original screen musical.

While one chord in musicals resonated with a nostalgia for small-town America in the 1940s and 1950s, an equally ubiquitous strain celebrated the urban landscape—one dominated by pulsing vignettes of the city instead of pastoral tableaux offering baseball fields and dance-shell gazebos. Both embraced the life of the mainstream, with musicals continuing to fuel a middle-class mythos of optimism and abundance.

The leading musical celebrant of urban America in these years was Leonard Bernstein—indeed, perhaps not since George Gershwin had anyone been so enraptured by the romance of the city. It had been Gershwin, after all, who proclaimed, "We are living in an age of staccato, not legato," and created a faster, brassier sound befitting the machine age of the metropolis. Like Gershwin, and often compared to him in his early career, Bernstein reveled in the rhythms of the city—its brassy rush, its reverence for the "new," and its dissonance.

Considered a musical wunderkind by such transcendent figures as Aaron Copland, Dimitri Mitropoulos, and Serge Koussevitzky, Bernstein by his early twenties began to collect around him the creative team that would impart a gritty urgency to the American musical voice. Just after graduating from Harvard in 1939, he moved to New York and roomed with Adolph Green, whom he had met when they both worked on a summer camp production of *The Pirates of Penzance*. A year earlier, Green and Betty Comden had formed a satirical group, "The Revuers," that also included Judy Tuvim (later, Judy Holliday). Bronx-born Green, the son of Hungarian immigrants, had worked as a Wall Street runner after graduating from high school in 1934. But his heart belonged to Broadway, and the extrovertish Green hung around casting offices hoping to find work as a character actor. Brooklyn-born Comden, daughter of a lawyer and a schoolteacher, was in New York to earn her degree in drama at New York University, with the intent ultimately to teach; yet she too was seriously bitten by the acting bug and met Green in 1938 as they were both optimistically—and unsuccessfully—doing the rounds of theatrical agents. They formed the Revuers with the up-and-coming Judy Holliday largely out of self-defense, thinking that at least they now had a real act to sell and that they might as well be unemployed together. The group was too poor to buy other people's material, so they wrote their own, consisting mostly of irreverent sketches that skewered icons of advertising, journalism, and Hollywood. One part of their act featured *Reader's Digest* versions of classic novels, such as their interpretation of *Gone with the Wind*, which went, in toto:

> Scarlett O'Hara's a spoiled pet,
> She wants everything that she can get,
> The one thing she can't get is Rhett.
> The End.

BETTY COMDEN AND ADOLPH GREEN, "READER'S DIGEST," C. 1940

When Bernstein arrived in New York, the Revuers were enjoying considerable vogue at the Village Vanguard nightclub in Greenwich Village. Betty Comden recalled that the first time the "very handsome and ebullient" Bernstein saw their act, he took over the piano after their last performance about 3:00 a.m. and "started to play and we were there till about six or seven in the morning. . . . That night I was so staggered by this marvelous man . . . and I knew that just knowing him would affect my life."[43] It would be another five years, though, before they would actually work together, as Bernstein spent two years in graduate study at the Curtis Institute in Philadelphia and then embarked on a career in New York as a pianist and conductor. In November 1943 he made front-page news in the *New York Times* when he replaced an ailing Bruno Walter as conductor of the New York Philharmonic for a Sunday matinee performance. The performance, broadcast from Carnegie Hall by CBS radio, catapulted Bernstein into fame as "an overnight sensation"; the *Times* ran an editorial the following Tuesday calling him "a good American success story. The warm, friendly tri-

Leonard Bernstein. By René Bouché, 1960.

National Portrait Gallery, Smithsonian Institution, Washington, D.C.; gift of Springate Corporation.

Leonard Bernstein (left) with Jerome Robbins, Betty Comden, and Adolph Green, 1944.

Photofest.

umph of it filled Carnegie Hall and spread over the airways."[44]

In the wake of this success, Bernstein soon met Jerome Robbins, a young dancer with the Ballet Theatre who would help entice the fledgling maestro from the classical podium to the Broadway stage. The son of Russian Jewish immigrants, Robbins had grown up in Weehawken, New Jersey, where his father ran a delicatessen and later became a corset manufacturer. Along with his sister, he had studied dance as a teenager and attended New York University in 1935–36 before deciding to undertake a career in dance. He encompassed a wide range of dance, from ballet with Antony Tudor to modern dance at the New Dance League, and appeared as a chorus boy in several Broadway shows in the late 1930s, at the same time attempting some initial choreographic work at Tamiment summer camp in Pennsylvania. In 1940 he joined the newly created Ballet Theatre and established himself as an important artist in his solo debut in 1942 as Petrouchka.

Robbins found his way to Bernstein's Carnegie Hall studio in late 1943, bringing along a story outline for a one-act ballet called *Fancy Free*. Just as Bernstein was determined to create music with an authentic *American* voice, Robbins wanted the ballet to be a modern, fast-paced story about life in wartime New York, with choreography that incorporated such

Jerome Robbins.

Photofest. © 1962 United Artists Corporation.

current popular dances as the boogie-woogie, the lindy-hop, and the soft-shoe shuffle; what he needed was a simpatico composer, and this he clearly discovered in Bernstein. Scenic designer Oliver Smith would become the third member of *Fancy Free*'s creative team. A recent graduate of Pennsylvania State University, Smith had a special affinity for dance, explaining once that dance and ballet were the real proving grounds for a designer, forcing him to be "abstract, conscious of the space on-stage, able to think in terms of physical movement, capable of eliminating fussy detail."[45] He had designed his first professional sets in 1941 for the Ballet Russe de Monte Carlo's production of Massine's *Saratoga*; in 1942 he did the evocative corral, ranch house, and sun-baked prairie sets for Agnes de Mille's ballet sensation *Rodeo*. By 1945, Smith would become codirector—along with Lucia Chase—of the American Ballet Theatre.

Fancy Free premiered in April 1944, with the tone of the ballet reflected in Smith's spare waterfront bar set. Bernstein's program notes describe how "the curtain rises on a street corner with a lamp post, a side street bar and New York skyscrapers pricked out with a crazy pattern of lights, making a dizzying back drop. Three sailors explode on the stage. They are on a 24-hour shore leave in the city and on the prowl for girls. The tale of how they first meet one, then a second girl, and how they fight over them, lose them, and in the end take off after still a third, is the story of the ballet."

Fancy Free was showered with acclaim—"Just exactly ten degrees north of terrific," raved the *New York Times*.[46] Designer Oliver Smith now encouraged Bernstein and Robbins to join him in a collaboration on a full-fledged musical comedy. With the addition of Bernstein's old "Revuer" friends Comden and Green as writers of the book and lyrics, *On the Town* emerged in the six months between June and December 1944. As they began, the creative team solemnly composed a credo listing the "dos" and "don'ts" that would guide their aims and ideals in writing a musical comedy: essentially, it outlined their desire to achieve a perfect "integration," or fusion, of song, dance, and dialogue. In September, with several drafts of the show written, the book was submitted to the legendary George Abbott, universally acknowledged as the era's greatest "show-doctor" and director. "Mr. Abbott," as everyone called him, quickly agreed to direct the show, and, as Comden and Green later wrote, "Our lives changed." Whereas all connected with the show—Bernstein, Comden and Green, Robbins, Smith—were in their mid-twenties, Abbott was thirty years older, and held in awe. His new colleagues respected his "patriarchal grandeur," his "puritanical aloofness," and, of course, his "authority." When there was a creative disagreement, they ultimately took Abbott's advice. The one time the disagreement was serious—concerning their desire to use a flashback device to open and close the show, and their director's insistence that they remove it bodily, and at once—they marched boldly into Abbott's office at Radio City and passionately presented their case; he quietly said, "O.K. You have either the flashback or me. Take your choice." And that was the end of that.[47] As it turned out, *On the Town*'s opening owed a debt to *Oklahoma!* the prototypic Americana musical: when the curtain went up on *Oklahoma!* rather than a big production number featuring a colorful barn dance, the audience saw a woman alone on stage, churning butter. A year later, *On the Town* opened not with a chorus of dancing sailors but with a single laborer singing on a dockside set.

On the Town premiered on December 28, 1944. The show told the story of three sailors

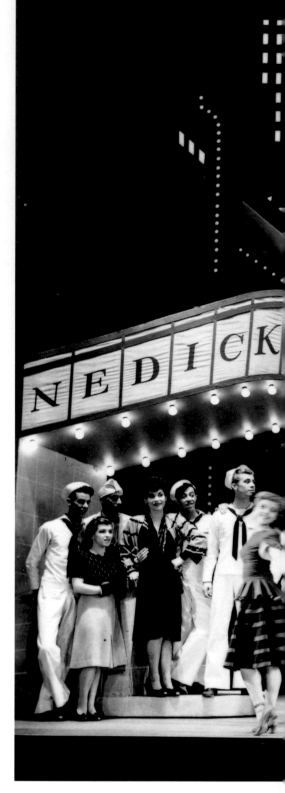

Act 1 finale, "Times Square" of *On the Town* (1944). By Van Damm Studio.

Van Damm Collection, New York Public Library for the Performing Arts, New York City.

and the three girls they "found" while on a twenty-four-hour shore leave in New York. The atmosphere was carefree and full of swirling New York locations, including the Brooklyn Navy Yard, Times Square, Central Park, and Coney Island. Set designer Oliver Smith later said the show was "a valentine to New York. We each adored New York in our own way, and it became a unifying theme."[48] Each of the sailors finds his date in some familiar New York surrounding: the subway, where one of them falls in love with the poster girl for that month's "Miss Turnstiles"; the Museum of Natural History, where another meets an anthropologist whose libido eclipses his own; and—in that most quintessential New York locale—a taxicab, whose man-hungry driver turns out to be the girl of the third sailor's dreams. As it happened, Green and Comden wrote two of the choicest roles for themselves—as the "carried away" sailor Ozzie and his new inamorata, the sex-crazed anthropologist Claire de Loon. To Betty Comden, there was also a strong emotional base to the story: "The fact there was a war on was working for us all the time; the fact that these boys had just twenty-four hours beginning with their coming off the ship and ending with their saying goodbye and getting on the ship going who knew where. The song 'Some Other Time,' which comes near the end of the show, is full of emotion. In wartime it had a tremendously poignant feeling."[49]

On the Town was a smash hit, although some were confused by the prominence of satire and dearth of homey warmth in this energetic urban romance, especially in the explosive Robbins choreography and in such songs as "New York, New York":

New York, New York, a visitor's place,
Where no one lives on account of the pace
But seven million are screaming for space.
New York, New York, it's a visitor's place!

BETTY COMDEN, ADOLPH GREEN, AND LEONARD
BERNSTEIN, "NEW YORK, NEW YORK," 1944

This was obviously a different kind of Broadway beast—savvy, sassy, and city bred. The show ran for 436 performances and grossed more than $2 million, with its run weakening only after the war ended in 1945 and public interest turned to more domestic issues.

A departure from anything seen before on Broadway, *On the Town* had been an exultation of the city, and that joyousness was present in all aspects of the production. Bernstein once said that "the essence of the whole production is contained in these dances"—and in every other creative element of the show. Jerome Robbins's kinetic choreography was as key as the music of Bernstein, the lyrics and book of Comden and Green, and the sets of Oliver Smith. "You have to remember the context of the time, the kind of musicals that were being done," Robbins recalled forty years later. "We didn't know what the rules were, but we knew what should and shouldn't be. We all threw our ideas into the pot."[50] And what emerged was what they had intended from the beginning of their collaboration, a revolutionary fusion of the elements of musical comedy.

It would be another seven years before Bernstein, Abbott, Comden and Green, and Robbins (though only unofficially, as a "show doctor" for the dance routines) were able to collaborate again—this time, on a musical version of *My Sister Eileen*. Originally an autobiographical book by Ruth McKenney, *My Sister Eileen* had appeared in several guises—a successful 1940 play by Joseph Fields and Jerome Chodorov, a movie, and a long-running radio program—when Fields and Chodorov decided to adapt it as a musical. George Abbott had signed on as a producer, and Rosalind Russell had already agreed to repeat her starring film role when Bernstein was approached to write the score and Comden and

Betty Comden as Claire de Loon and Adolph Green as Ozzie in *On the Town* (1944).

Museum of the City of New York.

Green the lyrics. Because the option on Russell was very short-term, Bernstein and Comden and Green had barely five weeks to complete the words and music; by cloistering themselves away in Bernstein's apartment, they managed to meet their deadline, and by mid-December 1952 there was an entire score for what was now called *Wonderful Town*.

The basic story tells of two sisters from Ohio who come to Greenwich Village in the 1930s to seek their fortune, Ruth as a writer and Eileen as an actress. To a much greater extent than in *On the Town*, *Wonderful Town* was a star vehicle rather than an ensemble work, creating enormous audience sympathy for Rosalind Russell's character. But, as in *On the Town*, the same throb of youthful exuberance pulsed through this production, especially in Bernstein's music, from the opening "Christopher Street" to the "Wrong Note Rag" finish; perhaps best known was "Ohio," a lament the homesick sisters sing about their small-town roots: "Why oh why oh why oh, / Why did I ever leave Ohio?"

Just before the show opened for Boston previews, Bernstein told the *Boston Morning Globe* that he felt the "real future of real American music lies in the theater. . . . The scores for such hits as *Carousel* and *South Pacific* are relatively simple, but they are alive, they are emotional and they make people respond to them. 'There's Nothing like a Dame' is one of the great moments of American music today. It says something to people. That, in brief, is why I want to concentrate on writing for the theater."[51]

Bernstein's passionate commitment to theater music was noted by several reviewers when *Wonderful Town* opened in New York at the Winter Garden on February 25. Olin Downes declared in the *New York Times* that the show was "utterly American in conception and execution from head to toe . . . current and characteristic of our people, and not paralleled by any other musical theater. . . . The electricity shoots back and forth over the footlights. . . . In days to come it may well be looked upon in some museum exhibit as the archetype of a kind of piece which existed peculiarly in the America of neon lights and the whir and zip of the twentieth century." Theater critic Brooks Atkinson wrote: "Sometimes gifted people never quite get attuned to each other in the composition of a musical circus. But in *Wonderful Town* everyone seems to have settled down joyfully to the creation of a beautifully organized fandango—the book, the score and the ballets helping each other enthusiastically."[52]

Wonderful Town won a number of Tony Awards, including that for best musical for the 1952–53 season, with Bernstein also winning for music, Comden and Green for lyrics, and Rosalind Russell for best actress in a musical. But despite its great success—and despite the joyful collaboration particularly between Bernstein and Comden and Green—another four years passed before Bernstein returned to theater music. And although many attempts were made over the years, *Wonderful Town* marked this team's last Broadway collaboration.

Never one to focus on a single pursuit, Bernstein struck out in several directions after *Wonderful Town*—composing the score for the 1954 film *On the Waterfront* (for which he was nominated for an Academy Award), becoming involved in November 1954 with the *Omnibus* television program, beginning work on both *Candide* (1956) and *West Side Story* (1957), and turning more to the conducting side of his career. And, as they had since they first collaborated as "Revuers," Comden and Green continued to work on projects that satirized modern city life—especially New York—and the world of show business. For some

Judy Holliday and
Jule Styne rehearsing
Bells Are Ringing
(1956).

Photofest.

time they had wanted to write a show for their old Revuer partner Judy Holliday, who had emerged as a popular star following her Oscar-winning performance as Billie Dawn in *Born Yesterday*. Holliday's "acting" career had been launched when she was hired as a switchboard operator for the Mercury Theater; Comden and Green were reminded of this auspicious beginning one day when they spotted an illustration of a telephone operator with tentacles stretched all over the city. Comden recalled that "this was a time when answering services were a new phenomenon. I asked Adolph, 'Have you ever seen your answering service?' He hadn't. With a little research, we discovered it was right around the corner from where he lived. We rushed over, and it was indeed a terrible, filthy little cellar room. Down a couple of steps there was this one huge woman sitting in front of a lone switchboard among the squalor saying, 'Gloria Vanderbilt's residence.' We just fell on the floor laughing. We said, 'That's it!'"[53]

To write the music for *Bells Are Ringing*, they chose Jule Styne, best known at that time for having written the score for *Gentlemen Prefer Blondes* (1949). Styne, born in London

to Ukrainian Jewish immigrants, came to the United States with his family at the age of seven. He grew up in Chicago as a prodigy on the piano, performing with the Chicago and Detroit Symphonies. But by the time he was fifteen, his taste had turned to jazz, and he would spend his early career traveling with such great bands as those of Benny Goodman and Glenn Miller. The thirties found him in Hollywood, first as a vocal coach for Shirley Temple, Alice Faye, and Tony Martin, and then as a songwriter for the cowboy pictures of Gene Autry and Roy Rogers; as he once said, "I wrote five or six songs for each picture. . . .

Play piano for Trigger? Sure." He also wrote some of the songs that fueled Frank Sinatra's stellar rise in the forties, including "I've Heard That Song Before," "Time after Time," "Saturday Night Is the Loneliest Night of the Week," and "I Fall in Love Too Easily." Styne's breakthrough Broadway show was *Gentlemen Prefer Blondes*, in which the saucer-eyed Carol Channing soared to stardom, propelled by "Diamonds Are a Girl's Best Friend" and "A Little Girl from Little Rock."

With *Bells Are Ringing*, Styne was paired again with Jerome Robbins, with whom he had worked in the 1947 Broadway production of *High Button Shoes*. Robbins, who had also worked so successfully with Comden and Green in *On the Town*, agreed to direct this story of a young woman who works for Susanswerphone. With Styne—more than in their collaborations with Bernstein—Comden, Green, and Robbins placed more emphasis on character development and less on dance: *Bells Are Ringing* was really a star vehicle for Judy Holliday. Her "Ella Peterson" is a remarkably appealing character, radiating an innate benevolence that is, as in the song "Hello, Hello There!" capable of reducing surly subway riders to cheerfulness. The music and lyrics of Styne and Comden and Green—including "Just in Time," "Long Before I Knew You," and "The Party's Over"—imbue this urban romance with a winsome quality that gentles it, creating a less aggressive atmosphere than in the harder-edged *Town* shows they had done with Bernstein.

After *Bells Are Ringing*, Jerome Robbins and Oliver Smith reunited with Bernstein in the landmark 1957 *West Side Story*. This show was the culmination of an idea that had been percolating since January 1949, when Robbins had called Bernstein to suggest that they refashion *Romeo and Juliet* and set it in New York's East Side slums at the time of celebrations for Easter and Passover; in this version, originally called *East Side Story*, the family antagonisms posed against one another were Jewish and Catholic. But both Robbins and Bernstein would be too involved in other projects to focus on this show for years— Robbins, with establishing himself as one of Broadway's leading director-choreographers in such productions as Irving Berlin's *Call Me Madam* (1950) and Rodgers and Hammerstein's *The King and I* (1951); and Bernstein, who aside from conducting, teaching at Brandeis, and riveting audiences with his *Omnibus* telecasts, composed *Trouble in Tahiti* (1952) and *Candide* (1956).

By the time Robbins and Bernstein rekindled the idea of their modern *Romeo* in 1955, the demographics of New York had changed enough to make the Jewish-Catholic antipodes outdated. Now, the newspapers were full of stories about juvenile delinquency and Puerto Rican–Anglo gang warfare on the West Side, and it was decided to refocus on what became *West Side Story*.

At first, Bernstein agreed to write both lyrics and music, but he was working on *Candide* at the same time and soon realized that "The music for *West Side Story* turned out to be extraordinarily balletic, and there was tremendously more music—symphonic and balletic music—than anything I had anticipated."[54] He would not be able to write both music and lyrics, and the search was on for a lyricist. Comden and Green were committed to a movie in Hollywood, so Oscar Hammerstein's young protégé Stephen Sondheim was approached. Sondheim, born into an upper-middle-class New York family in 1930, had lived a precocious life, spending much of his time at the Pennsylvania home of the Oscar Hammersteins after his own parents were divorced when he was ten. Their son Jimmy was his

Producers Robert E.
Griffith and Harold
Prince, director-
choreographer
Jerome Robbins,
lyricist Stephen
Sondheim, composer
Leonard Bernstein,
and others at
rehearsal of *West Side
Story* (1957). By
Martha Swope.

© Time, Inc.

own age, and Sondheim spent so much of his youth with the Hammersteins that he later said, "They gradually became surrogate parents for me."[55]

It was in this period that Hammerstein was composing *Oklahoma!* and the adolescent became enthralled with musical theater. At fifteen, he composed a school play called *By George:* "And when I finished it, I not only wanted Oscar to see it but I wanted him to be the first to read it, because I just knew he and Dick Rodgers would want to produce it immediately and I'd be the first fifteen-year-old to have a musical done on Broadway." Alas, Oscar took him at his word and read it objectively, telling him it was terrible. But he added that if he wanted to know *why* it was terrible, he would explain—and he did, song by song, scene by scene, line by line. Sondheim has said that "in that afternoon I learned more about songwriting and the musical theater than most people learn in a lifetime. . . . He taught me how to structure a song like a one-act play, how essential simplicity is, how much every word counts and the importance of content . . . how to build songs, how to introduce character, how to make songs relate to character, how to tell a story . . . the in-

Chita Rivera (b. 1933)

Chita Rivera (née Dolores Conchita del Rivero) has enjoyed a long and varied career as one of the musical theater's finest dancers. At its best, her dancing is hallmarked by an ageless, feline sensuality and vigorous athleticism, particularly when executing movements designed by masters such as Jerome Robbins, Gower Champion, and Bob Fosse.

Born in Washington, D.C., of Puerto Rican heritage, Rivera abandoned her dreams of becoming a ballerina and turned her attentions to the musical theater, making her New York debut at seventeen as a chorus replacement in the long-running *Guys and Dolls*. In 1957 she won critical plaudits for her portrayal of the explosive Anita in the original production of *West Side Story*. Stardom swiftly followed with the Broadway and London companies of *Bye Bye Birdie* (1960), and she was viewed by critics and audiences alike as a potential rival to Gwen Verdon as the musical theater's dancing darling.

Throughout the 1960s a series of indifferent roles in several so-so musicals temporarily dimmed the glowing promise of Rivera's early career.[1] In 1975 she essayed a riveting performance as a tough-as-nails murderess in Fosse's *Chicago*, although she decidedly played second banana to Verdon's showy star turn. A decade later, she won her first Tony Award for best actress in a musical in the flawed, commercially unsuccessful John Kander–Fred Ebb–Terrence McNally musical *The Rink*. If nothing else, the show confirmed that her dramatic skills were at least equal to her terpsichorean talents.

In 1993, under the guidance of Harold Prince and teamed again with Kander, Ebb, and McNally, Rivera reaffirmed her status as a brilliant Broadway luminary in *The Kiss of the Spider Woman*. As a sultry Latin American film star, she found perhaps her splashiest theatrical assignment thus far and made the most of a strenuous series of dance numbers, achieving a stunning coup de theatre with a dazzlingly eerie climb up a mammoth spider web that spanned the width and height of the stage. Her authoritative performance earned her a bundle of awards, including a second Tony. She remains one of the few stars who rose to fame during the musical theater's golden era to have successfully sustained the transition to the uncertain sensibilities of the contemporary musical stage.

1. Rivera starred on Broadway in 1964 in *Bajour*, a tale of gypsies in modern-day New York based by its authors Walter Marks and Ernest Kinoy on *New Yorker* short stories by Joseph L. Mitchell. She also appeared on the West Coast in two productions for impresario Edwin Lester's Los Angeles Civic Light Opera Association. The first was *Zenda* (1963), based on the *Prisoner of Zenda*, with music by Vernon Duke and costarring Alfred Drake, and the second was *1491*, a 1969 disaster by Meredith Willson based on the exploits of Christopher Columbus.

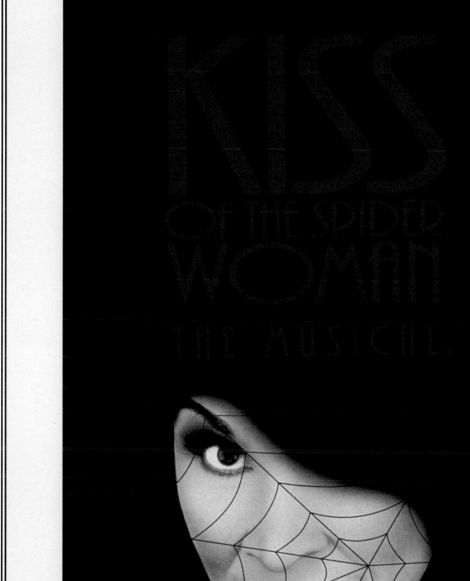

Portrait of Chita
Rivera on the poster
for *Kiss of the Spider
Woman* (1993).

Livent Inc.

LEFT: **Chita Rivera
in *West Side Story*
(1957). By Fred Fehl.**

Humanities Research
Center, The University of
Texas at Austin.

terrelationships between lyric and music. . . . Most people think of Oscar as a kind of affable, idealistic lunkhead. Instead, he was a very sophisticated, sharp-tongued, articulate man who did indeed have an idealistic philosophy which prompted him to be attracted to the kind of material he was attracted to."[56]

Sondheim majored in music at Williams College and then spent two years on a fellowship studying with avant-garde composer Milton Babbitt. His first job had nothing to do with music but with writing scripts for the new television series *Topper*—which he later described as good training for "compressed storytelling."[57] In 1955, when his name was broached to work on lyrics for *West Side*, Sondheim's first reaction was negative; when he went into music, he had hoped to establish himself as a composer as well as a lyricist. But Hammerstein convinced him that it was an opportunity not to be wasted—even though Bernstein was still intending to write some of the lyrics himself. Sondheim reluctantly accepted the assignment, though he also worried that "I've never been that poor and I've never even *known* a Puerto Rican!"[58]

The backbone of *West Side Story* was the book written by Arthur Laurents, a playwright at this point who had never been associated with a musical and whose greatest successes had been the screenplays for Alfred Hitchcock's *Rope* (1948) and the melodramatic *Anastasia* (1956), for which Ingrid Bergman won an Academy Award as best actress. Because of the amount of music and dance in *West Side*, Laurents wrote what Bernstein has called "one of the shortest books of any major Broadway musical." His considerable task was to convert Shakespeare into this modern major musical—to stay true to *Romeo and Juliet* while still communicating, as Robbins has said, "some of the poetry, the argot, the drives and passions of the 1950s."[59]

Just as every note of music had to resonate with meaning for Bernstein, so did every dance step for Robbins: "What's it about?" was his constant demand. Indeed, Robbins—who had, after all, conceived the idea for the show in 1949—envisioned the entire production as being driven by choreography. In this show, which Robbins directed as well as choreographed, the balance among music, drama, and dance shifted away from the equi-

Oliver Smith's design for the opening scene of *West Side Story* (1957).

Robert L. B. Tobin Collection, courtesy Marion Koogler McNay Art Museum, San Antonio, Texas.

**"Rumble Scene"
from *West Side Story*
(1957). By Fred Fehl,
1957.**

Harry Ransom Humanities
Research Center, The
University of Texas at
Austin.

librium established by *Oklahoma!* Here, dance clearly carried the burden. Remarkably, his colleagues generally acceded to the primacy of movement. Bernstein once recalled that, as originally scored, the "Prologue" was meant to be sung, but that there was general agreement that it did not work. Robbins "took over and converted all that stuff into this remarkable thing . . . all dancing and movement. . . . We learned how to relearn and to teach," according to Bernstein. "It was an extraordinary exchange." And not always silky smooth, either, as when, during its pre-Broadway run in Washington, D.C., Robbins began cutting Bernstein's music for the second-act ballet. He wanted to achieve a "rhythmless" sound. Sondheim has since said that he "expected there to be a big fight," but Bernstein instead simply disappeared. A while later, Sondheim followed him out into the street and walked into the first bar, where "there was Lenny, with three scotches lined up." Bernstein would do whatever possible to avoid confrontations, explaining only, "I hate scenes."[60]

In a BBC tribute following Bernstein's death in 1990, Jerome Robbins summed up the achievement of *West Side Story*, beginning with the assertion that it was "an American musical." The aim had been to "see if all of us—Lenny who wrote 'long-hair' music, Arthur who wrote serious plays, myself who did serious ballets, Oliver Smith who was a serious painter—could bring our acts together and do a work on the popular stage." Although Robbins is generally recognized as the prime mover behind this musical milestone, Bernstein never really relegated his own role. While *West Side* was playing its pre-Broadway run in Philadelphia, Bernstein wrote that "this show is my baby. . . . If it goes as well in New York as it has on the road we will have proved something very big indeed and maybe changed the face of American Musical Theater."[61]

When *West Side Story* opened in New York on September 26, 1957, there was general if not universal acclaim. It would run for almost two years (772 performances), go on the road for a year, and then return to New York for another 253 performances. But some critics found the pace of the show too dizzying and the streets too mean. In the *New York Herald Tribune*, the inestimable Walter Kerr reported that it was "rushingly acted" and characterized the dances as "savage, restless, electrifying." But "apart from the spine-tingling velocity of the dances," he found the show "almost never emotionally affecting." Nevertheless, he foresaw that "the radioactive fallout . . . must still be descending on Broadway this morning." In the *Times*, Brooks Atkinson called it "a profoundly moving show . . . as ugly as the city jungles and also pathetic, tender and forgiving. . . . The subject is not beautiful, but what *West Side Story* draws out of it is beautiful."[62]

In 1957 the "beauty" of the urban jungle was yet to be found in the eyes of all beholders. When that year's Tony Awards were announced, *West Side Story* garnered only two—for choreography and scenic design. The show that swept the awards was *The Music Man*, Meredith Willson's warm-hearted and nostalgic visit to small-town America at the turn of the century. Trouble in River City remained far more comprehensible and clearly more controllable than gang rumbles on the West Side, even—or perhaps especially—as the American social fabric began to rend in the late 1950s.

Increasingly in the 1960s, particularly as symbolized by the emergence of the civil rights, feminist, and antiwar movements, social dissonance disrupted the outwardly placid era of peace and prosperity that had dominated since the end of World War II. The mainstream version of the American Dream, based on optimistic notions of expanding middle-class affluence, faced an ominous reinterpretation that rejected the status quo. The culture that had worshipped the great god Conformity now found itself engulfed by an almost palpable sense of disaffection.

Much as *West Side Story*'s gang warfare served as a virtual metaphor for America's growing fragmentation, *Gypsy* would portray the hopeless dissolution of those caught by the juggernaut of change. Based on the memoirs of ecdysiast Gypsy Rose Lee, *Gypsy* was originally envisioned by producer David Merrick as a vehicle for Ethel Merman. Merman herself thought it could be an affectionate salute to the lost worlds of vaudeville and burlesque; Jerome Robbins, who had worked with her as the choreographer of *Call Me Madam*, agreed and began to hire veteran performers who could give him some historical perspective on these lost urban folk arts. He also suggested to Merrick that playwright Arthur Laurents—with whom Robbins had collaborated on *West Side Story*—write the book.

It would be Laurents who would transform the idea of the show from a nostalgic look at old-time Broadway to the more abrasive story of Rose, the quintessential stage mother who lived for—grasped at—the success she sought for her daughters, Baby June and Louise (a.k.a. Gypsy Rose Lee). And it was Laurents who suggested that the young Stephen Sondheim write the entire score for *Gypsy*—a suggestion Merman contradicted by saying that, clever as Sondheim was, "he can't write for me. He doesn't know who I am." Or, more to the point, she did not really know who Stephen Sondheim was. She insisted—and Merrick concurred—that an established composer be engaged to write the music, while Sondheim be retained as lyricist.

After Merrick was turned down by Irving Berlin and Cole Porter, he turned to Jule Styne. As it happened, the Styne-Sondheim partnership worked brilliantly: "Steve was the first lyric writer who understood what I was doing," Styne has said. "For me the music has

to come from the situation and has to capture it before the words are there."[63] The key was that they were writing for a star of Merman's caliber—the first time Sondheim had ever written for a star—so that the music and lyrics could be shaped directly to fit her character. And if anyone doubted Merman's luminosity, she would be quick to point out, as she once did on television, that "when I do a show, not to pat myself on the back, but when I do a show, the whole show revolves around *me*. . . . And if I don't show up, they can just

Barbara Cook (b. 1927)

A sassy lyric in a 1960s off-Broadway revue cleverly queries: "Why Julie Andrews instead of Barbara Cook?" Although Andrews solidified the image of the soprano leading lady primarily through appearances in blockbuster films, Barbara Cook remained ever faithful to the musical stage. Throughout the 1950s and 1960s she brightly bore the banner of the ingenue heroine, remaking and redefining the persona in a series of roles as individual and diverse as they were memorable. There is perhaps no other performer in the history of the American musical theater who has appeared in more fascinating (if commercially disappointing) shows, or whose work is more devoutly treasured by musical-comedy buffs.

Cook left her Atlanta home in the late 1940s to seek fame and fortune in New York City. She landed on Broadway in 1950 as the heroine of the E. Y. Harburg–Sammy Fain musical *Flahooley*, an endearing mess of a show with a lovely score that displayed her crystalline soprano and nascent acting skills. A number of conventional roles followed; however, her first real stretch as a performer came in 1956 with Bernstein's *Candide*. As its naively mercenary heroine Cunegonde, she gamely tackled a character and a score that would have sent many a traditional musical-comedy soprano in frantic

Barbara Cook as
Marian the librarian
and Robert Preston
as Harold Hill in *The
Music Man* (1957).

Photofest.

Daniel Massey and
Barbara Cook in *She
Loves Me* (1963).

Photofest.

search of a job in a road company of *Oklahoma!*
or *Rose Marie.* For the few who witnessed
Candide's brief Broadway run (seventy-nine
performances), or the many who have since
heard the show's cast album, her performance
of the aria "Glitter and Be Gay" is a classic
moment.

Cook's biggest commercial success was as
Marian the librarian in *The Music Man* (1957),
with her artfully artless projection of tender
strength tempering the brash braggadocio of
Robert Preston's Harold Hill. The role that was
perhaps her most expansive was that of Amalia
Balash, the shopgirl heroine of *She Loves Me*
(1963)—yet another commercial failure that has
amassed (chiefly through its cast recording)
ardent admirers. Here was a role that gave her
ample opportunities to reconfirm her depth as
an actress and in the delightful song-aria "Ice
Cream" gave her a showstopping eleven o'clock
number.

By the early 1970s Cook felt increasingly
disillusioned and displaced with a musical
theater in unsteady transition. A decade later,
she became a cabaret singer of the first rank,
attaining a level of stardom that had eluded her
in all her years on Broadway. The musical
theater has, however, remained the source for
much of her concert repertoire, proving her
affection for the medium. "I wish that I had
known that I was living through a golden era in
the musical theater," she has mused. "I might
have enjoyed it more."

forget it!"[64] As for David Merrick, his genius had been to bring together the show's creative team, but he managed to alienate himself from everyone by the time *Gypsy* opened. A difficult and acerbic presence, Merrick was said to combine "the delicacy of the Marquis de Sade, the humanity of Attila the Hun, the generosity of Ebenezer Scrooge and the sophisticated taste of Yogi Berra."[65]

The Styne-Sondheim score would include "Let Me Entertain You," "Some People," "Small World," "If Mama Was Married," "Everything's Coming Up Roses," "Together Wherever We Go," "You Gotta Have a Gimmick," and the remarkable "Rose's Turn," in which Mama Rose steps out onto the deserted Minsky stage and vents her years of frustration—unblinking in her belief that she could have been a bigger star than anyone. Her character unravels in a veritable mad scene:

Gangway, world, get offa' my runway!
Startin' now, I bat a thousand!
This time, boys, I'm takin' the bows.
And ev'rything's coming up Rose!
Ev'rything's coming up roses!
Ev'rything's coming up roses this time for me!
For me!
For me!
For me!
For me!!
For me!!!
FOR ME!!!

STEPHEN SONDHEIM AND JULE STYNE,
"ROSE'S TURN," 1959

Gypsy marquee at the Broadway Theatre, 1959. By Friedman-Abeles.

Friedman Abeles Collection, New York Public Library for the Performing Arts, New York City.

Gypsy opened at the Broadway Theatre on May 21, 1959, and enjoyed a solid run of 702 performances. For Sondheim, it marked the last Rodgers and Hammerstein–style show that he would do— one that told a story through character and song, with the characters causing the story to move forward in a song-scene, song-scene progression. Oscar Hammerstein had once told him not to imitate other people's emotions, but to "speak your own."[66] After *Gypsy*, Sondheim agreed, saying, "Now, let's try different things."[67]

Frank Loesser (1910–1969)

Composer-lyricist-librettist-producer-publisher Frank Loesser, a pint-sized torrent of talent and temperament, was a major force in the Broadway musical theater of the 1950s and 1960s. Although he experimented (with some success) with the retro romanticism of the Rodgers and Hammerstein tradition (*The Most Happy Fella*, 1956; *Greenwillow*, 1960), Loesser's finest work was firmly entrenched in the sweetly cynical soot and sparkle of urban asphalt—a world he knew and loved well from his childhood days on West 107th Street in New York City.

Loesser grew up in a household where classical music and the performing arts were revered. His Prussian-born father was an accomplished pianist and teacher who often accompanied opera diva Lilli Lehmann on her concert tours. Frank's half-brother Arthur was a noted concert pianist, music critic, and arts administrator. In contrast, Frank had a long-running, self-described "rendez-vous with failure" until he won his earliest fame in the late 1930s as the lyricist of such Hollywood song hits as "Two Sleepy People" and "Small Fry" (both written with composer Hoagy Carmichael).[1]

In the 1940s Loesser vigorously assumed the tandem tasks of writing words and music for the wartime hit "Praise the Lord and Pass the Ammunition" and the Academy Award–winning "Baby, It's Cold Outside." His Broadway debut as a composer-lyricist was the well-received *Where's Charley?* a 1948 musical version of the British farce *Charley's Aunt*, which gave him a chance to work with comic dancer Ray Bolger and the venerable director George Abbott.

Two years later, Loesser wrote the score for *Guys and Dolls*, which endures as his crowning achievement in the musical theater. Freely adapted by ex-radio scriptwriter Abe Burrows (and others) from characters and incidents in stories by journalist-author Damon Runyon, this self-described "musical fable of Broadway"

Frank Loesser painted this self-portrait to hang on his office door when he was working.

Courtesy Mrs. Frank Loesser.

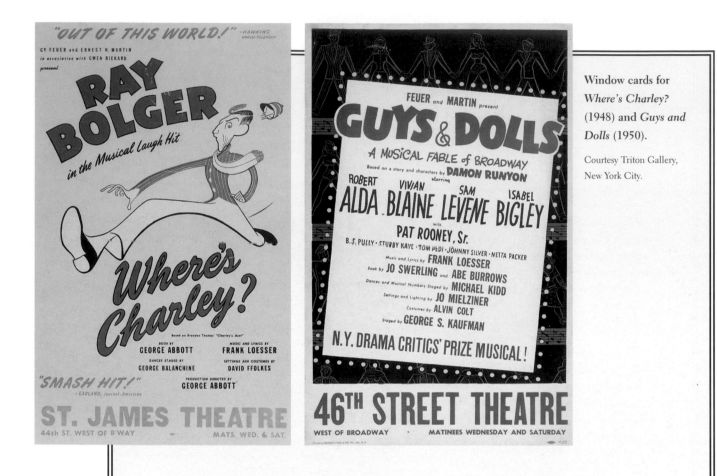

Window cards for *Where's Charley?* (1948) and *Guys and Dolls* (1950).

Courtesy Triton Gallery, New York City.

is the American musical theater's ultimate fantasia on that urban playground known as New York City. Even more than the Bernstein-Comden-Green *On the Town*, *Guys and Dolls* relied on warmhearted caricatures of the cityscape for much of its effectiveness, not only because of its colorful (and colorfully named) cast of characters and Burrows's witty narrative, but also because of Loesser's score, which masterfully translates Runyon's curious but strangely appropriate patois into catchy and touching music and lyrics.[2] The songs range in scope from traditional Broadway ballads ("I'll Know," "I've Never Been in Love Before") and comic character numbers ("Adelaide's Lament," "Sue Me") to moody and poetic evocations of city life: "When the smell of the rainwashed pavement / Comes up clean and fresh and cold / And the streetlamp fills the gutter with gold" (Frank Loesser, "My Time of Day," 1950).

Columbia Records executive Goddard Lieberson pronounced Loesser's music and lyrics for *Guys and Dolls* "so perfectly integrated that it was impossible, afterwards, to recall which was song and which was book in furtherance of the plot."[3]

The expansively titled *How to Succeed in Business without Really Trying* (1961) returned Loesser to an urban milieu. This time, the setting was the ruthless and fast-paced world of American big business. Giving him the chance to reteam with Abe Burrows, *How to Succeed* gave Loesser his greatest commercial and critical success in the musical theater, achieving a run of 1,417 performances and amassing a bundle of awards, including the 1962 Pulitzer Prize for drama. Although Loesser reportedly was disappointed with his own work, the score—brassy, satiric, and appealingly abrasive—is a perfect fit for the comically heartless cartoon of a plot about a window washer's swift ascent on the corporate ladder through shameless wile and guile.

Frank Loesser's best work is hallmarked by a beguiling unpretentiousness—a word that may well have described the man himself. "I don't write for posterity," he insisted. "I write for entertainment." It is a tribute to his talents that he skillfully managed to do both.

1. Susan Loesser, *A Most Remarkable Fella* (New York).

2. Among the Runyon characters included in *Guys and Dolls* are gamblers Sky (né Obadiah) Masterson, Nicely-Nicely Johnson, Big Jule, and Harry the Horse, to name just a few.

3. Loesser, *A Most Remarkable Fella*, 102.

Window cards for *The Most Happy Fella* (1956), *Greenwillow* (1960), and *How to Succeed in Business without Really Trying* (1961).

Courtesy Triton Gallery, New York City.

Frank Loesser.

Courtesy Mrs. Frank Loesser.

REDEFINITION AND REVIVAL, 1960–PRESENT

Where is style?
Where is skill?
Where is forethought?
Where's discretion in the heart,
Where's passion in the art,
Where's craft?
STEPHEN SONDHEIM, "LIAISONS," 1973

"Side by Side by Side"

In the early 1960s America entered a period of social disquiet and dissonance. This uncertainty—in the social, political, and artistic climates—forced a jarring transition in the American musical: the time-tested formulas that had once vitalized the genre revealed themselves to be timeworn. This brought about the virtual demise of the splashy, spectacular Hollywood musical, at least in the original dimensions that it had once achieved.[1] Meanwhile, the stage musical was forced to enter a new phase of redefinition and revival, combining the familiar with the experimental in an effort to seek various new patrons to replace the rapidly disappearing broadly based, middle-class audience.

Many of the composers, authors, directors, and performers of the musical's belle epoque were continuing to contribute to the medium, albeit with fluctuating degrees of success.

RIGHT: Jerry Herman. By Al Hirschfeld, 1980. Collection of Jerry Herman.

© Al Hirschfeld. Drawing reproduced by special arrangement with Hirschfeld's exclusive representative, The Margo Feiden Galleries, Ltd., New York City.

LEFT: Carol Channing in *Hello, Dolly!* (1964). By Mark Kauffmann for *Life* magazine.

© Time Inc.

Richard Rodgers, Leonard Bernstein, Jule Styne, Alan Jay Lerner, Betty Comden and
Adolph Green, George Abbott, Agnes de Mille, Joshua Logan, Alfred Drake, Mary Martin, and Ethel Merman, to name a few, maintained a presence in the early and middle
parts of the era but uniformly failed to deliver work that superseded their past glories.

In these years of transition, the best of a new generation of those working in the traditional mold were composer-lyricist Jerry Herman and director-choreographer Gower
Champion, who, in tandem with librettist Michael Stewart and producer David Merrick,
created the wildly popular and critically embraced *Hello, Dolly!* (1964).

"To me, the most important thing a theater composer can do is write songs that audiences can leave the theater humming. I call them take-home songs," asserted Jerry Herman in a 1985 interview.[2] Indeed, the hallmark of Herman's music and lyrics is their immediate accessibility in a way that recalls the output of his inspiration, Irving Berlin. In
fact, Herman credited a teenage viewing of Ethel Merman in the original Broadway production of *Annie Get Your Gun* as the impetus for his desire to write for the musical theater. Another important influence in his early years was his mother Ruth Sax, who was a
singer, pianist, and local radio personality in his hometown of Jersey City.

After completing his undergraduate studies in drama at the University of Miami, Herman first supported himself playing piano in Manhattan cocktail lounges. While playing at a small Greenwich Village club called The Showplace, he persuaded its owner to finance and present there an intimate revue that he had written called *Nightcap*. The show was a surprise hit and ran for more than four hundred performances. Its score contained a song that seemed a vital affirmation of its composer's commitment to his chosen profession:[3]

Hello, Dolly! (1964).
Sheet music.

Alice Becker Levin.

There's just no tune as exciting
As a show tune in 2/4.
When it's played, you can just tell
There's footlights everywhere.
When it's played, you can just smell
The greasepaint in the air.

JERRY HERMAN, "SHOW TUNE (IN 2/4)," 1958

Herman first made his mark on Broadway in 1961 as the composer-lyricist of *Milk and Honey*, a musical comedy set in contemporary Israel. His score, a clever marriage of pseudo-Israeli folk rhythms and Tin Pan Alley ballads, was judged the show's chief virtue and earned him his first Tony Award nomination. In early 1963, when he learned that impresario David Merrick was planning a musical version of Thornton Wilder's play *The Matchmaker* as a vehicle for Ethel Merman, he campaigned actively to be its composer-lyricist. He obtained a copy of the adaptation from its author, Michael Stewart, and over the course of a weekend, he composed four songs to audition for Merrick. The volatile producer, known as "the abominable showman" to his foes, was impressed with Herman's eagerness and obvious talent, and, on the spot, announced, in characteristic Broadway lingo, "Kid, the show is yours."[4]

When Merman abandoned the project early in its development, Merrick instructed Herman to redesign his score for the talents of Carol Channing. One of the most distinctive comediennes of her generation, Channing made her first impression on New York audiences in 1941 in Marc Blitzstein's labor opera *No for an Answer*. Seven years later, she won favorable notice for her gamboling in the Broadway production of the West Coast revue *Lend an Ear*. One year later, she catapulted to stardom as the baby-voiced Amazon Lorelei Lee in the Jule Styne musical *Gentlemen Prefer Blondes*. For the next decade, she tried in vain to find another vehicle that was its equal.

When David Merrick offered her the chance to play the resourceful mistress-of-all-trades Dolly Gallagher Levi, she seized the opportunity to reestablish her standing as a prominent member of the Broadway community. Her performance was greeted with huzzahs and hat-tossing and lifted her to the status of theatrical superstar.

Along with Herman, Channing, and Merrick, there was one more star who shone in the original production of *Hello, Dolly!*—its director-choreographer Gower Champion. He had launched his professional career as a dancer in the early 1940s, appearing in a progression of forgettable musicals.[5] After serving with the Coast Guard during World War II, he formed a nightclub act with dancer Marjorie Bell. In 1947 they married, and as Marge and Gower Champion, they won their first kudos for appearances on television and in several MGM movies, including Arthur Freed's 1951 production of the Kern-Hammerstein *Show Boat*.

Champion attracted his earliest attention on Broadway in 1948 for his Tony Award–winning choreography for the revue *Lend an Ear* (which gave him his first opportunity to work with Carol Channing). Eleven years later, his direction and dances for *Bye Bye Birdie* (1960) energetically captured the zestful innocence of the burgeoning rock 'n' roll generation and established him as a promising figure in the musical theater. *Carnival*, a 1961 musical stage adaptation of the MGM film *Lili*, added further luster to his career and gave him his first opportunity to work for David Merrick. With his dominant role in molding the look and sensibilities of *Hello, Dolly!* Champion solidified his claim as the logical successor to Jerome Robbins. Moreover, his work was instrumental in affirming the director-choreographer as the theater professional most directly responsible for shaping and conjoining all the elements of the Broadway musical into a glossy final product. As Robbins had done with his staging for *West Side Story*, Champion infused virtually every scene of *Hello, Dolly!* with stylized movement, from simple solos and duets to electric, energetic full-stage numbers. Conveying Dolly's celebratory return to the Harmonia Gardens, a favorite haunt of her youth, Champion's staging of Herman's celebrated title song ranks as one of the most memorable moments in the American musical theater. The number began with Dolly's stately descent down the red-carpeted, balustraded stairs of Oliver Smith's elegant setting and built steadily to a riotous conclusion, with the heroine and the energetic ensemble (dressed as waiters) practically dancing in the audience's lap as they pranced in line on a circular runway that jutted out into the theater. In the words of *New York Herald Tribune* critic Walter Kerr, the effect was one of the "most exhilaratingly straight-forward, head-on, old-fashioned, rabble-rousing numbers since Harrigan and Hart rolled down the curtain."[6]

Hello, Dolly! was a phenomenal hit, both on Broadway and in international tours. Aside from Carol Channing, whose performance remains definitive, Dolly was portrayed by such musical comedy matriarchs as Mary Martin, Ethel Merman, Ginger Rogers, and Pearl Bailey, just to name a few. The show spawned at least two multimillion-selling recordings, the 1964 LP by the original cast and a 45-rpm single of the title tune by Louis Armstrong, both of which temporarily unseated the complete domination of rock 'n' roll in the recording industry with the sounds of theater music.

Jerry Herman immediately followed his success with *Hello, Dolly!* with another whopping hit, *Mame*. Based on Patrick Dennis's novel about a free-living socialite who be-

Window card for
Mame (1966).

Dwight Blocker Bowers.

comes a mentor for her young nephew, the show was, like *Dolly!* another tour de force vehicle for a female performer. In this instance, the star was Angela Lansbury, taking on the role that confirmed her status as one of the great musical comedy finds of the decade. The score boasted another showstopping title number and a superb ballad, "If He Walked into My Life," the latter of which allowed the outrageous heroine an effectively rare moment of introspection.

Herman's next three shows (*Dear World*, 1968; *Mack and Mabel*, 1974; *The Grand Tour*, 1979) failed to achieve commercial or critical prosperity; however, *Mack and Mabel*, based on the lives of silent film greats Mack Sennett and Mabel Normand, gave him the chance for a reunion with the *Dolly!* team of Merrick, Champion, and Stewart and contains what he considers to be his finest score to date. His most recent theatrical effort was the remarkably successful *La Cage aux Folles* (1984), based on the play and film of the same name. Although Harvey Fierstein's libretto, which centered on the rocky union of a middle-aged drag queen and his impresario lover, was hardly conventional in theme, the show bore the comfortingly traditional vigor of the Herman style, with a tuneful parade of showstopping production numbers and ballads. Herman's detractors tend to assess his work as being too commercial. "Too commercial?" he responds. "What is that? I think being accused of too much commerciality is like saying the bride is too pretty. To me the ultimate compliment is being called commercial."[7]

Following *Hello, Dolly!* Gower Champion continued a long, if often adversarial, relationship with David Merrick, culminating in a final, bittersweet joint triumph—a 1980 stage version of the classic 1933 Warner Bros.–Busby Berkeley film, *42nd Street*. Billed as "a musical extravaganza," the show more than fulfilled the promise of Merrick's promotional hoopla and provided Champion with myriad opportunities for creating the kind of theatrical excitement that resided in his finest work. Its marathon engagement of more than three thousand performances gave both Champion and Merrick their longest run on Broadway. But Champion did not live to see its success. He died on the morning of the

Choreographer Gower Champion, surrounded by the chorus from *42nd Street* (1980). By Martha Swope.

© Time, Inc.

RED, HOT & BLUE

show's Broadway premiere. Merrick announced his death onstage to a shocked audience and cast immediately following the rapturously received opening night performance.

"When I started out I wanted to be a Fred Astaire, and after that a Jerome Robbins," confessed Bob Fosse. "But then I realized there was always somebody a dancer or choreographer had to take orders from. So I decided I wanted to become a director, namely George Abbott. But as I got older I dropped the hero-worship thing. I didn't want to emulate anyone. I just wanted to do the things I was capable of doing—and have some fun doing them."[8] Fosse's career paralleled a significant trend in the 1950s and 1960s musical theater that sidled away from the traditional Rodgers and Hammerstein story-song structure to a more loosely constructed modus operandi built more upon stylized movement than on linear narrative structure. The best of his work is marked by a staccato angularity and a jazzy, sensual cynicism.

Robert Louis Fosse became a professional dancer at the age of fifteen, appearing in variety shows, clubs, and burlesque houses in his hometown of Chicago. The seediness and sensuality he encountered in these third-rate arenas of American show business would later exert a profound influence on his choreographic style. After a hitch in the Navy during World War II, he devised a club act with a young dancer named Mary-Ann Niles, who became his wife in 1945. By his own description, they were "a second-rate Marge and Gower Champion";[9] however, their regional popularity soon propelled them to New York and appearances on various television shows, including "Your Hit Parade," and in the Broadway revue *Dance Me a Song*. In the latter, Fosse met (and later married) its star, Joan McCracken. McCracken, a former Agnes de Mille protégée and alumna of the original productions of *Oklahoma!* and *Bloomer Girl*, encouraged him to refine his theatrical skills by studying dance and dramatic technique at the American Theatre Wing and at Sanford Meisner's esteemed Neighborhood Playhouse. McCracken urged him to participate in *Talent '52*, a one-night showcase of young Broadway performers sponsored by the stage managers' union. Fosse's satiric send-up of the balletic mannerisms of de Mille and Robbins earned him a contract at MGM. Ultimately, his sojourn in Hollywood proved static and disappointing;[10] however, his work for one sequence in the MGM film version of the stage hit *Kiss Me, Kate* provided a spectacular display of those elements of movement that would become distinctive of the Fosse style. Designed as an extended coda for the song "From This Moment On," Fosse's scenario paired him with Carol Haney, Gene Kelly's assistant and a disciple of choreographer Jack Cole, in a sizzling progression of out-and-out hoofing, acrobatic leaps and slides, sultry burlesque bumps and grinds, rhythmic finger-snaps, and elbows-locked-at-the waist, open-palmed, splayed-finger hand gestures.[11] A complete rejection of the de Mille-Robbins classically derived traditions, Fosse's choreographic patterns were founded entirely on the rhythms of African American and Latin jazz.

Citing the "From This Moment On" sequence as evidence of her husband's skills, Joan McCracken persuaded director George Abbott to hire him as choreographer for his new show, *The Pajama Game*. Coproducer Harold Prince insisted that Jerome Robbins be hired as a backup, giving Robbins his first status as codirector; nonetheless, Fosse's debut as a Broadway choreographer was spectacular. Standing out was his movement for "Steam Heat," a lively number that opened the second act and featured his *Kiss Me, Kate* partner Carol Haney, who scored a personal triumph with her performance in the show, and fellow dancers Buzz Miller and Peter Gennaro.[12] The song, by the show's composers Richard Adler and Jerry Ross, was an ingenious series of brassy explosions and stringed-bass vamps that underscored Fosse's rhythmic patterns of movement. Even the costuming, by veteran Lemuel Ayers, presented vaudeville-inspired components that became part and parcel of Fosse's bag of tricks: androgynous tight black suits, white gloves, and, above all, derby hats.

Damn Yankees (1955), a musical version of the novel *The Year the Yankees Lost the Pennant*, reteamed Fosse with many members of the company that constructed *The Pajama Game*.[13] The show also marked the beginning of a lifelong professional, as well as personal, association with Gwen Verdon, cast in the star role of Lola, a temptingly beautiful agent of the Devil. With *Damn Yankees*, Verdon became the most acclaimed musical comedy dancer since Ziegfeld's Marilyn Miller. Over the next two decades, she would establish herself as the ultimate interpreter of Fosse's choreographic vision.

Gwen Verdon and Stephen Douglass in *Damn Yankees* (1955). By Peter Stackpole for *Life* magazine.

© Time, Inc.

Verdon had grown up in Culver City, California, in proximity to MGM Studios, where her English-born father was an electrician. Plagued with a variety of infantile diseases, she was instructed in dance by her ex-vaudevillian mother, who hoped that it would prove therapeutic in straightening her weak, bent legs. Billed as "the world's fastest tapper," she performed as a child in stage shows at various Los Angeles movie theaters. By the time she reached sixteen, she had amassed a sheaf of professional credits ranging from professional ballroom dancer to member of the corps de ballet at the Hollywood Bowl. Marriage and motherhood brought about a five-year hiatus to her career; however, in 1947, she dusted off her dancing shoes and succeeded Carol Haney as assistant to choreographer Jack Cole. Following her divorce and near-anonymous appearances in several stage and screen musicals, Verdon became "an overnight sensation" as the second female lead in the Cole Porter musical *Can-Can* (1953).[14] Her triumph in that show led directly to her being cast in *Damn Yankees*, the work that would launch her career.

The number in *Damn Yankees* that solidified the Fosse-Verdon collaboration was the predatory tango "Whatever Lola Wants." Combining Latin dance movements with the unbridled bravado of burlesque, the number was exhilaratingly sensual, albeit satirically so. Verdon assigned complete credit for its effectiveness to Fosse, asserting that it "was staged right down to the minute I touched my hair":[15]

> Whatever Lola wants
> Lola gets
> And little man
> Little Lola wants you.

RICHARD ADLER AND JERRY ROSS, "WHATEVER LOLA WANTS (LOLA GETS)," 1955

Their next joint effort was *New Girl in Town* (1957), an uneasy musical adaptation of *Anna Christie*, Eugene O'Neill's dour drama about a prostitute and her redemption.

During its out-of-town tryouts, star and choreographer quarreled with director George Abbott and coproducer Harold Prince about an erotic second-act dance sequence set in a bordello. Prince deemed it "crotch-dancing" and Abbott found it "just plain dirty," while Verdon and Fosse defended it as decadent art of the first order.[16] By the time of the Broadway opening, Prince and Abbott had succeeded in effecting its censorship, but their victory was a temporary one. Fosse eventually restored most of the deleted material during the show's run. *Redhead*, a musical deftly fashioned to capitalize on Verdon's gamine appeal, marked Fosse's Broadway debut as a director-choreographer.[17] If his direction of the dialogue scenes was hardly exceptional, the dances and musical numbers were distinctive, rooted as they were in his own affection for the eccentric movements of vaudeville and variety entertainment, which suited the show's 1907 London setting. Although mildly diverting in script and score, *Redhead* was decidedly a triumph of style over substance.

Fosse and Verdon married in 1960 while on a national tour of *Redhead*. With *Sweet Charity* (1966), they returned to Broadway in style, revealing the finest fusion of their talents thus far. Sleek, urban, and adamantly contemporary, *Charity* revealed Fosse in a state of transition, taking one step away from the pseudorealistic trappings of the conventional musical and jumping one leap ahead toward a new style of musical—one filtered through his showbiz–surrealist choreographic perspective. Freely adapting the plot from the Fellini screen classic *The Nights of Cabiria*, Fosse and scriptwriter Neil Simon structured the entire show around Verdon's Chaplinesque persona, keeping her onstage almost constantly in the role of a waiflike, put-upon dance-hall hostess ironically named Charity Hope Valentine.[18] Propelled by Cy Coleman and Dorothy Fields's hard-driving score, Fosse made all the elements of the production "breeze by, whiz by, strut by, and fly by like a galaxy of comets on the loose."[19] Nearly every number became a showstopping event, from the languid, lean-on-the-bar come-on of the taxi dancers in "Big Spender" to Verdon's ebullient solo turn, "If They Could See Me Now," which cleverly elaborated on the vaudeville panache suggested years earlier in "Steam Heat."

If the stage version of *Sweet Charity* pointed to a new direction for Fosse, its 1969 screen adaptation almost stopped his career cold. With Shirley MacLaine gamely attempting to perform a role exquisitely tailored for Verdon (who selflessly acted as Fosse's assistant and MacLaine's coach), the film, skewed by an obsession with cinematic pyrotechnics, was lambasted by critics and ignored by audiences.[20] Curiously enough, Fosse's next project was not only the finest film musical of its generation, but it also endures as perhaps his most consistently superlative work in the genre of the American musical. *Cabaret* (1972) offers an unsentimental, uncompromising portrait of 1930s Berlin. Loosely based on the 1966 stage hit (and its source, Christopher Isherwood's *Berlin Stories*), the film restricts all but one of its musical numbers to the tawdry nightclub that is the principal setting, using the superb songs by John Kander and Fred Ebb as acrid metaphors for the dramatic action. Centering on the evocation of sensuality, sexual ambiguity, and show business seediness—all vital components of the Fosse style—the film depicts a seamy underworld enveloped in a spirit of decadence that is not moribund and soporific but, instead, thrillingly, even horrifyingly, alive. In the words of *New Yorker* critic Pauline Kael, "The picture has the distortions and the exaggerations and the grinning vividness of Expressionist art."[21]

As he had aided Verdon in developing her distinctive stage persona, Fosse guided

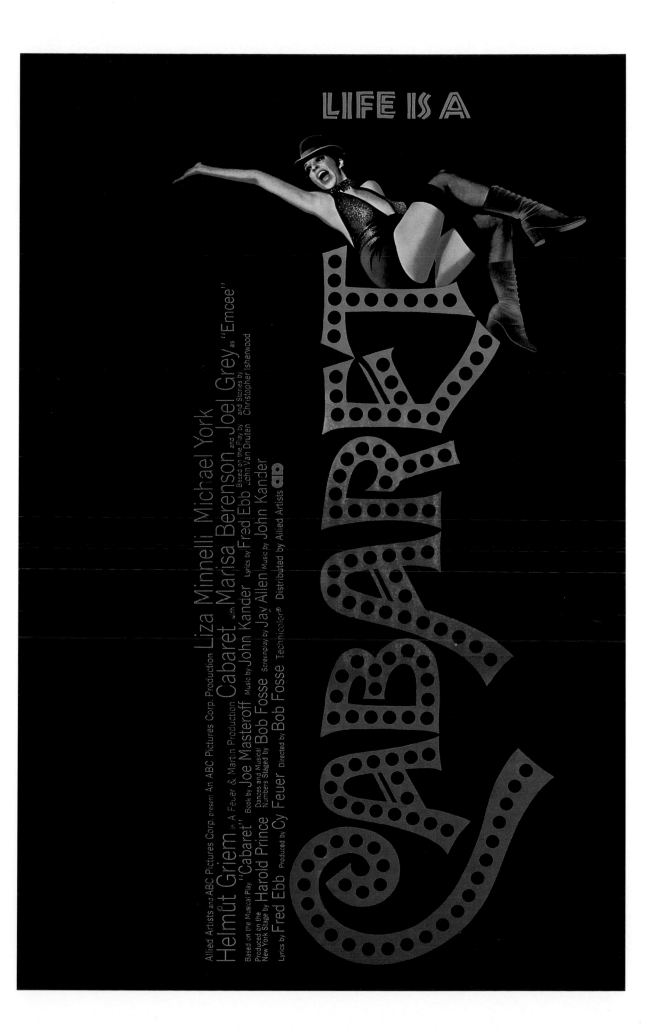

Cabaret's star Liza Minnelli in synthesizing her singing, dancing, and acting talents into a strikingly unified screen presence. As tender-tough entertainer Sally Bowles, she is nothing short of electrifying, especially in her performance of the sybaritic title tune. In a nightmarish, chiaroscuro limbo of piercing white light and murky shadow, she and Fosse remake the number into a glittering psychodrama. Minnelli's work in the film earned her an Academy Award and placed her in the vanguard of a new generation of musical stars.

Liza Minnelli spent her childhood on the perimeters of Hollywood soundstages, observing the work of her mother Judy Garland and father Vincente Minnelli. At sixteen, she won kudos from theater critics for her performance as the comic lead in a 1963 off-Broadway revival of the 1941 musical comedy *Best Foot Forward.* Two years later, as a result of her exultant Broadway debut in the musical *Flora, the Red Menace,* she became the youngest female performer to win the Tony Award for best actress in a musical (a record that still stands). Although the show itself had a brief life, she formed an enduring collaboration with its composer-lyricist team, John Kander and Fred Ebb, who wrote both the stage and screen versions of *Cabaret* with her in mind.

In 1973 Bob Fosse won a show business triple crown, receiving an Oscar for his direction of *Cabaret,* an Emmy for his staging of Liza Minnelli's television concert *Liza with a Z,* and a Tony for his ingenious directorial sleight-of-hand on the otherwise mediocre *Pippin.* The 1975 musical *Chicago,* a final Broadway teaming with Verdon, represented the theatrical apotheosis of Fosse as auteur. Infused with a venal worldview reminiscent of Bertolt Brecht, the show, co-written by Fosse and lyricist Fred Ebb, made the decadence portrayed in *Cabaret* seem tame by comparison. The plot portrayed the depravity and political corruption of 1920s Chicago through the character of Roxie Hart (Verdon), a whorish "jazz-slayer" who kills her lover, gets acquitted by a shady lawyer (Jerry Orbach), and goes into show business in partnership with another murderess (Chita Rivera).

As he had hinted at in *Sweet Charity* and realized in *Cabaret,* Fosse built the entire show around a production concept; in this instance, that of "a musical vaudeville," using each number in Kander and Ebb's sour, brassy score as both ironic commentary on the action and flashy pastiches of variety acts. In a progression of gaudily staged turns, he evoked such bygone luminaries as Bert Williams, Marilyn Miller, Sophie Tucker, and Jeanette MacDonald. *Chicago* was not for everyone; its tinseled bleakness destroyed any suggestion of the sunny resolution typical of the commercial musical comedy. But for those willing to be adventurous, it presented a spectacularly heartless amalgamation of the entertainment forms—burlesque, vaudeville, nightclubs—that influenced the evolution of Fosse's technique. One song in Kander and Ebb's score, aptly titled "Razzle Dazzle," might well provide the most accurate voicing of Fosse's theatrical credo:

> Give 'em the old razzle dazzle
> Razzle dazzle 'em.
> Give 'em an act with lots of flash in it
> And the reaction will be passionate
> Give 'em the old hocus pocus
> Bead and feather 'em
> How can they see with sequins in their eyes?
> FRED EBB AND JOHN KANDER, "RAZZLE-DAZZLE," 1975

Liza Minnelli in
Cabaret (1972).

Fosse/Verdon Collection,
Music Division, Library of
Congress, Washington,
D.C.

When Joe Papp originated the New York Shakespeare Festival in 1956, his intent was to cultivate a far broader audience than the middle-class mainstream that flooded Broadway theaters in the mid-1950s. Born in the tough Williamsburg section of Brooklyn in 1921 to a trunkmaker from Poland and a seamstress from Lithuania, Joseph Papirofsky gave little hint early in his life of an interest in theater; the only glimmer had been his discovery, at the age of twelve, of a love for Shakespeare. But the fire caught during his Navy service in World War II, when he helped to organize an entertainment unit and staged shows on the decks of aircraft carriers, eventually meeting another young sailor named Bob Fosse in 1945. Using the GI Bill after the war, he went to school at the Actors' Laboratory Workshop in Los Angeles. Founded by several members of the Group Theater, the Actors' Lab aimed at developing a permanent acting ensemble and an indigenous American technique. Theirs was to be "art for the people"—a priority that Joe Papp would take as his own.[22]

In the early 1950s Papp went to New York and became a CBS television stage manager for such shows as *Studio One*, *Omnibus*, and the *Jackie Gleason Show*. At the same time, he began to produce and direct plays, organizing productions of Shakespeare at the Emmanuel Church in the Village. Papp's theater was free, as he "wanted to reach audiences who might never have seen a play before and who were unable or unwilling to pay."[23] He aimed to develop both interracial casts and multiracial audiences—clearly not the norm on Broadway in the mid-1950s. Aside from some "all-Negro musicals" and integrated Federal Theatre casts from the 1930s on, mainstream theater—casts and audience—had remained white.

Driven by an intense desire to reform and reshape America's theater, Papp was an inveterate innovator, at once charming, visionary, and mercurial. When he launched his free Shakespeare Festival in Central Park in 1956, he wanted to showcase an American version of Shakespeare rather than the kind of British "singing tradition, declamatory, oratorical" that he found "pompous" and "horribly artificial." By the early 1960s, he had also funded a Mobile Theater, which would caravan its forty-foot-long stage and other vehicles carting equipment, props, chairs, and bleachers through downtrodden borough neighborhoods. "There is a special hunger in all true people of the theater," he once said, "not just to play for the dressed-up society audience but to engage in a form of theater that is much more basic and immediate—the itinerant circus, the *barracas* of Garcia Lorca's day. The Mobile satisfied that hunger." The caravan theater particularly targeted black and Hispanic audiences, with several tours devoted to Spanish-language performances.[24]

Papp's theater became a cultural lightning rod for alternative theater in the sixties—perhaps most successfully exemplified by the "American tribal love-rock musical," *Hair.* "I am looking for plays that have some passionate statement to make that is commensurate with the times we are living in," he said in 1966.[25] That year, 285,000 Americans were in Vietnam, while the antiwar student protest movement burgeoned. A year earlier, Watts had exploded, igniting an urban summer ritual of angry rampage that would last until the late 1960s. In the midst of such social upheaval, Joe Papp opened his new Public Theater to the flower-power strains of Gerome Ragni and James Rado's *Hair.* The reviews posted in October 1967 were mixed; some focused on the innocence and charm of this "first hippie

ABOVE: Joseph Papp. By Alice Neel, 1964.

National Portrait Gallery, Smithsonian Institution, Washington, D.C.

RIGHT: Poster for *Hair* (1967).

Courtesy Triton Gallery, New York City.

musical," while others noted the show's lack of story and overall structure. However, its score—including "Age of Aquarius" and "Good Morning Starshine"—marked a turning point in American musicals: as one critic wrote, "nothing that has happened in popular music since World War II—the folk fad, the rise of rock (much less the numerous developments in jazz)—had effectively reached the musical theater. But now *Hair* . . . has plunged into this vacuum."[26]

Few vacuums enveloped Papp in the next several years, as he carved five new theaters under the Public Theater's roof on Lafayette Street; ironically (but appropriately), the Public was housed near the former Astor Place Opera House, the site of an infamous 1849 incident—the Astor Place Riot—that had been occasioned by a long-standing feud about the superiority of American versus English acting; twenty to thirty people had been killed, and scores more wounded in a chauvinistic battle over the merits of America's most celebrated actor, Edwin Forrest, and his English counterpart, the tragedian William Macready.[27] By 1971 at the Public, Papp was presiding over rock musicals, classic and contemporary theater, jazz workshops, chamber music, puppet shows, and Samuel Beckett readings. That year, he enjoyed his biggest theatrical success since *Hair*, with a racially integrated rock musical production of Shakespeare's *Two Gentlemen of Verona*. A lighthearted romp with a decided New York cadence that blended a Latin beat with jazz and blues, the show won that year's Tony for best musical, with playwrights John Guare and Mel Shapiro sharing honors for best book.[28] By 1975 Papp was being hailed by none other than Bernard Jacobs, head of the Shubert Theatre organization, as "the most important force in the English-speaking theater today."[29]

The single most successful venture of Papp's career was *A Chorus Line*—a phenomenon that marked a transition in American musical theater. This show was the brainchild of choreographer-director Michael Bennett. Born Michael Bennett DiFiglia in Buffalo,

Choreographer
Michael Bennett
(center) with Marvin
Hamlisch (left) at
rehearsal for A
Chorus Line, 1975.
By Martha Swope.

© Time, Inc.

he began dance lessons at the age of three. Even as a boy, he once said, "I wanted to choreograph. . . . I used to arrange marbles as dancers—people thought I was playing with marbles, but I was actually staging musicals. What I wanted to work at was putting on big shows—not just dancing, but singing, acting, dancing shows."[30] Theatrically, he would become a direct descendant of the de Mille-Robbins-Fosse tradition of director-choreographers, with his particular hero being Robbins. In fact, Bennett dropped out of high school to become "Baby John" in the 1960 international tour of *West Side Story* so that he could work with Robbins firsthand. After the tour, he returned to New York and appeared in the choruses of several Broadway shows, including *Subways Are for Sleeping* (1961) and *Here's Love* (1963); his debut as choreographer was in the short-lived *A Joyful Noise* (1966)—for which, though the show itself lasted only twelve performances, Bennett received a Tony nomination for best choreography. He did the choreography for the 1968 hit *Promises, Promises*, an adaptation of Billy Wilder's film *The Apartment;* the next year, he worked on the Alan Jay Lerner–André Previn musical *Coco*, based on the life of Coco Chanel and starring Katharine Hepburn in her only musical role. Indeed, in the number "Ohrbach's, Bloomingdale's, Best & Saks," he devised a can-can that managed a good facsimile of Hepburn dancing. The finale, "Always Mademoiselle," showcased beautiful women in dazzling shades of red descending a mirrored staircase—mirrors had become and would endure as a Bennett hallmark—with more women floating by on a revolving double staircase, and Hepburn/Coco strutting in front of the whole montage.

By this time, Bennett was being noticed by the critics: John Simon, the acerbic reviewer for *New York* magazine, reported that "Michael Bennett has again come up with wonderfully sculptural and suggestive movements for the dances and fashion sequences. His choreography is mostly the heightenings of the tempos of everyday goings-on, the embellished groupings of social intercourse, but the telling details add up to the perfect orthography of evocation and delight."[31]

Bennett's next step was to pair with producer-director Harold Prince and composer-lyricist Stephen Sondheim on two major works: *Company* (1970) and *Follies* (1971). For *Company*, an examination of marriage and mores in contemporary Manhattan, Bennett triumphed over the challenge of working with a cast consisting primarily of nondancing, singing actors. As Sondheim said, Bennett wanted the actors to function "not only as people who were each other's company, but . . . a company of semi-amateur singers and dancers."[32] For *Follies*, Bennett served as both choreographer and codirector, sharing the responsibilities for the latter with producer Prince. For this dark tale of a reunion of aging showgirls, Bennett was integral in achieving the almost cinematic transitions the complex show demanded. His Tony-winning choreography captured the spectacle of earlier Follies, while also functioning as a psychological exploration into the characters the women had become. This was best evoked in the number "Who's That Woman?" in which the retired women re-create a legendary tap number downstage while their younger ghosts—in mirror-laden costumes—perform an exact mirror image of the number upstage.

After scoring a Robbinsesque coup with *Seesaw* (1972), in which he functioned as its director, choreographer, and scriptwriter, Bennett began a collaboration with Joe Papp. Their project grew out of Bennett's disgust with the 1973 Watergate hearings: Bennett often said that after watching hours of cover-ups and deceit on television, he felt compelled to create something truthful for the stage, and to say something positive about the innate goodness of American values. But the show that became *A Chorus Line* was also the product of Bennett's realization that the Broadway of his dreams was changing, that the economics of the theater had come to dictate the end of the era of the big, splashy "dance musical." Indeed, sensing that the role of the dancer in musical theater was seriously threatened, Bennett decided to create a show in which the dancers themselves—as an ensemble of virtual unknowns—would be the stars.

In January 1974 Bennett hosted an all-night talkfest with eighteen dancers with whom he had worked over the years; these conversations—covering their careers, childhoods, lifestyles, goals—became the basis for *A Chorus Line*. He approached Joe Papp, who offered to help fund the project and also gave Bennett space at his Public Theater to develop the show in a workshop. Bennett would serve as director-choreographer, while Marvin Hamlisch—who had never written a musical before—was hired to compose the score, and Edward Kleban to write the lyrics. The songs convey the dancers' stories, including "I Can Do That," describing one dancer's childhood; "At the Ballet," telling of a young dancer's ballet school period; and "Dance: Ten, Looks: Three," depicting a career's beginnings. "What I Did for Love" and the anthem-like "One" became the show's best-known numbers, but "The Music and the Mirror" captured the chorus line's reason for being: "Give me a chance to come through / All I ever needed was the music and the mirror, and the chance to dance for you" (Edward Kleban and Marvin Hamlisch, "The Music and the Mirror," 1975).

Theoni V. Aldredge, Broadway's top costume designer, became part of the *Chorus Line* team. Greek-born Aldredge had studied at Chicago's Goodman School of Design before making her Broadway debut in Elia Kazan's 1959 production of Tennessee Williams's *Sweet Bird of Youth*. She considered Joe Papp her mentor and worked extensively with

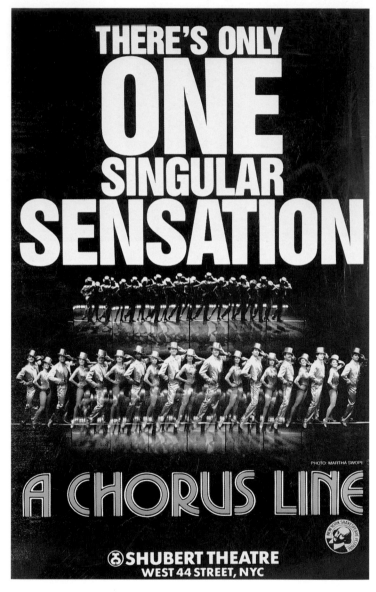

Poster for *A Chorus Line* (1975).

National Museum of American History, Smithsonian Institution, Washington, D.C.

The company in *A Chorus Line* (1975). By Martha Swope.

© Time, Inc.

him over the years, including designing the counterculture costumes for *Hair*. Papp called her "the first lady of the New York Shakespeare Company" and credited her with having "an incomparable sense of what is psychologically and dramatically appropriate."[33] With *A Chorus Line*, she found that it was "much more difficult to do a rehearsal garment than . . . a beaded dress. To find a character in each dancer took us six months. I was in rehearsal every day with my Polaroid, and I watched the kids because they brought their own personalities, and I just borrowed from what they brought."[34]

Bennett's choreography descended in a direct line from Agnes de Mille and Jerome Robbins: like de Mille, he used dance to convey the emotion of character; like Robbins, he made the work a seamless integration in which all the show's elements were choreographed. He also employed his hallmark "mirror" effect: the set by Robin Wagner consists mainly of tall, revolving panels of mirrors at the back of the stage. The lights first come up on the full company of dancers at a final audition for a razzle-dazzle Broadway musical, and the audience—reflected back to itself from the mirror panels—instantly becomes integrated into the action and emotions of the chorus line itself. The show unfolds as each of the twenty-seven dancers—competing for eight roles—not only performs but speaks of the ambitions of the lowly "gypsy" chorus dancer battling for a place in the sun. Yet instead of being depressing, the show pulses with an abundance of exuberant energy.[35] As theater historian Ken Mandelbaum has argued, *A Chorus Line* was a hybrid of old and new musicals: as with older musicals in the Rodgers and Hammerstein tradition, it had an emotional impact often lacking in contemporary shows that made stagecraft technology more of a priority than human emotion; and like *Company*, it can also be considered a "concept musical," in that it lacked a linear plot and substituted the show's characters for any conventional book—the entire premise of the show was organized around the concept of an audition. By focusing on the dancers' world, this backstage show became a metaphor for life itself.[36]

After five weeks of previews that had electrified the New York theater community, *A Chorus Line* opened on May 21, 1975, at Papp's 299-seat Newman Theater in the Public Theater complex on Lafayette Street. The response was tumultuous: even the *New York Times* critic Clive Barnes could barely contain himself, writing that "the conservative word for *A Chorus Line* might be tremendous, or perhaps terrific . . . the reception was so shattering that it is surprising if, by the time you read this, the New York Shakespeare Festival has got a Newman Theater still standing. . . . It is a show that must dance, jog and whirl its way into the history of the musical theater."[37] Like other backstage musicals of earlier generations—notably *42nd Street* and *Singin' in the Rain*—*A Chorus Line* told its own era's show business saga: here, the emphasis on the ensemble rather than on any particular "star" told a story more congruent to an era that had stopped believing in heroes.

On July 25 the show moved to Broadway to standing-room audiences at the Shubert Theatre. It won nine Tonys and the Pulitzer Prize that year; eventually more than six million people on Broadway, and millions more across the country and around the world, saw *A Chorus Line*. Although Papp himself made nothing on this show, the New York Shakespeare Festival would ultimately earn approximately $40 million—making it the most affluent institutional theater in America.

Papp's commitment to a theater embracing multiculturalism reflected a significant trend in American musicals from the sixties on, as musicals registered the postmodern phenomenon of cultural fragmentation—a period when, as historian Arthur Schlesinger Jr. has said, the cultural balance has tilted more often toward the "pluribus" than the "unum."

The issue of multiculturalism on Broadway reached center stage in the seventies and eighties. Michael Bennett, following the phenomenal *Chorus Line* and then an unsuccessful 1978 show called *Ballroom*, next turned to a story focusing on three black women—backup singers who leave the group's "star" to go out on their own. Aimed at a nontraditional audience, *Dreamgirls* was conceived by writer Tom Eyen, and Bennett eagerly collaborated as director-choreographer: joined by his colleagues Theoni V. Aldredge (costumes) and Robin Wagner (sets), Bennett again had a show about one of his favorite topics—the backstage musical.

Dreamgirls (1981) opens as the three singers try to win a talent contest at Harlem's Apollo Theater; they lose, but gain a manager who helps them begin their ride to the top. The rest of the story centers on the toll taken by fame. It was not only about Diana Ross and the Supremes, Bennett said at the time, but also about Stevie Wonder, the Temptations, and a lot of other Motown stars of the 1960s. Asked why he chose this subject, Bennett replied, "I approached the material as if cultural assimilation is something that has happened in America. . . . *Dreamgirls* is not about being black, it's about being human. It's a black musical, but it's about people. It's not a black version of a white show."[38] The latter comment was a direct jibe at earlier white attempts to produce black shows, notably David Merrick's 1967 all-black production of *Hello, Dolly!* Opening in a climate of na-

Principal cast of
Dreamgirls (1981). By
Martha Swope.

© Time, Inc.

tional racial turmoil, this *Dolly* struck many in the civil rights movement as little more than a minstrel show. Although it provided jobs for many black performers—including Pearl Bailey, Morgan Freeman, and Clifton Davis—it clearly was not a product of indigenous black culture.

Indigenous black culture did find its Broadway voice in two strong proponents, Geoffrey Holder and Gregory Hines. Born in Trinidad in 1931, the six-foot, six-inch Holder—artist, designer, dancer, choreographer, and singer—began his career as a member of his brother's dance troupe. By 1948 he had taken over the troupe; three of his revues—"Ballet Congo," "Bal Creole," and "Bal Nègre"—won great success in the early 1950s. Agnes de Mille saw a documentary film of the troupe, and encouraged young Holder to come to New York.

Holder made his Broadway debut in the 1955 Harold Arlen–Truman Capote musical, *House of Flowers*, playing "a cigar-smoking tough, The Champion," and "the voodoo Baron of the Cemetery." The critics were impressed with his "distinctive, Carib-flavored dancing," staged principally by George Balanchine.[39] In the fifties, as a craze for calypso music swept the country, Holder was at the forefront, writing in the *New York Times* in 1957 that calypso's appeal came from its simple and basic rhythm: "It makes the body want to move like true American jazz. . . . True calypso tells a story very close to the everyday lives of the people. It is spontaneous, improvised, timely; it is the music of strugglers struggling."[40]

Holder's work, whether in art, design, or dance, grows out of his fascination with Caribbean popular culture—particularly that of Trinidad and Haiti—and of the region's African-derived religious beliefs, including the religion known as voodoo. He once said that he "used Haitian legend like Martha Graham used Greek myth."[41] His best-known Broadway effort, the 1975 musical *The Wiz*, was an exuberant, Caribbeanized version of the L. Frank Baum book and the MGM movie. Critics called this all-black musical an "Oz with soul"—a jazzy, urban ghetto setting that "sizzles with vitality, and flaunts the gaudy hues of an exploding rainbow." Holder, as director-choreographer-designer, was credited with giving the show its "breathtaking flamboyance of design and color."[42] His

1978 *Timbuktu!* followed a similar pattern in a colorful retelling of the *Kismet* fable—here, set in Africa rather than Baghdad, but again essentially Caribbean in musical mood.[43]

While Geoffrey Holder was invigorating Broadway with a vibrant and highly colorful Caribbean flavor, Gregory Hines revivified the moribund world of tap dancing. In 1978 he joined with his brother Maurice to star in the musical revue *Eubie!* based on the career of Eubie Blake; Blake, with Noble Sissle, had brought *Shuffle Along* to Broadway in 1921. The Hines brothers were two-thirds of an act called "Hines, Hines, and Dad"; they had grown up

in Harlem and New York, and their mother had steered them toward tap dancing as a way out of the ghetto. By the time Gregory was six, he and his brother were performing at the Apollo Theater. They had a successful act for several years, until public interest in tap dancing waned; at one point, Gregory Hines put away his tap shoes for seven years.

After the Hines brothers' success in *Eubie!* Gregory Hines's career went into high gear. In 1981 he starred in Broadway's *Sophisticated Ladies*, a celebration of the music of Duke Ellington. *New York Times* critic Frank Rich said of Hines, "he may be the best tap dancer of our day, but he's never had a chance to show himself to quite the advantage that he does here. Wearing slicked-back hair, a series of sleek evening outfits and a raffish smile, he's more than a dancer; he's the frisky Ellington spirit incarnate." The show is set as a Saturday-night party at the Cotton Club, with Duke Ellington's son Mercer onstage leading the orchestra; designer Tony Walton's set featured a floating bandstand, a Deco frame, and high-flying explosions of neon. Hines presided over it all with insouciance, singing the title song "Don't Get Around Much Anymore" and "Something to Live For" and bringing down the house with a phenomenal Bill Robinson–like stair dance. He was, to one reviewer, "human lightning."[44]

In 1992 Gregory Hines starred in playwright George C. Wolfe's biography of composer-performer Jelly Roll Morton, *Jelly's Last Jam.* The show is as much a glaring look at Morton's racial and ethnic attitudes as at his musical contributions as the self-proclaimed "inventor of jazz." Key to the play is the depiction of Morton as a mixed-race Creole, priding himself on his relative whiteness while immersing himself in black music. *Jelly's Last Jam* opens with Morton at the brink of Heaven or Hell; a flashback returns the scene to Jelly's childhood—his beginnings as a jazz pianist in the brothels of Storyville, then on to his unfolding career in Los Angeles and Chicago, where he formed his own band, the Red Hot Peppers. To one reviewer, the performers became virtual "sounding boards in which a heritage reverberates." It was not an easy life, and Morton here is characterized as an embittered racist who denigrates his Creole heritage. The sweet-tempered Hines found it a difficult role, though one that clearly highlighted the uniquely American art form of tap dancing: "I feel that when I go onstage and dance it's not just me dancing, it's Honi Coles and Sandman Sims and Teddy Hale and Baby Lawrence"—the legendary black tap dancers who were Hines's role models.[45] With *Jelly's Last Jam*, Gregory Hines joined the pantheon as a preeminent Broadway leading man.

For more than four decades, Harold Prince has been one of musical theater's marquee figures, from his early career in Broadway's golden age through the modern era of redefinition and revival, in which he has played a pivotal role in the transformation of American musical theater. Born in New York in 1928, Prince remembers fantasizing about life in the theater from a young age, playing with a cardboard theater model and using toy soldiers as his actors. He wrote, acted, and directed at the University of Pennsylvania and attempted to make a living writing plays in New York after he graduated in 1948. Instead, he was soon working as a scriptwriter for the legendary producer-director George Abbott, who was then planning a small experimental production unit at ABC-TV—a venture that ultimately failed. Prince was next about to become assistant stage manager for the new Irving Berlin show, *Call Me Madam*, when he was drafted for service in the Korean War and sent to join an antiaircraft battalion near Stuttgart, Germany. Here, he later said, the evenings he whiled away at sleazy nightclubs eventually proved useful when he tried to re-create that same mood for the 1966 stage production, *Cabaret*, which he would produce and direct.

When Prince returned home in 1952, Abbott put him to work as assistant stage manager on the Leonard Bernstein musical, *Wonderful Town*, where he would first work as well with Betty Comden, Adolph Green, and Jerome Robbins. The success of this show—which ran for more than 500 performances—plus Abbott's continued mentoring, gave Prince a solid foothold on Broadway. He sought Abbott's help for his next project, a show based on Richard Bissell's *7½ Cents*, a novel about a strike in a pajama factory. At first Abbott was unenthusiastic about the subject matter, though he admitted there was "a certain novelty in that there had never been a kind of romantic show about a labor union."[46] Abbott thought of the show's title—*The Pajama Game*—while walking down Fifth Avenue.

Harold Prince (far right) with George Abbott (standing), 1954.

Courtesy Joy Abbott.

He then began to assemble the creative team: he would direct, with Bob Fosse as choreographer and Richard Adler and Jerry Ross writing the words and music. Opening in New York on May 13, 1954, *The Pajama Game*—including such songs as "Hey There," "Hernando's Hideaway," and "Steam Heat"—won effusive reviews: Walter Kerr in the *New York Herald Tribune* called it a show "that takes a whole barrelful of gleaming new talents, and a handful of stimulating ideas as well, and sends them tumbling in happy profusion over the footlights."[47] Prince, at the age of twenty-six Broadway's youngest producer, found himself associated with a sensational hit: *The Pajama Game* won that year's Tony Award as best musical, and the show went on to an eventual run of 1,063 performances.

Over the next decade Prince would produce seven more shows directed by George Abbott; except for a comedy called *Take Her, She's Mine*, all were musicals, including *Damn Yankees* (1955), *New Girl in Town* (1957), *Fiorello!* (1959), *Tenderloin* (1960), *A Funny Thing Happened on the Way to the Forum* (1962), and *Flora, the Red Menace* (1965). Director Abbott shaped most productions in the sleek Rodgers and Hart style he had been associated with in the thirties. Each featured a variation of the boy-meets-loses-wins-girl formula, although many of these shows touched on characters and situations that promised something different, such as factory workers (*The Pajama Game*), baseball players (*Damn Yankees*), communists (*Flora*), and Roman slaves (*Forum*).[48]

Two shows that Prince produced without George Abbott in the late 1950s and sixties were indicative of the direction he would take without the "Abbott touch." *West Side Story* (1957) and *Fiddler on the Roof* (1964), both staged by Jerome Robbins, contain the seeds of what would become the Prince trademark—the "concept musical," which has expanded the modern musical's thematic and theatrical possibilities and has given Prince a reputation as "the architect of the dark or anti-musical." According to theater critic Frank Rich, the concept musical, which came into vogue in the late 1960s, essentially meant that a traditional story line was being eschewed for a theme (or "concept") that was in turn illustrated by songs and dances put forward for ironic commentary as much as for dramatic action.[49]

Unlike his earlier shows, which functioned within a traditional and sometimes sentimental musical comedy framework, *West Side* and *Fiddler* ventured into darker territory. In *West Side Story*, the ravages of ghetto life deplete individual efforts to surmount an unrelenting impoverishment of spirit; *Fiddler on the Roof* is given a somber cast by posing the constant threat of a pogrom against the love stories and rituals of the shtetl community. In both of these shows, everyday lives are confronted not only by daily hardships but by a potentially overwhelming historical juggernaut.

Poster from the original Broadway production of *Cabaret* (1966), directed by Harold Prince.

Courtesy of Triton Gallery, New York City.

Prince's transitional status between traditional and modern Broadway is apparent in his digression, in 1963, to produce and direct *She Loves Me*, with book by Joe Masteroff and music and lyrics by Jerry Bock and Sheldon Harnick — the latter his collaborators on the Pulitzer Prize–winning *Fiorello!*, as well as *Tenderloin* and *Fiddler on the Roof*. Starring perennial ingenue Barbara Cook, *She Loves Me* reverted to a Middle European setting and a heartwarming mood, but the temper of the times — which Prince has called "the peak of the noisy heavy-sell musical" — worked against it, and it ran only nine-and-a-half months. It remained a favorite of Prince's, however, who has called it "a style piece, an unsentimental love story. . . . It had irony and an edge to it. It was funny, but not hilarious. It was melodic, but not soaring. There were only two dances, and they were small. No one came to the edge of the footlights and gave it to you. It was soft-sell."[50]

Prince returned in 1966, producing and directing the stage version of *Cabaret*, a transitional work in the evolution of the concept musical. He and Joe Masteroff had just finished working together on *She Loves Me* when Prince suggested they develop a musical based on Christopher Isherwood's *Berlin Stories*. With Masteroff writing the book, Prince then hired John Kander and Fred Ebb — with whom he had worked on *Flora, the Red Menace* — to write the score.

Prince's production of *Cabaret* — as Bob Fosse's later screen version would do — delineated a society in disarray. Prince saw a parallel between what he called "the spiritual bankruptcy of Germany in the 1920s and our country in the 1960s."[51] On the first day of rehearsal, he showed his cast a photograph from *Life* magazine "of a group of Aryan blonds in their late teens, stripped to the waist, wearing religious medals, snarling at the camera like a pack of hounds. I asked the identity, the time and the place of the picture. It seemed obvious I'd lifted it from Munich in 1928. In fact, it was a photograph of a group of students in residential Chicago fighting the integration of a school."[52] Prince thought that this play

Set designer Boris Aronson. By Robert Galbraith.

Courtesy Lisa J. Aronson.
© Robert Galbraith.

about the rise of Fascism was "the best kind of show," because it "makes an important state-ment . . . and it provides entertainment." It was, in fact, "more than a musical."[54]

Cabaret used the decadent Kit Kat Club and its grotesque emcee (played by Joel Grey) as metaphors for Weimar Germany's careening journey into a Nazi apocalypse. As the model for his emcee, Prince harkened back to his Stuttgart days during the Korean War and the dwarf emcee that he had seen at Maxim's, a seedy nightclub in the rubble of an old church basement: the emcee had "hair parted in the middle and lacquered down with brilliantine, his mouth made into a bright-red cupid's bow." He "wore heavy false eye-lashes and sang, danced, goosed, tickled, and pawed four lumpen Valkyries waving di-aphanous butterfly wings."[54]

Boris Aronson designed the sets, beginning with the idea that in Germany before World War II, "coexisting with the predominant sense of order was the bizarre defiance of the Berlin cabarets. Neither theater nor vaudeville, political cabaret was improvisational satire, and the German performers were masters of it."[55] Theatergoers to *Cabaret* entered to find no show curtain, and a trapezoid-shaped mirror in a vertical position to reflect back on them. The theater goes black, and, to a drumroll, each letter of the "Cabaret" sign in front of the mirror lights up; with the entire sign illuminated, the emcee emerges from the dark-ness singing "Wilkommen," and the mirror rises to become the ceiling. To emphasize even more the mirror that became *Cabaret*'s essential metaphor, lighting designer Jean Rosen-thal created a curtain of light—with lights embedded downstage that could be swiveled up to form a "curtain"—that replaced the usual painted curtains for set changes. The overall purpose, for Aronson, was to expose the artifice of the theater directly to the audience.

Born in 1898 as one of ten children of the Grand Rabbi of Kiev, Boris Aronson became transfixed by theater when he wandered into an opera house at the age of eight and was awed by a peacock painted on a stage curtain. He studied set design with Alexandra Exter, the visionary Constructivist scenic and costume designer; immigrating to America in 1923, Aronson—because he spoke no English—initially worked with avant-garde Yiddish

theater companies in New York. His Broadway debut came with a 1927 show called $2 x 2 = 5$; through the mid-1970s, Aronson would design more than one hundred productions for the American stage.

The latter part of his career, when he collaborated with producer Harold Prince, would be the most spectacular.[56] According to Prince, he and Aronson would begin a play by talking about "characters, period, philosophy, the play in relation to its times." He found that "Boris is comfortable with fanatics. He is one. He is also domineering. And selfish. Impatient. Even monomaniacal. And . . . persistently entertaining. . . . It is likely no author has engaged my mind, lit a fuse which ignites my imagination, tempted me to inch ahead more than Boris."[57]

After *Cabaret*, Prince forged a partnership with Stephen Sondheim that virtually changed the course of the American musical. They had met decades earlier at the Broadway opening of *South Pacific* (1949), worked together on *West Side Story* and *A Funny Thing Happened on the Way to the Forum* (1962), the former marking Sondheim's debut as a composer-lyricist of a Broadway musical.

The landmark *Company* cemented the Prince-Sondheim union. "So extraordinary in execution that it defies comparison with any musical that has come before it," raved WNEW-TV critic Stewart Klein after witnessing its momentous Broadway premiere. In its own way, *Company* would mark as large a leap in American musicals as had *Show Boat*, *Oklahoma!* and *West Side Story*.

Company's source was found in an unproduced series of eleven one-act plays that actor-playwright George Furth had written for actress Kim Stanley. "I was knocked out by them," Prince later reflected, "seeing a potential musical which could examine attitudes toward marriage, the influence of life in the cities, and collateral problems of especial interest to those of us in our forties."[58] For his mostly plotless libretto, Furth merged three of his existing plays and created two more. He combined the intertwined narratives with a

Harold Prince and Stephen Sondheim. By Martha Swope, 1984.

© Time, Inc.

Tony Walton (b. 1934)

For the past forty years, English-born Tony Walton has embellished many an American musical on stage and on screen with his imaginative, witty costumes and scenic decor. Trained at London's Slade School of Fine Arts, he began his career while still a student, apprenticing as an assistant designer. Upon his first trip to the United States in the 1950s, he was enchanted by a musical theater aglow with what he recalls as "the painterly, vigorous work of Jo Mielziner, Oliver Smith, and Boris Aronson." Unlike these illustrious predecessors, however, Walton has refused to impose a readily identifiable, distinctive "look" on his theatrical design, adopting instead a brilliantly chameleon-like approach that allows him "to see through the eyes of the director and playwright." He maintains that his intent is always "to serve the material, as opposed to looking for an opportunity to shine."

The range of Walton's production designs for the American musical reflects this striking versatility, whether it is the soft pastels and sedate Edwardian sensibilities of the 1964 Disney film *Mary Poppins* or the flamboyantly neon-hued and cartoonish Broadway backdrops for the acclaimed 1992 Broadway revival of *Guys and Dolls*. Some of his finest work to date was done in partnership with Bob Fosse. For their first shared triumph, the 1972 rock musical *Pippin*, Walton earned his first Tony Award for his funky progression of stylized medieval tapestries and trendy macramé facades of English castles that acted as stunning visual metaphors for Fosse's sexily anachronistic view of Charlemagne's court. Similarly, his work for both *Chicago* (1975) and the film *All That Jazz* (1979) vividly illustrated Fosse's acrid perspective on the enticingly sinister sensuality of American show busi-

Tony Walton. By
Roddy McDowall.

ness, from the harsh neon and art deco dimensions of the former to the psychedelic phantasmagoria evident in the latter (which brought Walton his first Oscar).

What appeals the most to Walton is the challenge of determining the totality of a production's design. For the 1996 Broadway revival of *A Funny Thing Happened on the Way to the Forum*, he created virtually every visual aspect of the show, from a fresh rethinking of his sets and costumes for the show's legendary original 1962 presentation down to its props. While wildly accomplished at creating settings for films, he remains a creature of the theater, ready and willing to take on "any new play that embraces theatricality." Ultimately, for Tony Walton, "the set without the characters in it is nothing. I mean it's the whole point of theater. The set isn't a separate artwork or display object; it's only a complete and animated thing when the characters and costumes . . . are part of the overall picture."

Scene from the revival of *Guys and Dolls* (1992). By Martha Swope.

new central character, a bachelor named Robert, who would catalyze and connect the unrelated vignettes. Sondheim's music was the aural quintessence of modern urbanism—staccato, propulsive, and aggressively electronic in orchestration. Complementarily, his lyrics were literate and emotionally complex in their depiction of Manhattan:

> It's a city of strangers.
> Some come to work, some to play
> A city of strangers
> Some come to stare, some to stay,
> And every day some go away.

STEPHEN SONDHEIM, "ANOTHER HUNDRED PEOPLE," 1970

To enmesh his score with Furth's nonlinear script and his songs, Sondheim consciously discarded "the Rodgers and Hammerstein kind of song in which the characters reach a certain point and then sing their emotions" and instead used music and lyrics "in a Brechtian way as comment and counterpoint."[59] In his supervisory roles as impresario and director, Prince strove to make every element of the production feed into a central concept: to evoke the neurotic dynamism and ambivalence of contemporary upper middle-class urban life, where constant agitation made the idea of "connecting"—of establishing permanent relationships or making commitments—seem all but hopeless. New York itself became not simply a backdrop, but a central presence in the psychological landscape, a Manhattanscape with Boris Aronson's sets brilliantly embodying the show's themes. The cramped, mile-high warrens and labyrinths of the New York skyline were expressed as a Constructivist chrome and glass jungle gym, which evoked, through its various levels, platforms, and elevators, a postmodern pattern of separation and isolation. Aronson also intended to convey the idea that "in New York, people sit stacked on top of each other in transparent cages. We live in a Plexiglas world now."[60] Similarly, Michael Bennett's choreography, for a cast made up mostly of singing actors rather than musical comedy performers, echoed the tension and physical awkwardness of big-city life more through stylized patterns of movements than in out-and-out dance numbers.

Disintegration rather than ambivalence was the theme of the next Sondheim-Prince collaboration—*Follies*—which opened on Broadway in April 1971. Sondheim and librettist James Goldman had started writing the show in the mid-1960s, when it was first titled *The Girls Upstairs* and centered on a reunion of *Ziegfeld Follies* showgirls. When Prince assumed responsibilities as producer-director, he exerted considerable influence in determining the show's final form, urging its authors "to consider the simultaneity of past and present" and to create "a Proustian fracturing of time."[61] Sondheim and Goldman's tight little melodrama of two former chorines and their former stage-door-johnny husbands was

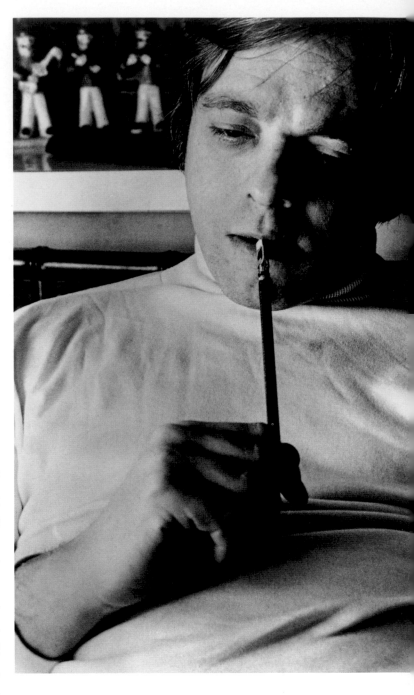

Stephen Sondheim, c. 1959.

Museum of the City of New York; gift of Mary Bryant.

Scene from *Company*
(1970) showing Boris
Aronson's set design.
By Martha Swope.

© Time, Inc.

transformed into an epic exercise in surrealism, with the principal figures mirrored by a second cast of actors (clad in black and white costumes and makeup) playing the ghosts of their youthful selves. In the final twenty minutes of the work, past and present collided in a nightmarish, Felliniesque variety show that embodies the show's themes of self-confrontation, doubt, and loss.

In Prince's vision, the shambles of the central characters' lives became representative of a national loss of innocence and the collapse of the American dream in modern society. The references to "follies" were various, ranging from Ziegfeld's glittering spectacles "glorifying the American girl" earlier in the century, to the follies of youth and dreams deferred, to, finally, the French word "folie," or "madness." Throughout, the metaphor of

Boris Aronson's
maquette (set model)
for *Follies* (1971).

Courtesy Lisa J. Aronson.

LEFT: *Follies* poster, designed by David Edward Byrd, 1971.

National Museum of American History, Smithsonian Institution, Washington, D.C.

RIGHT: Gloria Swanson in the ruins of the Roxy Theatre. By Eliot Elisofon for *Life* magazine, 1960.

© Time, Inc.

show business was invoked: the original *Ziegfeld Follies* represented an America that loved glamour and glitz and believed in itself; *Follies* showed the hollowness of that be-spangled vision, and suggested that standards built out of sequins and tinsel had inevitably led to the kind of disillusion that hovered over the country in 1971.

Prince found his visual concept for the production in a 1960 Eliot Elisofon *Life* magazine photograph, in which screen star Gloria Swanson, elegantly attired in black chiffon and marabou, stands glamorously with arms upraised amid the sun-bleached ruins of a de-molished New York movie palace, the fabled Roxy Theatre. Boris Aronson's set brilliantly embodied the show's fragmented emotional landscape. His cavernous unit set depicted a

theater building in decay, with the scattered detritus of scaffolding, rubble, and exposed brick. In the show's final moments, when the *Follies* metaphor became literal, the surroundings transformed magically into the remarkable "Loveland" setting, a candy box of "valentines and lace" depicting the naïveté of a bygone era, in which all is "symmetrical, sweet, rosy."[62] In complement to the show's visual and intellectual stances, its cast consisted of a group of show business survivors—Alexis Smith, Dorothy Collins, Gene Nelson, Yvonne DeCarlo, Fifi D'Orsay—whose glorious pasts on stage and screen enriched its pervading atmosphere of ironic nostalgia and the ravages of time.

Stephen Sondheim's score of twenty-two songs was brilliantly schizoid, ranging from mordant solos and ensembles for the show's principal characters, to extraordinary, nonsentimental pastiches of the works of such great musical comedy songsmiths as Jerome Kern, Sigmund Romberg, Cole Porter, George Gershwin, and Dorothy Fields. In scope, volume, and complexity, it represented a major step forward from the music and lyrics for *Company* and reaffirmed the value of his collaboration with Prince.

A Little Night Music (1973) and *Pacific Overtures* (1975) illustrated the Sondheim-Prince partnership at extremes. An adaptation of Ingmar Bergman's film *Smiles of a Summer Night, A Little Night Music* proved immensely popular and even produced a hit song in "Send in the Clowns," a rarity for both Sondheim and the contemporary musical theater. For all of its astute psychological layerings and adult stance, the show was a modern operetta, reminiscent in milieu, if not in execution, of the elegant, refined, fairy-tale world conjured by Lehár, Romberg, and the Shuberts. As in *Follies*, the script centered on the foolishness of love and romantic delusion; however, it did so without the former's darkness and hopelessness, managing even to muster an unequivocally happy ending. Sondheim's music, composed completely in three-quarter time, recalled the sounds of Brahms, Rachmaninoff, and Ravel—ingenious, but hardly typical referents for a Broadway musical. The lilting melodies were equipped with highly sophisticated lyrics, which had become the hallmark of his art.

On the other hand, *Pacific Overtures*, a pageant-like chronicle of the corruption of Japanese culture by the encroachment of Western civilization, proved too emotionally esoteric and too icily cerebral to engender much interest beyond a cult intelligentsia. Sondheim's score was perhaps his least accessible, and the high point of the original production was Prince's remarkable staging, which drew upon the ancient techniques of Japanese Kabuki and Noh theater, and his manipulation of Boris Aronson's ingenious scenic decor.

Sweeney Todd, the Demon Barber of Fleet Street (1979) represented Sondheim and Prince at their most audacious, centering as it did on mass murder, cannibalism, and other horrors of the Industrial Revolution. Its genesis began with Sondheim, who saw musical theater possibilities in the penny-dreadful horror story of a bloodthirsty, vengeful barber and his matronly accomplice who baked their victims into meat pies. Sondheim envisioned an adaptation that would capitalize on the stock elements of nineteenth-century melodrama to tell a monumentally tragic tale of revenge. Prince was reluctant at first, but found the show's "motor," as he called it, in interpreting the dark narrative as commentary on the demeaning caste system in Victorian England and "the incursion of the industrial age on souls, poetry, and people."[63] His conceptual metaphor for the show was strikingly visualized in Eugene Lee's cavernous setting, which surrounded the grisly proceedings with the grimy, sunless transoms and dank walls of a factory.

In creating a musical identity for the piece, Sondheim achieved an extraordinarily rich and expansive score that was, by his own admission, "unsettling, scary, and very romantic."[64] To many, the show's extensive use of recitative, full-scale arias, and choral pieces approached the realm of opera. Sondheim responded by asserting that his musical expansiveness was "not because I wanted to do an opera, but because I realized that the only way to sustain tension was to use music continually."[65]

As the sinister yet comic Nellie Lovett, Sweeney Todd's cockney partner in crime, Angela Lansbury found the role that coalesced her years of experience as a dramatic actress and as a front-ranking star of the American musical theater. The daughter of British char-

Angela Lansbury with
George Hearn in
Sweeney Todd (1979).
By Martha Swope.

© Time, Inc.

acter actress Moyna McGill, she came to America in 1940 to escape the destruction of the
German blitz. Her earliest successes were on the screen, where she was often cast in sup-
porting roles that were considerably older than her chronological age. Although primarily
a dramatic actress in this period, she did appear in two well-remembered movie musicals:
The Harvey Girls (1946), in which she played a tough dance-hall girl (and had her singing
voice replaced unsettlingly by a studio contralto), and the Arthur Freed–produced *Till the
Clouds Roll By* (1947), in which, in her own voice, she warbled Jerome Kern's "How'd You
Like to Spoon with Me?" She made her Broadway musical debut in 1964, playing the humorously conniving mayoress, Cora Hoover Hooper, in Stephen Sondheim's short-lived
Anyone Can Whistle. Her fine work in that ill-fated endeavor convinced Jerry Herman that
she was the top candidate to play the title role in his 1966 musical *Mame.* Lansbury's performance as the beldame of Beekman Place ensured her theatrical immortality, earning
her the first of four Tony Awards for best actress in a musical. Her next two musicals, *Dear
World* (1968) and *Prettybelle* (1971), were ambitious failures; however, in 1974 she returned to Broadway (via London's West End) as the indomitable Rose in a highly praised
revival of *Gypsy.* After the Broadway run, national tour, and television adaptation of
Sweeney Todd, Lansbury announced plans to star in a stage musical version of the film
Sunset Boulevard, with score by Sondheim and staging by Prince.[66] When the project
failed to materialize, she turned to network television, winning legions of new fans as the
star of CBS-TV's series, *Murder, She Wrote.*

The Prince-Sondheim partnership soured and came to a halt in 1981 with the disastrous *Merrily We Roll Along*, which reteamed them with George Furth, the librettist for *Company*. Rather freely adapted from a play of the same title by George Kaufman and Moss Hart, the show was about compromise—moral, artistic, filial—and its destructive effect on the relationships among a composer, a lyricist, and a writer. As in the Kaufman-Hart play, the plot was revealed in reverse order, taking the three principal characters from the conflict that ends their friendship to their first encounter twenty-five years earlier. Topping the list of its attributes was Sondheim's score, a surprisingly brassy, "hummable" collection of musical comedy songs that recalled the pure Broadway sound of such composers as Jule Styne and Irving Berlin. On the other hand, Prince neither succeeded in finding a suitable production concept for the piece, nor was he well served by his decision to have the show performed by a cast of energetic but inexperienced teenagers and young adults. Lambasted by critics and avoided by audiences, *Merrily* closed after only sixteen performances. Over the next several years, Sondheim experimented with its revision at various regional theaters. Prince abandoned the work and stepped away from his long-standing professional association with Sondheim, seeking new collaborators to assist in redefining his own vision of musical theater.

Emerging from the disappointment of *Merrily We Roll Along*, Stephen Sondheim formed a new partnership with dramatist-director James Lapine. Unlike Prince and Sondheim, who were products of the commercial Broadway musical, Lapine, a former graphic designer, came from the world of university and off-Broadway theater. His only previous association with the musical theater was as director of the wildly unconventional *March of the Falsettos* (1981) by composer-lyricist-librettist William Finn. *Sunday in the Park with George* (1984), the first Sondheim-Lapine effort, comprised essentially two one-act musicals that probed the rewards and solitariness of the creative process. The two halves of the production were tenuously linked by a fictional reinterpretation of the career and legacy of French postimpressionist painter Georges Seurat and his most famous painting, "Sunday Afternoon on the Island of the Grande Jatte."

Sunday in the Park with George evolved in a manner quite different from that to which Sondheim had become accustomed in his work with Prince. It was developed in stages through readings and minimalist workshops presented at Playwrights Horizons, a nonprofit off-Broadway theatrical organization where Lapine had worked previously and happily as both a director and author. Although Sondheim asserted that the various Playwrights Horizons experiments were "not a way station to Broadway," the show eventually moved uptown to Broadway's Booth Theatre in spring 1984.[67] Greeted with mixed reviews, the show was taken up by *New York Times* critic Frank Rich, an ardent admirer of the Sondheim canon. For the rest of the season and into the next, Rich launched an extensive campaign to trumpet the production's merits in his columns for the *Times*. All but shut out of the year's Tony Awards (Herman's *La Cage aux Folles* was the grand-slam winner), *Sunday* was bestowed with a Pulitzer Prize for the season's best play.

If Lapine's direction lacked Harold Prince's epic pizzazz and theatrical wizardry, his stage pictures were often highly effective in their emotional intimacy and richness in

character shadings. Sondheim's often brilliant score was founded on an intricate series of leitmotifs, which were developed within the course of the score and melded in the show's final number, prophetically titled "Move On":

> I want to move on.
> I want to explore the light.
> I want to know how to get through,
> Through to something new,
> Something of my own—
> Move on.

STEPHEN SONDHEIM, "MOVE ON," 1987

Into the Woods, a second collaboration with Lapine that followed two seasons later, gave Sondheim his greatest commercial success since the original Broadway production of *A Funny Thing Happened on the Way to the Forum*. Though hardly conventional in theme, design, and structure, *Into the Woods* possessed an accessibility and emotional warmth that made it appealing to an audience diverse in both tastes and ages. The show was a stylish, ingeniously clever, and often moving reinterpretation of Grimm's fairy tales, vaguely filtering them through the psychological analyses of Carl Jung and Bruno Bettelheim. "I thought it would be interesting and exciting to see how people react to stories they already know," explained Lapine, "but told from a different angle."[68]

Despite their Disneyesque associations and permutations, the tales became, in Sondheim and Lapine's hands, considerably more than mere moral fables. Intertwining the stories of such familiar characters as Jack (and his beanstalk), Cinderella, and Little Red Riding Hood, and adding two new figures—a baker and his wife—of their own, the authors used their "quest musical" to explore such timely and timeless issues as wish-fulfillment, loss of innocence, individual and community responsibility, and the relationship between parent and child (or mentor and pupil).[69] Sondheim's music and lyrics, perhaps his most felicitous and buoyant since the days of *Forum*, consisted of a constantly flowing progression of different short phrases of melody that suited perfectly the tongue-in-cheek innocence of the production as a whole.

Both *Sunday in the Park with George* and *Into the Woods* were invigorated by the presence of Bernadette Peters, the leading musical theater artist of her generation. In the former she brought a sensual glamour and warmth to the dual roles of George Seurat's model-mistress Dot and their daughter, and in the latter she made a beguiling witch, whether masked in old-age mufti or looking ravishing in a form-fitting Ann Hould–Ward creation. Peters started performing professionally at the age of four. At thirteen, she was cavorting as Baby June in a national tour of *Gypsy*. She made her Broadway debut in 1967, playing vaudevillian Josie Cohan in the musical biography *George M!* A year later, she won praise for her performance as the tap-dancing heroine of the off-Broadway Busby Berkeley spoof *Dames at Sea*. Her next appearances were in the short-lived musicals *La Strada* (1969) and *Mack and Mabel* (1974), although in the latter she made a strong impression as silent-screen comic Mabel Normand. A nine-year hiatus in Hollywood followed, distinguished only by her appearance in the imaginative but commercially unsuccessful movie musical *Pennies from Heaven* (1978). Returning to New York in the early

1980s, she established herself as a musical star of the first order in Andrew Lloyd Webber's *Song and Dance* (1985).

In 1991 Sondheim vacationed briefly from his association with Lapine to pair with director Jerry Zaks and *Pacific Overtures* librettist John Weidman on the daring *Assassins*. Mounted off-Broadway at Playwrights Horizons (where *Sunday in the Park with George* and *Into the Woods* premiered), this mordant revue about the infamous murderers of presidents was vaguely reminiscent in tone, if not in production, of *Chicago*, the 1975 Fosse-Kander-Ebb "musical vaudeville." Even in its experimental, one-act form, *Assassins* was a strikingly original, if wildly uneven, work; however, many expressed moral outrage at its narrative focus and it became Sondheim's first theatrical endeavor not to make the transfer from a formal tryout stage to a Broadway presentation.

In his next work, *Passion* (1994), Sondheim tried to show "how the force of somebody's feelings for you can crack you open, and how it is the life force in a deadened world."[70] With Lapine as its author and director, the show, stated in one long act, told of an unseemly, almost pathological romance between Giorgio, a handsome soldier, and Fosca, an unattractive woman haunted by emotional and physical demons. For this chamber musical, Sondheim composed some of his loveliest music and mated it to spare, unadorned lyrics that eschewed the verbal pyrotechnics of his earlier efforts. Lapine's script, however, was often talky and stilted, and the decision to reveal much of the action through letters sung by the principals imbued the production with a lethargy that undermined its thematic stance of obsessive, selfless love. Curiously enough, *Passion* captured all the Tonys that had eluded the more worthy *Sunday in the Park with George* and *Into the Woods*. Its victory was more a rejection of its competitor, a stage version of the Disney film *Beauty and the Beast*, than it was a lapsed recognition of Sondheim's long-term commitment to the American musical stage.

"Art isn't easy," asserts a Stephen Sondheim lyric. In a career that spans more than forty years, Sondheim has been associated with some of the most adventurous, challenging, and artful efforts ever created for the American musical theater. His musicals are marked by a probing intelligence and a vigorous disregard for convention, both in style and content. And yet much of his work has remained remote to the masses, failing to achieve the commercial prosperity or audience adulation showered on his mentor, Oscar Hammerstein. Nonetheless, his commitment is genuine to the troubled world of the American musical. "The theater is a place where I really love to work," he has asserted. "It's a place where I hope to work until Broadway packs up and goes away."[71]

Instead of retreating, Broadway in the last several seasons has been festooned by revivals of such shows as *Guys and Dolls* (1992), *She Loves Me* (1993), *The King and I* (1996), and *A Funny Think Happened on the Way to the Forum* (1996). In addition, there have been a number of "revisals," notably the 1992 *Crazy for You*, a loose remake of the 1930 Gershwin hit *Girl Crazy* with a zany new script by Ken Ludwig. Looking over Broadway's dominance by its own history, in April 1995 the *New York Times* proffered: "Right now much of Broadway is a Museum of the American Musical staffed by busy curator-directors eager to put their stamp on every show they mount."[72]

Although his career has been primarily devoted to directing new musicals, Harold Prince has ironically become a pivotal force in musical theater's recent love affair with its own past, including successful revivals of *Candide* (1973, 1982) and *Cabaret* (1987). The most spectacular example of musical theater's backward gaze is Prince's 1994 production of *Show Boat*. This version of the 1927 classic has been adapted by Prince to conform to a more "politically correct" nineties sensibility, while retaining the grandeur that was originally intended: "I have a perception," Prince once said, "that what everybody likes to see is an old-fashioned musical done in a new-fashioned way. And that is probably the most difficult assignment in the world."[73]

Show Boat was "born big and meant to stay that way," lyricist Oscar Hammerstein II once said. This huge $12-million-dollar production—the cast numbers seventy-one—boasted choreography by Susan Stroman (who won a Tony for *Crazy for You*) and sets by Eugene Lee (Tony Award winner for *Candide* and *Sweeney Todd*). It was originally conceived as an epic narrative about five couples whose lives interconnect from the 1880s to the 1920s. Set in the American heartland, *Show Boat* courses from Natchez, Mississippi, to Chicago, with the boat—a floating theater palace called the *Cotton Blossom*—functioning as a backdrop to a family chronicle that includes Captain Andy, proprietor of the show boat, his wife Parthy and their daughter Magnolia, riverboat gambler Gaylord Ravenal, and Julie, the leading lady on the *Cotton Blossom* whose melodrama forms a key part of the story.

In reconstructing this musical, Prince has focused on what remains a central paradox of America's democracy—its inherent racial ambivalence. He has substantially rewritten the show, going back through several versions of the scripts, adding some songs originally cut (the 1927 version ran more than four hours), and excising others. And while Prince has given the show a darker edge—a tone that theater historian Ethan Mordden has termed "musical noir"—*Show Boat* still radiates what one critic has called "the idealistic chutzpah of Kern and Hammerstein. Their work is full of love—for a romantic ideal that's gone, for a fraternal ideal that never arrived."[74]

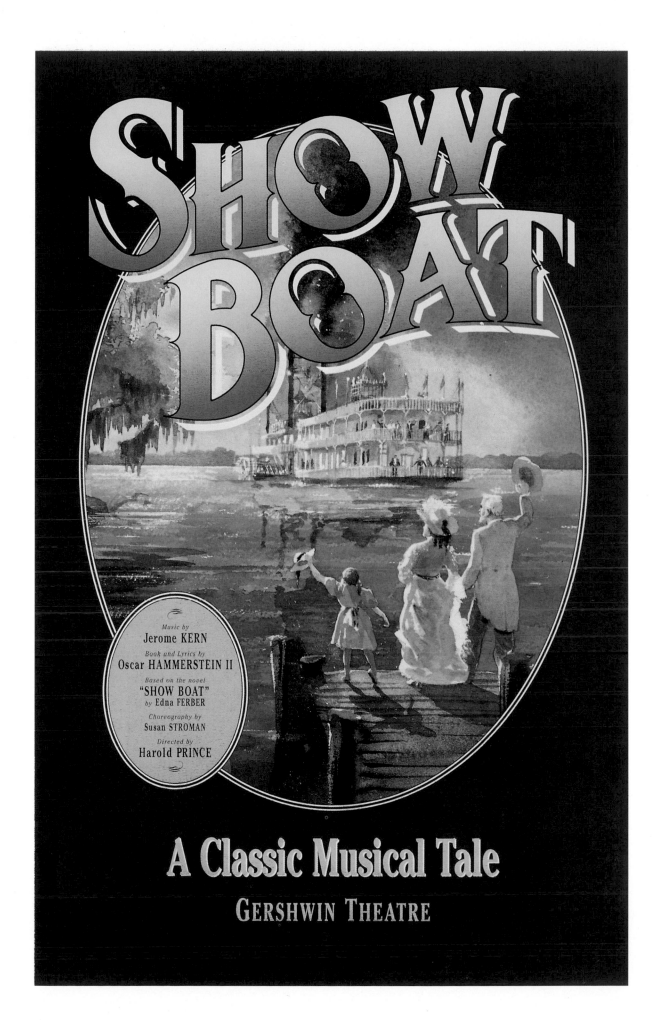

SHOW BOAT

Music by
Jerome KERN

Book and Lyrics by
Oscar HAMMERSTEIN II

Based on the novel
"SHOW BOAT"
by Edna FERBER

Choreography by
Susan STROMAN

Directed by
Harold PRINCE

A Classic Musical Tale

GERSHWIN THEATRE

Show Boat production shot. By Catherine Ashmore, 1994.

The rage for historical redefinition reflects a hunger for the tried and true—for days when the many voices of American culture were fused into a national audience by the entertainment industry. Musicals played a formative role in our collective myth-making for nearly a century, giving us the words and music for the American Dream—the dream celebrated by Walt Whitman in his 1885 poem, "Broadway": "Thou portal—thou arena—thou of the myriad long-drawn lines and groups! . . . Thou, like the parti-colored world itself—like infinite, teeming, mocking life!"[75] But the American mosaic has come under rigorous scrutiny in the last forty years, and, as theater historian John Lahr has written, "As America's Dream becomes increasingly threadbare, so has the art form that best promoted it. In this, at least, the musical remains the perfect metaphor for the time."[76]

When *Show Boat* premiered in 1927, American musical theater was at a crossroads, confronted not only by the advent of "talkies" that year, with the screening of *The Jazz Singer* starring Al Jolson, but by a transformation in the style of Broadway musicals themselves, as vaudevillian revues began to lose favor to the kind of cogent storytelling that ultimately triumphed in the landmark 1943 production of *Oklahoma!* Now, after a golden age of musical theater in the 1940s and 1950s, the Prince revival of *Show Boat* has arrived in the midst of an era when musicals have lost their unifying voice. Yet, more than any other show in America's musical canon, *Show Boat* retains an epic quality, remaining "eternal and unconquerable—like the River."[77] Perhaps it is still possible for this show to be what Florenz Ziegfeld originally intended—the "all-American musical."

NOTES

PREFACE: "A FINE ROMANCE"

1. See Robert Sklar, *Movie-Made America: A Cultural History of the Movies* (New York: Vintage Books, 1975), chap. 1; Cynthia Hoover, *Music Machines—American Style* (Washington, D.C.: Smithsonian Institution Press, 1971), esp. 23–33; Benjamin B. Hampton, *A History of the American Film Industry from Its Beginnings to 1931* (New York: Dover Press, 1970), 7.

SETTING THE STAGE

1. Armond Fields and L. Marc Fields, *From the Bowery to Broadway: Lew Fields and the Roots of American Popular Theater* (New York: Oxford University Press, 1993), 5. The best discussion of Broadway's evolution is Mary C. Henderson, *The City and the Theatre: New York Playhouses from Bowling Green to Times Square* (Clifton, N J.: James T. White, 1973). See also John W. Frick, *New York's First Theatrical Center: The Rialto at Union Square* (Ann Arbor, Mich.: UMI Research Press, 1985).

2. Cited in John D. McCabe, *New York by Gaslight* (New York: Greenwich House, 1984), 191.

3. See William R. Taylor, ed., *Inventing Times Square: Commerce and Culture at the Crossroads of the World* (New York: Russell Sage Foundation, 1991), esp. 36–146.

4. Ibid., 191.

5. Boucicault quoted in E. J. Kahn Jr., *The Merry Partners: The Age and Stage of Harrigan and Hart* (New York: Random House, 1955), 30.

6. *New York Tribune*, 17 September 1866; cited in George C. D. Odell, *Annals of the New York Stage*, 15 vols. (New York: Columbia University Press, 1927–41), 8: 155.

7. See Robert W. Snyder, *The Voice of the City: Vaudeville and Popular Culture in New York* (New York: Oxford University Press, 1989), 8–12; Fields and Fields, *From the Bowery to Broadway*, 3–7; Parker Zellers, *Tony Pastor: Dean of the Vaudeville Stage* (Ypsilanti: Eastern Michigan University Press, 1971), xv–xviii.

8. Zellers, *Tony Pastor*, xi, xix. For a description of vaudeville as deriving from the eighteenth-century French phrase "voix de ville," see Snyder, *The Voice of the City*, 12. Others trace the term to "vaux-de-Vire," named for popular satirical songs of fifteenth-century French valleys, "vaux"—near the town of Vire. See Charles W. Stein, ed., *American Vaudeville as Seen by Its Contemporaries* (New York: Alfred Knopf, 1984), xi.

9. From "Tony Pastor, 39 Years a Manager," *New York World*, 26 March 1904, quoted in Zellers, *Tony Pastor*, 4.

10. Advertisement for "American Concert Hall," *New York Clipper*, 9 (27 April 1861): 14; Zellers, *Tony Pastor*, 9, 15.

11. Harry S. Sanderson, "Reminiscences of Tony Pastor, Vaudeville's Dean," *Variety*, 12 (12 December 1908): 50.

12. Handbill for Tony Pastor's Opera House, Tony Pastor Collection, New York Public Library (NYPL)—Billy Rose Theatre Collection, n.d.

13. *New York Herald*, 2 October 1865, reprinted in Odell, *Annals of the New York Stage*, 8: 85–86.

14. Quoted in Robert C. Toll, *On with the Show: The First Century of Show Business in America* (New York: Oxford University Press, 1976), 183.

15. Richard Harding Davis, "Edward Harrigan and the East Side," *Harper's Weekly* 35 (21 March 1891): 210.

16. Quoted in David C. Ewen, *American Songwriters* (New York: H. W. Wilson, 1987), 62.

17. Quoted in Kahn, *The Merry Partners*, 64.

18. Isaac Goldberg, *Tin Pan Alley: A Chronicle of American Popular Music* (New York: Frederick Ungar, 1961), 74, 77.

19. Kahn, *Merry Partners*, 58; Toll, *On with the Show*, 185–87.

20. Kahn, *Merry Partners*, 27, 69; Toll, *On with the Show*, 186.

21. Fields and Fields, *From the Bowery to Broadway*, 50.

22. Quoted in Kahn, *Merry Partners*, 3.

23. Joe Laurie Jr., *Vaudeville: From Honky-Tonks to the Palace* (New York: Henry Holt, 1953), 81.

24. Cited in Fields and Fields, *From the Bowery to Broadway*, xiii.

25. O. J. Gude, "Art and Advertising Joined by Electricity," *Signs of the Times*, November 1912, 3.

26. The quotation is from investment banker Paul Mazur, 1928, in Taylor, *Inventing Times Square*, 99. See also pp. 2–65 for a description of the entertainment industry's centralization around Times Square.

27. Fields and Fields, *From the Bowery to Broadway*, 137.

28. Ibid., 203.

29. Ibid., 199.

30. Ibid., xiv.

31. Ibid., chaps. 10 and 11, "The King of Musical Comedy," "The King of Musical Comedy (Part Two)," 206–75.

32. See, e.g., Frank Dumont, *The Witmark Amateur Minstrel Guide and Burnt Cork Encyclopedia* (London: M. Witmark & Sons, 1899).

33. Robert C. Toll, *Blacking Up: The Minstrel Show in Nineteenth-Century America* (New York: Oxford University Press, 1974), chap. 8.

34. Thomas L. Riis, *Just before Jazz: Black Musical Theater in New York, 1890–1915* (Washington, D.C.: Smithsonian Institution Press, 1989), 44.

35. Thomas L. Morgan and William Barlow, *From Cakewalks to Concert Halls: An Illustrated History of African American Popular Music from 1895 to 1930* (Washington, D.C.: Elliott & Clark Publishing, 1992), 66.

36. Riis, *Just before Jazz*, 91.

37. Ibid., chap. 7; Toll, *On with the Show*, 130–31.

38. Riis, *Just before Jazz*, "Preface."

39. Will Marion Cook, "Clorindy, The Origin of the Cakewalk," *Theatre Arts*, September 1947, 65. Songwriter Bob Cole was another major African American contributor to Broadway, perhaps best known for the 1897 *A Trip to Coontown*, the first full-length musical entirely written, performed, produced, and owned by African Americans. See Riis, *Just before Jazz*, chap. 3.

40. Toll, *On with the Show*, 128; Riis, *Just before Jazz*, "Epilogue"; Williams quoted in Riis, *Just before Jazz*, 161.

41. Riis, *Just before Jazz*, xxi.

42. Sissieretta Jones file, Moorland-Spingarn Collection, Howard University, n.d.

43. Willa Daughtry, "Sissieretta Jones: A Study of the Negro's Contribution to Nineteenth Century American Concert and Theatrical Life," Ph.D. diss., Syracuse University, 1968, 94–95.

44. James Weldon Johnson, *Black Manhattan*, repr. ed. (Salem, N.H.: Ayer, 1990), 101.

45. Mercer Cook Papers, Box 157–9, folder 12, Moorland-Spingarn Collection.

46. Johnson, *Black Manhattan*, 99.

47. Sophie Tucker, *Some of These Days: The Autobiography of Sophie Tucker* (Garden City, N.Y.: Garden City Publishing, 1946), 10–11. By the turn of the century, Adler and Thomashefsky ran the two major Yiddish theaters on the Lower East Side—the area that itself had become the center for Yiddish theater in America. See Nahma Sandrow, *Vagabond Stars: A World History of Yiddish Theater* (New York: Limelight Editions, 1986), 86 ff.

48. See Sophie Tucker, *Some of These Days*, passim.

49. Sophie Tucker Scrapbook, Book II, 1909, Billy Rose Theatre Collection, New York Public Library at Lincoln Center.

50. Ibid., bk. III, 1909–10.

51. Ibid.; Sophie Tucker, *Some of These Days*, 95.

52. Sophie Tucker, *Some of These Days*, 114.

53. Snyder, *The Voice of the City*, 54.

54. John Burke, *Duet in Diamonds: The Flamboyant Saga of Lillian Russell and Diamond Jim Brady in America's Gilded Age* (New York: Putnam, 1972), 32.

55. Ibid., 45.

56. New York *Dramatic Mirror*, 27 July 1895, 2.

57. Fields and Fields, *From the Bowery to Broadway*, 214.

58. Israel Zangwill, *The Melting Pot: A Drama in Four Acts* (New York: 1908–1909). Also see Philip Gleason, "The Melting Pot: Symbol of Fusion or Confusion?" *American Quarterly* (Spring 1964): 20–46; and Nathan Glazer and Daniel Patrick Moynihan, *Beyond the Melting Pot* (Cambridge, Mass.: MIT Press, 1963).

59. Edwin Milton Royle, "The Vaudeville Theater," in Stein, ed., *American Vaudeville as Seen by Its Contemporaries*, 33.

CURTAIN UP

1. Harry B. Smith, *First Nights and First Editions* (Boston: Little, Brown, 1931), 260.

2. Richard Ziegfeld and Paulette Ziegfeld, *The Ziegfeld Touch* (New York: Harry N. Abrams, 1993), 176.

3. Billie Burke, with Cameron Shipp, *With a Feather on My Nose* (New York: Crowell-Collier), 242.

4. In their book *The Ziegfeld Touch*, biographers Richard and Paulette Ziegfeld report that Florenz Ziegfeld Sr. was born in Jever, Germany, on June 10, 1841, and his wife Rosalie de Hez, of Belgian heritage, was born in 1848, day, date, and location unknown.

5. Smith, *First Nights and First Editions*, 70.

6. Smith wrote the libretti for 123 Broadway musicals. In addition to serving as the primary sketch writer for the 1907, 1908, 1909, 1910, and 1912 editions of the *Follies*, Smith wrote the scripts for such major works as *Robin Hood* (1891), *The Fortune Teller* (1898), and *Watch Your Step* (1914). The original company of the *Follies of 1907* included the team of Harry Watson Jr. and George Bickel, singer Grace LaRue, and dancer Mlle. Dazie.

7. Smith, *First Nights and First Editions*, 242.

8. George Jean Nathan, *The Theatre, the Drama, the Girls* (New York: Knopf, 1921), 146.

9. Gregory Gilmartin, "Joseph Urban," in William R. Taylor, ed., *Inventing Times Square* (New York: Russell Sage Foundation, 1991), 272.

10. Eddie Cantor, and David Freedman,

"Ziegfeld and His Follies," *Collier's*, 10 February 1934.

11. Joseph Urban, *Theatres* (New York: Theatre Arts, 1929), n.p.

12. Ibid.

13. Jerry Stagg, *The Brothers Shubert* (New York: Random House, 1968), 141.

14. Brooks McNamara, *The Shuberts of Broadway* (New York: Oxford University Press, 1990), 5.

15. Founded in 1896, the Syndicate consisted of six members. In addition to Klaw and Erlanger, the executive board included producer-theater owner Charles Frohman, theater owner Al Hayman, and theater managers J. Fred Zimmerman and Sam Nixon (né Nirdlinger).

16. Brooks Atkinson, *Broadway* (New York: Macmillan, 1974), 12.

17. Robert Grau, cited in McNamara, *The Shuberts of Broadway*, 6.

18. McNamara, *The Shuberts of Broadway*, 52.

19. In 1894 American impresario George Lederer presented *The Passing Show* at his Casino Theatre in Manhattan. With its penchant for burlesque, topicality, and elaborate scenic decor, it is generally credited by historians as the prototypical Broadway revue.

20. McNamara, *The Shuberts of Broadway*, 96.

21. Ibid., 38

22. Florenz Ziegfeld Jr., "Stars in the Making," *Theater Magazine*, November 1926, 9.

23. McNamara, *The Shuberts of Broadway*, 96.

24. Fanny Brice, as quoted by Ethan Mordden, *Broadway Babies* (New York: Oxford University Press, 1983), 42.

25. Eddie Cantor, with Jane Kesner Ardmore, *Take My Life* (New York: Doubleday, 1957), 7.

26. The song reflected a then-current "Salomania" in the wake of Richard Strauss's opera.

27. Fanny Brice, as quoted by Stanley Green, *The Great Clowns of Broadway* (New York: Oxford University Press, 1984), 4.

28. Warren G. Harris, *The Other Marilyn* (New York: Arbor House, 1985), 24.

29. Ibid., 72.

30. Billie Burke, *With a Feather on My Nose*, 175.

31. Program, *Ziegfeld Follies of 1919*, Billy Rose Theatre Collection, New York Public Library at Lincoln Center, n.p.

32. Eddie Cantor, with Jane Kesner Ardmore, *Take My Life* (New York: Doubleday, 1957), 201.

33. Cantor, *Take My Life*, 119.

34. Herbert G. Goldman, *Jolson: Legend Comes to Life* (New York: Oxford University Press, 1988), 12.

35. James Weldon Johnson, *Black Manhattan*, repr. ed. (Salem, N.H.: Ayer, 1990), 170.

36. It would not remain so. By the early 1920s Harlem nightspots like the *Cotton Club* and *Connie's Inn* presented black performers to an exclusively white clientele. See James Haskins, *The Cotton Club* (New York: Random House, 1977).

37. Hollis Alpert, *Broadway* (New York: Arcade, 1991), 82.

38. Florence Mills, as quoted by Allen Woll, *Black Musical Theatre* (Baton Rouge: Louisiana State University Press, 1989), 97.

39. Ibid., 97.

40. Program, *Dixie to Broadway*, Billy Rose Theatre Collection, NYPL, n.p.

41. Theophilus Lewis, *Messenger* 7 (January 1925): 18; as quoted by Woll, *Black Musical Theatre*, 13.

42. Alpert, *Broadway*, 82.

43. Other noted *Shuffle Along* alumni included Josephine Baker and Elisabeth Welch.

44. Robert Kimball and William Bolcom, *Reminiscing with Sissle and Blake* (New York: Viking Press, 1973), 80.

45. Flournoy Miller, Noble Sissle, and Eubie Blake, *Shuffle Along*, typescript, Eubie Blake Collection, Maryland Historical Society.

46. Englishman Leslie Stuart was a leading composer of the late nineteenth- and early twentieth-century London musical stage, working often in tandem with producer George Edwardes. Stuart's greatest artistic and commercial success was *Florodora*, for which he provided the musical score. It premiered in London in 1899 and one year later proved a transcontinental hit in its New York production.

47. Al Rose, *Eubie Blake* (New York: Schirmer Books, 1979), 77.

48. Woll, *Black Musical Theatre*, 73.

49. Laurence Bergreen, *As Thousands Cheer: The Life of Irving Berlin* (New York: Viking, 1990), 19.

50. He used only the black keys, pecking out all his tunes in the key of F-sharp major. He insisted, "The black keys are right there under your fingers. The key of C is for people who study music." Ibid., 57.

51. Berlin's earliest songs for the theater were written in partnership with Ted Snyder. Among them are "She Was Only a Dear Little Girl," introduced by comedienne Marie Cahill in *The Boys and Betty* (1908); "Oh, How That German Could Love," sung by Berlin himself in *The Girl and the Wizard* (1909); and "Sadie Salome, Go Home," performed by Fanny Brice in burlesque in 1909.

52. Englishman Vernon Castle (Blythe) launched his career as a comedian with Lew Fields's company, appearing with him in the musical comedies *About Town* (1906), *Old Dutch* (1909), *The Summer Widowers* (1909), and *The Hen Pecks* (1910). In 1910 Castle married and formed a professional union with dancer Irene Foote. Together, they became internationally renowned as the preeminent ballroom dancers of their era. Vernon was killed in action during World War I. Irene's autobiography, *Castles in the Air*, became the basis for the 1939 RKO film *The Story of Vernon and Irene Castle*, which starred Fred Astaire and Ginger Rogers.

53. Bergreen, *As Thousands Cheer*, 101.

54. Ibid., 110.

55. Bergreen, *As Thousands Cheer*, 122.

56. Gerald Bordman, *Jerome Kern* (New York: Oxford University Press, 1980), 149.

57. Ibid., 87. Kern actually acquired the phrase from musical comedy star Irene Bentley, wife of librettist Harry B. Smith.

58. The phrase "musical play" was used by Ziegfeld in his advertising campaigns to describe *Show Boat*. The term, popularized by Rodgers and Hammerstein in defining their own collaborative works, has generally become adopted in theater parlance to describe a type of musical entertainment, with roots in the operetta form, which combines a dramatic

story of scope and depth with extensive use of song elements that define character and locale and are integrally involved in propelling the narrative.

59. Bordman, *Jerome Kern*, 10.

60. Ibid., 28–29.

61. George Edwardes's work is discussed in Sheridan Morley, *Spread a Little Happiness: The First Hundred Years of the British Musical* (London: Thames and Hudson, 1987), 16–31.

62. Michael Freedland, *Jerome Kern* (New York: Stein and Day, 1978), 34.

63. Kern's Princess Theatre musicals are *Nobody Home* (1915), *Very Good Eddie* (1915), *Oh, Boy!* (1917), and *Oh, Lady! Lady!* (1918). Though not presented at the Princess Theatre, the following Kern shows are in the spirit of the productions that he and his associates perfected there and are recognized as being composed in the Princess Theatre style: *Leave It to Jane* (1917), *Have a Heart* (1917), and *Sitting Pretty* (1924).

64. Hugh Fordin, *Getting to Know Him* (New York: Random House, 1977), 79.

65. Florenz Ziegfeld, as quoted by Miles Kreuger, *Show Boat: The Story of a Classic Musical* (New York: Oxford University Press, 1977), 20.

66. Kern and Hammerstein had conceived the role of Joe with Paul Robeson specifically in mind. Although Robeson was clearly set for the part, the yearlong delay in the production of *Show Boat* forced him to withdraw because of other commitments. Robeson eventually played Joe in the 1928 London production, the 1932 Broadway revival, and the classic 1936 film version.

67. Bordman, *Jerome Kern*, 292.

68. The first Broadway production to be clearly modeled on the pattern established by *Show Boat* was the 1928 musical *Rainbow*, by Oscar Hammerstein II, Laurence Stallings, and Vincent Youmans. Attempting to do for the era of the California gold rush what *Show Boat* did for the late nineteenth-century South, *Rainbow* was a work of considerable promise marred, and eventually destroyed, by an inadequate production. It was lambasted by critics for its shoddiness and rejected by audiences after a mere twenty-eight performances.

LIGHT THE LIGHTS

1. Ted Sennett, *Hollywood Musicals* (New York: Harry N. Abrams, 1981), 31 ff.; John Kobal, *Gotta Sing, Gotta Dance: A History of Movie Musicals* (New York: Exeter Books, 1971), 290 ff.

2. Peter Hay, *MGM: When the Lion Roars* (Atlanta: Turner Publishing, 1991), 63 ff.; Sennett, *Hollywood Musicals*, 32 ff.

3. J. M., "The Dance: New Musical Comedy Talent," *New York Times*, 22 July 1928, 6.

4. Ibid.

5. Quoted in Tony Thomas and Jim Terry, *The Busby Berkeley Book* (Greenwich, Conn.: New York Graphic Society, 1973), 24–25.

6. Parsons cited in Thomas and Terry, *Busby Berkeley Book*, 26; *New York Herald* quotation is in ibid., 54.

7. Thomas and Terry, *Busby Berkeley Book*, 70.

8. Ibid., "Epigraph."

9. Arlene Croce, *The Fred Astaire–Ginger Rogers Book* (New York: Galahad Books, 1972), 75. The dance director was Dave Gould, but Hermes Pan—who would become Astaire's chosen choreographer throughout his movie career—was auditioning in this film to be Gould's assistant.

10. Morton Eustis, "Fred Astaire: The Actor-Dancer Attacks His Part," *Theatre Arts Monthly* 21 (May 1937): 379–80.

11. Ibid., 380–81.

12. "Dancing with Astaire and Rogers," *Literary Digest* 122 (12 December 1936): 20–21.

13. Ginger Rogers, *Ginger, My Story* (New York: HarperCollins, 1991), 139–40; authors' interview with Ginger Rogers, 23 February 1993.

14. Brooks McNamara, "The Entertainment District at the End of the 1930s," in William R. Taylor, ed., *Inventing Times Square* (New York: Russell Sage Foundation, 1991), 179–80.

15. Frederick Lewis Allen, *Only Yesterday* (New York: Harper & Row, 1964), 64.

16. Ira Gershwin lyric, "I Got Rhythm," in Robert Kimball, ed., *The Complete Lyrics of Ira Gershwin* (New York: Knopf, 1994), 166. It is also interesting to read Ethel Merman's own account of the audience reaction to her high C

note: see Merman with George Eells, *Merman* (New York: Simon & Schuster, 1978), 11.

17. Alan Jay Lerner, *The Musical Theatre: A Celebration* (New York: McGraw-Hill, 1986), 117. The pit orchestra for *Girl Crazy* included Red Nichols, Benny Goodman, Jack Teagarden, Gene Krupa, Jimmy Dorsey, and Glenn Miller.

18. Quoted in Kimball, *The Complete Lyrics of Ira Gershwin*, 173.

19. Deena Rosenberg, "Strike Up the Gershwins!" *Washington Post*, 14 June 1992.

20. Cited in Philip Furia, *Poets of Tin Pan Alley* (New York: Oxford University Press, 1990), 140.

21. Robert Kimball and Alfred Simon, *The Gershwins* (New York: Atheneum, 1975), xxxviii; Brooks Atkinson is also quoted in "George Gershwin," *Time-Life Records* booklet, 1982, 17.

22. "George Gershwin," booklet, 17.

23. Quoted in Deena Rosenberg, *Fascinating Rhythm: The Collaboration of George and Ira Gershwin* (New York: Dutton, 1991), 265. The best biography of the Gershwins remains Edward Jablonski and Lawrence D. Stewart, *The Gershwin Years* (New York: Doubleday, 1973).

24. Quoted in Rosenberg, *Fascinating Rhythm*, 273.

25. Quoted in Charles Schwartz, *Gershwin: His Life and Music* (New York: Bobbs-Merrill, 1973), 245.

26. Ira Gershwin to Yip Harburg, 12 June 1936. Harburg was already in Hollywood writing songs. Quoted in Rosenberg, *Fascinating Rhythm*, 323.

27. Authors' interviews with Ginger Rogers and Mrs. Vincenté Minnelli.

28. Rosenberg, *Fascinating Rhythm*, 325–94. Ira Gershwin would work on the final Astaire-Rogers film, MGM's 1949 *The Barkleys of Broadway*, as well as two outstanding 1954 films, *A Star Is Born* and *The Country Girl*.

29. George S. Kaufman, in the introduction to Kaufman and Moss Hart, *Six Plays* (New York: Random House, 1942), xxix.

30. Laurence Bergreen, *As Thousands Cheer: The Life of Irving Berlin* (New York: Viking, 1990), 323 ff.

31. Review from the Philadelphia *Public Ledger*, 17 September 1933, n.p., in Moss Hart collection, "Scrapbook, 1922–1962," State Historical Society of Wisconsin.

32. Quoted in Bergreen, *As Thousands Cheer*, 293.

33. Interview with Hermes Pan, quoted in Bergreen, *As Thousands Cheer*, 347.

34. Quoted in Bergreen, *As Thousands Cheer*, 367.

35. Robert Kimball, ed., *The Complete Lyrics of Cole Porter* (New York: Knopf, 1983), xviii.

36. Quoted in Furia, *Poets of Tin Pan Alley*, 153.

37. Gerald Mast, *Can't Help Singin'* (New York: Overlook Press, 1987), 195.

38. For early Merman memories see Ethel Merman with George Eells, *Merman* (New York: Simon & Schuster, 1978), chaps. 1–5.

39. Indeed, Porter later said that he "would rather write songs for Ethel Merman than anyone else in the world." Merman and Eells, *Merman*, 11. She would prove the perennial Porter heroine, electrifying such scores as *Red, Hot, and Blue* (1936), *DuBarry Was a Lady* (1939), and *Panama Hattie* (1940).

40. Quoted in Furia, *Poets of Tin Pan Alley*, 95. See also Frederick Nolan, *Lorenz Hart: A Poet on Broadway* (New York: Oxford University Press, 1994).

41. Richard Rodgers, *Musical Stages* (New York: Random House, 1975), 20.

42. Quoted in David Ewen, *Richard Rodgers* (New York: Henry Holt, 1957), 65.

43. Rodgers, *Musical Stages*, 64–65.

44. Quoted in Ewen, *Richard Rodgers*, 146–47.

45. Quoted in Benny Green, *Let's Face the Music: The Golden Age of Popular Song* (London: Pavilion Books, 1989), 201.

46. Quoted in Eric A. Gordon, *Mark the Music; The Life and Work of Marc Blitzstein* (New York: St. Martin's Press, 1989), 119.

47. John Houseman, *Run-through* (New York: Simon & Schuster, 1972), 268–69.

48. Walter Winchell, *Mirror*, 15 December 1937; Atkinson, *New York Times*, 6 December 1937.

49. John Updike, "Foreword" to Robert Kimball, ed., *The Complete Lyrics of Cole Porter* (New York: Vintage Books, 1984), xiv.

50. Moss Hart to Dore Schary, c. 1940 and c. 1941, Schary Collection, State Historical Society of Wisconsin, Box 99, folder 8.

51. Quoted in Sheridan Morley, *Gertrude Lawrence* (New York: McGraw-Hill, 1981), 151.

52. Quoted in Hay, *MGM: When the Lion Roars*, 19.

53. Sennett, *Hollywood Musicals*, 119.

54. Fred Astaire, *Steps in Time* (New York: Harper & Brothers, 1959), 241.

55. Dissatisfied with Warners, Berkeley was to remain at MGM.

56. The song was written originally for the 1937 stage musical *Hooray for What?* starring comedian Ed Wynn.

57. Sennett, *Hollywood Musicals*, 162.

58. Quoted in ibid., 114.

59. See Shirley Temple Black, *Child Star* (New York: McGraw-Hill, 1988), passim.

60. See James Haskins, *Mr. Bojangles: The Biography of Bill Robinson* (New York: William Morrow, 1988), passim; James Meehan, "Bojangles of Richmond: 'His Dancing Feet Brought Joy to the World,'" *Virginia Cavalcade* 27 (Winter 1978): 101; "Bill 'Bojangles' Robinson," *Vanity Fair*, December 1987, 110.

61. See Kobal, *Gotta Sing*, 175.

62. Quoted in *Current Biography* (1944), 310.

63. The first was Madame Sul-Te-Wan, who signed with D. W. Griffith in 1915. "Lena Horne," *Notable Black American Women* (Detroit: Gale Research Staff, 1992), 520.

64. Stephen Harvey, *Directed by Vincente Minnelli* (New York: Harper & Row, 1989), 39–40.

65. Ibid., 42–43; *Notable Black American Women*, 520; *Current Biography* (1944), 311–12.

66. Richard Schickel, *The Disney Version: The Life, Times, Art and Commerce of Walt Disney* (New York: Simon & Schuster, 1985), 213–27. To get a good understanding of the production of *Snow White*, see Stephen Ison, *Walt Disney's 'Snow White and the Seven Dwarfs': An Art in Its Making* (New York: Hyperion, 1994).

67. David Shipman, *Judy Garland: The Secret Life of an American Legend* (New York: Hyperion, 1992), 79.

68. "New Acts," *Variety*, 21 November 1934, quoted in Shipman, *Judy Garland*, 42.

69. Shipman, *Judy Garland*, 44.

70. Harold Meyerson and Ernie Harburg, *Who Put the Rainbow in the Wizard of Oz?* (Ann Arbor: University of Michigan Press, 1993), 129. In fact, there was not even a rainbow in the original book by L. Frank Baum.

71. Quoted in ibid., 84.

72. Quoted in ibid., 93.

THE HEIGHTS

1. Oscar Hammerstein II and Richard Rodgers, "Oklahoma!" (New York: Williamson Music, 1943).

2. Theresa Helburn, *A Wayward Quest* (New York: Little, Brown, 1960), 282.

3. Since the mid-1930s, Hammerstein had authored a relentless series of Broadway flops. Shortly after the triumphant opening of *Oklahoma!* he wrote an advertisement that he placed in the 4 January 1944 issue of *Variety*. The ad listed the titles of five failed shows (*Sunny River*, *Very Warm for May*, *Three Sisters*, *Ball at the Savoy*, and *Free for All*) and the brief number of weeks each had played and then ended with the mordant comment, "I've done it before and I can do it again!"

4. Strictly speaking, Rodgers and Hammerstein's first collaboration was writing the music and lyrics, respectively, for the song "There's Always Room for One More," which was interpolated into the 1920 Columbia University varsity musical *Fly with Me*. Most of the show's lyrics were composed by Lorenz Hart.

5. Among Mamoulian's accomplishments in *Applause* was his innovative use of a sound-track with two audio channels. The film is discussed at length by Richard Barrios in his book *A Song in the Dark: The Birth of the Musical Film* (New York: Oxford University Press, 1995), 314–16.

6. Agnes de Mille, as quoted by Ethan Mordden, *Rodgers and Hammerstein* (New York: Harry N. Abrams, 1993), 33.

7. Max Wilk, *O.K.!: The Story of Oklahoma!* (New York: Grove Press, 1993), 120.

8. Ibid.

9. Burns Mantle, Review, *New York Daily News*, 1 April 1943.

10. Jack Kapp's earliest efforts in recording theater music were a series of 78 rpm recordings released on the Brunswick label. The first of these were recorded in 1928 and consisted of four single 78 rpm discs of songs from *Blackbirds of 1928*, featuring original cast members Adelaide Hall, Bill Robinson, Elisabeth Welch, and the original theater orchestra. In 1932, in tandem with Ziegfeld's hit Broadway revival of *Show Boat*, Kapp produced an album of four 12-inch 78s featuring original revival cast members Helen Morgan and Paul Robeson. The *Show Boat* album was the first attempt to assemble selections from a single Broadway musical under one cover with artists who originally performed the songs in a Broadway production. In the strictest sense, the discs were not true original cast recordings (Victor Young's orchestra was used in lieu of the theater musicians, and two Brunswick contractees, Countess Albani and Frank Munn, filled in for the Broadway leads); however, the album's success pointed the way for other efforts in recording theater music.

One number in the Decca original cast recording of *Oklahoma!* was not sung on disc by the actor who introduced it in the theater. Leading man Alfred Drake recorded Jud Fry's song "Lonely Room," which was performed onstage by Howard da Silva, who created the role of the disturbed farmhand.

11. Technically speaking, the first full-fledged American original cast album was a limited pressing of 78s devoted to Marc Blitzstein's *The Cradle Will Rock*, recorded on the Keynote label in 1938 with members of the New York production.

12. Mordden, *Rodgers and Hammerstein*, 47.

13. Hammerstein, as quoted by Hugh Fordin, *Getting to Know Him: A Biography of Oscar Hammerstein II* (New York: Random House, 1977), 254.

14. Jo Mielziner, *Designing for the Theatre* (New York: Bramhall House, 1965), 243.

15. Ibid.

16. Hammerstein first addressed the issue of race prejudice in his libretto for *Show Boat* in his treatment of the principal character of Julie Laverne, a mulatto whose life is destroyed by the effects of bigotry.

17. It was Logan who, after first securing the rights to Michener's novel in tandem with his agent Leland Hayward, recognized the musical theater possibilities in the work and suggested it to Richard Rodgers.

18. Although Pinza appeared in one more Broadway musical (*Fanny*, 1954) and three film musicals (*Strictly Dishonorable*, 1951; *Mr. Imperium*, 1952; and *Tonight We Sing*, 1954), none came close to his triumph in *South Pacific*.

19. Martin's initial career in Hollywood was a series of disappointments and dead ends, in which she functioned as a dance coach and as a vocal double for, among others, French star Danielle Darrieux. She discusses this era in her professional development in her autobiography, *My Heart Belongs* (New York: Morrow, 1976), 58–67.

20. *Me and Juliet*, which Hammerstein called "a theatrical valentine," is set within the confines of a theater in New York City. Both *Pipe Dream* and *Flower Drum Song* take place in California: the former in the cannery rows of Monterey and the latter in a brightly synthetic version of San Francisco's Chinatown. The locales for *The King and I* and *The Sound of Music* are remote and exotic. They are, respectively, nineteenth-century Siam and late-1930s Austria.

21. *Bloomer Girl*, with music by Harold Arlen, lyrics by E. Y. Harburg, and script by Sig Herzig and Fred Saidy, centered on a fictional view of the Civil War era, contributing revisionist perspectives on women's rights, slavery, abolition, and the underground railroad. Aside from its nostalgia for America's past, it shared with *Oklahoma!* several members of the same production team (choreographer Agnes de Mille, costumier Miles White, set designer Lemuel Ayers, orchestrator Robert Russell Bennett) and cast (Celeste Holm, Joan McCracken).

Finian's Rainbow (1947), set in the mythical state of Missitucky, employed the Rodgers and Hammerstein formula of American regionalism to provide atmosphere to a modern fairy tale with leftist political overtones. Its score was composed by Burton Lane and E. Y. Harburg. Harburg also coauthored its libretto with Fred Saidy. The original production was further distinguished by a series of whimsical ballets by Michael Kidd, done in homage to those designed by Agnes de Mille.

The Golden Apple, the first and only commercial musical to date that was created as a result of a grant from the Guggenheim Foundation, was an audacious, inventive retelling of the *Iliad* and the *Odyssey* reset in early twentieth-century Washington State. Through-sung in arias, ensembles, and recitatives ranging from traditional musical comedy and modern opera to pastiches of American folk songs, its impressive score was by composer Jerome Moross and lyricist-librettist John Latouche.

Bandleader Meredith Willson wrote the book, music, and lyrics (the last in collaboration with Franklin Lacey) for *The Music Man*. A colorful fable about a charming con man redeemed by the love of a spinster librarian, the show made stars out of its principal players Robert Preston and Barbara Cook.

22. Dorothy Fields and Ethel Merman first worked together as the lyricist and star, respectively, of the 1939 Broadway musical, *Stars in Your Eyes*. Ethel Merman discusses their professional association and their personal friendship in her autobiography, *Who Could Ask for Anything More?* with Pete Martin (New York: Doubleday, 1955), 138–40.

Fields first pitched the Annie Oakley idea to producer Mike Todd, who had presented the most recent Merman-Fields project, the 1943 Broadway musical *Something for the Boys*, with the score by Cole Porter. Todd rejected the idea immediately.

23. Dorothy and Herbert Fields wrote the libretti for three shows with scores by Cole Porter (*Let's Face It!* 1941; *Something for the Boys*, 1943; and *Mexican Hayride*, 1944).

24. Alan Jay Lerner, *The Street Where I Live* (New York: Norton, 1978), 135.

25. As reported in Gene Lees's *Inventing Champagne: The Worlds of Lerner and Loewe*

(New York: St. Martin's Press, 1990), among the other actresses mentioned for the role were Deanna Durbin and Dolores Gray.

26. Irving Berlin, as quoted in Hugh Fordin, *The World of Entertainment: The Freed Unit at MGM* (Garden City, N.J.: Doubleday, 1975), 526.

27. Joseph Andrew Casper, *Stanley Donen* (London: Scarecrow Press, 1983), 8.

28. Six of the seven surviving Freed children chose careers in music. Aside from Arthur, Sydney and Clarence were recording company executives. Walter became an organist. And Ralph and Ruth, like their brother Arthur, were songwriters. Further biographical data on the Freed family is documented in Hugh Fordin, *The World of Entertainment*, ix.

29. Roger Edens came to MGM in 1934 to act as musical supervisor for the Jean Harlow film *Reckless*. He and Freed first worked together on the MGM movie *Broadway Melody of 1936*, for which Freed and Nacio Herb Brown supplied two songs.

30. One of Edens's earliest assignments was as onstage pianist for Ethel Merman in *Girl Crazy*. He and Merman remained friends throughout their respective careers, and when she launched a club act in the 1950s, he composed its opening number, "A Lady with a Song."

31. Sally Benson, as quoted in Hugh Fordin, *The World of Entertainment*, 91.

32. Freed, quoted in Fordin, *The World of Entertainment*, 91.

33. Ibid., 94.

34. Vincente Minnelli, with Hector Arce, *I Remember It Well* (Garden City, N.Y.: Doubleday, 1974), 13.

35. Ibid.

36. Stephen Harvey, *The Films of Vincente Minnelli* (New York: Museum of Modern Art/Harper and Row, 1989), 12.

37. Minnelli, *I Remember It Well*, 28.

38. Brooks Atkinson, as quoted in ibid., 73.

39. Arthur Freed, as quoted in Fordin, *The World of Entertainment*, 33.

40. John Kobal, *Gotta Sing, Gotta Dance* (New York: Exeter Books, 1971), 76.

41. Gene Kelly, as quoted in Tony Thomas, *That's Dancing* (New York: Harry N. Abrams, 1984), 178.

42. Alan Jay Lerner, as quoted in Donald Knox, *The Magic Factory: How MGM Made "An American in Paris"* (New York: Praeger, 1973), 40.

43. Quoted in Humphrey Burton, *Leonard Bernstein* (New York: Doubleday, 1994), 58.

44. Ibid., 117.

45. Oliver Smith, quoted in *Dance Magazine*, March 1967, 51.

46. Burton, *Leonard Bernstein*, 128.

47. From liner notes by Comden and Green, *On the Town*.

48. Interview in Otis L. Guernsey Jr., ed., *Broadway Song & Story* (New York: Dodd, Mead, 1985), 11.

49. Quoted in ibid., 11.

50. Burton, *Leonard Bernstein*, 136; Guernsey, *Broadway Song & Story*, 6.

51. Bernstein, quoted in Cyrus Durgin, "Bernstein Gives Up Conducting to Compose Music for Theater," *Boston Morning Globe*, 1 February 1953.

52. Olin Downes, "Wonderful Time: Bernstein's Musical Is Brilliant Achievement," *New York Times*, 10 May 1953. Brooks Atkinson, *New York Times*, 26 February 1953.

53. Quoted in David Zippel, "Together Again . . . and Again . . . and Again," *New York Times*, 20 June 1993.

54. Bernstein, quoted in Joan Peyser, *Bernstein, A Biography* (New York: Beech Tree Books, 1987), 257–58.

55. Quoted in Craig Zadan, *Sondheim & Co.*, 2d ed. (New York: Harper and Row, 1989), 3.

56. Sondheim, quoted in Zadan, *Sondheim & Co.*, 3–4.

57. Stephen Sondheim interview, Museum of Television and Radio, 27 October 1993.

58. Quoted in Zadan, *Sondheim & Co.*, 14.

59. Guernsey, ed., *Broadway Song and Story*, 44.

60. Peyser, *Bernstein*, 268 ff.; Burton, *Leonard Bernstein*, 275.

61. Quoted in Burton, *Leonard Bernstein*, 275–76.

62. Kerr, *New York Herald Tribune*, 27 September 1957; Atkinson, *New York Times*, 27 September 1957.

63. Howard Kissel, *David Merrick: The Abominable Showman* (New York: Applause, 1993), 161 ff.

64. Merman, quoted in Zadan, *Sondheim and Co.*, 49.

65. Dick Schaap, "Imp in a Monster Mask," *Life*, 13 December 1968, 43–44.

66. Quoted in Fordin, *The World of Entertainment*, 241.

67. Sondheim, quoted in Guernsey, ed., *Broadway Song and Story*, 229.

"SIDE BY SIDE BY SIDE"

1. Of these screen adaptations of Broadway musicals, only *My Fair Lady* (1964), *The Sound of Music* (1965), *Cabaret* (1972), and *Grease* (1978) were commercial successes. The lone winner among original film musicals in the 1960s was *Mary Poppins* (1964).

2. Jerry Herman, as quoted in Stephen Holden, "Jerry Herman, From 'Dolly' to 'La Cage,'" *New York Times*, 15 December 1985, sec. 2, 24.

3. The song was subsequently heard in Herman's 1960 off-Broadway revue *Parade* and elements of its melody were reused in the song "It's Today," written for the score of *Mame* (1966).

4. Howard Kissel, *David Merrick: The Abominable Showman* (New York: Applause Books, 1993), 288.

5. Gower Champion appeared in the musicals *Streets of Paris* (1939)—which introduced Carmen Miranda to U.S. audiences—*The Lady Comes Across* (1942), and *Count Me In* (1942).

6. Walter Kerr, Review of *Hello, Dolly! New York Herald Tribune*, 17 January 1964.

7. Jerry Herman, quoted in Al Kasha and Joel Hirshhorn, *Notes on Broadway: Conversations with Great Songwriters* (Chicago: Contemporary Books, 1985), 181.

8. Bob Fosse, *Dance Magazine*, February 1969, 25.

9. Bob Fosse, as quoted in Martin Gottfried, *All His Jazz: The Life and Death of Bob Fosse* (New York: Bantam, 1990), 56.

10. Fosse's first MGM film, *Give a Girl a Break* (1952), also starred Marge and Gower Champion. He and Champion would become

the preeminent theatrical director-choreographers of the 1960s.

11. Cole Porter composed "From This Moment On" for his 1950 musical *Out of This World*; however, George Abbott, who unofficially replaced Agnes de Mille during the pre-Broadway tryout, dropped the number from the show. Frank Sinatra's recording of the song established it as a pop hit and when *Kiss Me, Kate* was filmed, the number was added to its already bountiful score.

12. Aside from *The Pajama Game*, Peter Gennaro danced in the chorus of such Broadway productions as *Make Mine Manhattan; Kiss Me, Kate; Guys and Dolls;* and *Bells Are Ringing*. After serving as co-choreographer (with Jerome Robbins) for *West Side Story*, he devised the dances for such hits as *Fiorello!* (1959), *The Unsinkable Molly Brown* (1960), and *Annie* (1977).

13. In addition to Fosse, the principal members of *The Pajama Game* company who reunited to create *Damn Yankees* were producers Frederick Brisson, Robert E. Griffith, and Harold S. Prince; director George Abbott; composers Richard Adler and Jerry Ross; musical director Harold Hastings; and orchestrator Don Walker.

14. Verdon appeared in minor roles in the stage musicals *Bonanza Bound* (1947), *Magdalena* (1948), and *Alive and Kicking* (1950) and in the screen musicals *The Farmer Takes a Wife* (1951), *On the Riviera* (1952), and *The Merry Widow* (1952).

15. Gwen Verdon, quoted in Rex Reed, "Gwen Verdon," *New York Times*, 6 February 1966, sec. II, 1.

16. Harold Prince, *Contradictions: Notes on Twenty-Six Years in the Theater* (New York: Dodd, Mead & Co., 1974); George Abbott, *Mister Abbott* (New York: Random House, 1963).

17. *Redhead* began its life in 1951 under the title *The Works*. Dorothy and Herbert Fields had originally planned their script, a spoof of Victorian murder mysteries, for comedienne Beatrice Lillie with a score made up of unpublished melodies by Jerome Kern. When Lillie rejected the idea, they redesigned it for several prospective stars, including Celeste Holm and Ethel Merman. After hearing the story and songs (by Fields and composer Albert Hague), Verdon agreed to do the show.

18. Several years earlier, Oliver Smith tried unsuccessfully to persuade Betty Comden and Adolph Green to convert *The Nights of Cabiria* into a stage musical for their *On the Town* costar Nancy Walker.

19. Walter Kerr, Review of *Sweet Charity*, *New York Herald Tribune*, 31 January 1966.

20. Shirley MacLaine first worked for Fosse as a member of the chorus and understudy for Carol Haney in the 1954 Broadway production of *The Pajama Game*. When Haney broke her ankle and temporarily left the show, MacLaine replaced her, earning a Hollywood contract and eventual stardom for her efforts.

21. Pauline Kael, Review of *Cabaret*, *New Yorker*, 19 February 1972, 25.

22. Helen Epstein, *Joe Papp; An American Life* (Boston: Little, Brown, 1994), 56 ff.

23. Quoted in ibid., 92.

24. Ibid., 180.

25. Quoted in ibid., 102.

26. Quoted in ibid., 214. *Hair*, at its height earning $330,000 in one week, would contribute a million dollars to the Shakespeare Festival through 1971 and serve as Papp's "cash cow" until the 1976 production of *A Chorus Line*. See ibid., 490.

27. See Vera Brodsky Lawrence, *Strong on Music: The New York Music Scene in the Days of George Templeton Strong, 1836–1875* (New York: Oxford University Press, 1988), vol. 1, 576 ff.

28. See Roy Bongartz, "Pitchman for a Free (And Freewheeling) Theater," *New York Times*, 15 August 1971, 12–13; *New York Times*, 14 April 1972, 40.

29. Quoted in Mel Gussow, "A Playwright's Invention Named Papp," *New York Times*, 9 November 1975, 18.

30. Quoted in Ken Mandelbaum, *A Chorus Line and the Musicals of Michael Bennett* (New York: St. Martin's Press, 1989), 22.

31. Quoted in ibid., 51.

32. Quoted in ibid., 59.

33. Quoted in "Theoni V. Aldredge," *Architectural Digest*, May 1993, 200–201.

34. In *Playbill*, June 1982, quoted in Mandelbaum, *A Chorus Line*, 135.

35. See "Michael Bennett and the Making of *A Chorus Line*," *Dance Magazine*, June 1975, 62–65; *Time*, 28 July 1975, 47–48.

36. Mandelbaum, *A Chorus Line*, 189 ff.

37. Clive Barnes, *New York Times*, 22 May 1975.

38. Bennett is quoted in Mandelbaum, *A Chorus Line*, 217. Bennett would earn another Tony in this, his last show. He would die in 1987.

39. Emory Lewis in *Cue*, 22 January 1955, quoted in "Geoffrey Holder," *Current Biography* (1957), 263–64.

40. Geoffrey Holder, "That Fad from Trinidad," *New York Times*, 21 April 1957, 14, 60.

41. Quoted in *Spirits: Selections from the Collection of Geoffrey Holder and Carmen de Lavallade* (Katonah, N.Y.: Katonah Museum of Art, 1991), 12.

42. "The Wiz," *Time*, 20 January 1975; *Newsweek*, 20 January 1975; *New York Daily News*, 6 January 1975; *New York Times*, 6 January 1975.

43. *Time*, 13 March 1978.

44. "*Eubie!*" *Time*, 22 September 1978; *New York Times*, 6, 24 November 1978; "Sophisticated Ladies," *New York Times*, 2 March 1981.

45. William A. Henry III, "Triple Threat," *Time*, 4 May 1992, 78.

46. Abbott quoted in Carol Ilson, *Harold Prince: From Pajama Game to Phantom of the Opera and Beyond* (New York: Limelight Editions, 1989, 1992), 13–14.

47. Walter Kerr, "Theatre," *New York Herald Tribune*, 14 May 1954; NYPL Critics' Reviews, vol. 15, 324.

48. For an extremely incisive discussion of George Abbott's influence on Harold Prince see Foster Hirsch, *Harold Prince and the American Musical Theater* (Cambridge: Cambridge University Press, 1989), chap. 2 and passim.

49. Frank Rich and Lisa Aronson, *The Theatre Art of Boris Aronson* (New York: Alfred A. Knopf, 1987), 85.

50. Prince, *Contradictions*, 99–100.

51. Ibid., 125.

52. Ibid., 125–26.

53. Quoted in ibid., 1.

54. Ibid., 126.

55. Boris Aronson first worked with Prince on the original Broadway production of *Fiddler on the Roof* (1964), where his settings were heavily influenced by the art of Marc Chagall. Aronson quoted in Rich and Aronson, *Boris Aronson*, 188.

56. Beginning in 1964, Aronson and Prince collaborated on *Fiddler on the Roof*; they also worked together on *Cabaret* (1966), *Company* (1970), *Follies* (1971), *A Little Night Music* (1973), and *Pacific Overtures* (1976).

57. William Zimmer, "Stage Designs by Aronson, a Master of Visual Metaphor," *New York Times*, 22 October 1989, sec. 22, 5; Rich, *The Theatre Art of Boris Aronson*, ix–31, 218–30.

58. Prince, *Contradictions*, 143.

59. Craig Zadan, *Sondheim and Co.*, 2d ed. (New York: Harper & Row, 1989), 117.

60. Boris Aronson, as quoted in Rich, *The Theatre Art of Boris Aronson*, 220.

61. The first quotation is Stephen Sondheim, in Hirsch, *Harold Prince and the American Musical Theatre*, 93. The second quotation is Harold Prince, in ibid., 93.

62. Boris Aronson quoted in Rich and Aronson, *Boris Aronson*, 237.

63. Harold Prince quoted in Mel Gussow, "*Sweeney Todd*: A Little Nightmare Music," *New York Times*, 1 February 1979, sec. C, 15.

64. Sondheim, quoted in Zadan, *Sondheim and Co.*, 246

65. Ibid., 248.

66. *Sunset Boulevard* eventually reached the musical stage in 1994 in an adaptation by British composer-producer Andrew Lloyd Webber, librettist Christopher Hampton, and lyricist Don Black.

67. Sondheim, quoted in Zadan, *Sondheim and Co.*, 300.

68. James Lapine, quoted in Zadan, *Sondheim and Co.*, 337.

69. Sondheim, quoted in *New York Magazine*, 21 September 1987, 50.

70. Sondheim, quoted by Michiko Kakutani in liner notes, *Passion* (New York: Angel/EMI, 1994), 3.

71. Sondheim, quoted in Zadan, *Sondheim and Co.*, 394.

72. Margo Jefferson, "Strolling along Broadway's Museum Mile," *New York Times*, Arts & Leisure, 2 April 1995, 1. Yet a short year later, *Rent* and *Bring in 'da Noise, Bring in 'da Funk* infused Broadway with the sound and fury of a new generation.

73. Prince speaking at the 1988 New York Festival of the Arts describing the director's greatest challenge. Quotation courtesy of Harold Prince.

74. See Ethan Mordden, "A Proud Flagship Keeps on Rolling in Deeper Currents," *New York Times*, 25 September 1994, sec. 2, 1, 22; and Jack Kroll, "Stormy Trip for *Show Boat*," *Newsweek*, 1 November 1993, 76–77.

75. Walt Whitman, "Broadway, 1885," in *Leaves of Grass* (Signet Classic: New York, 1964), 393.

76. John Lahr, *Automatic Vaudeville* (New York: Limelight Editions, 1985), 6.

77. Conclusion to Edna Ferber's novel, *Show Boat* (New York: Doubleday & Co., 1926), 398.

SELECTED BIBLIOGRAPHY

PRIMARY SOURCES

Academy of Motion Picture Arts and Sciences
  Script files
  MGM Collection
Columbia University
  Joseph Urban Collection
Howard University
  Moorland-Spingarn Collection
Library of Congress
  Leonard Bernstein Collection
  Bob Fosse–Gwen Verdon Collection
  Victor Herbert Collection
  Rodgers & Hammerstein Collection
Los Angeles County Museum of Natural
  History
  RKO Studio Collection
Maryland Historical Society
  Eubie Blake Collection
Marion Koogler McNay Museum
  The Tobin Collection
Museum of the City of New York
Museum of Television and Radio
New York Public Library at Lincoln Center
  Billy Rose Theatre Collection
Harry Ransom Research Center, University of
  Texas at Austin
Shubert Archive
State Historical Society of Wisconsin
  Pandro Berman Collection
  Marc Blitzstein Collection
  Edna Ferber Collection
  Moss and Kitty Carlisle Hart Collection
  Herman Levin Collection
  Lindsay and Crouse Collection
  Stephen Sondheim Collection
UCLA Film and Television Archive
University of Southern California
  Arthur Freed Collection
Wisconsin Center for Film and Theater
  Research

INTERVIEWS

Kitty Carlisle Hart
Geoffrey Holder
Ken Ludwig
Liza Minnelli
Mrs. Vincenté Minnelli
Harold S. Prince
Debbie Reynolds
Ginger Rogers
Kay Thompson
Tony Walton

SECONDARY SOURCES

Abbott, George. *Mister Abbott*. New York: Random House, 1963.

Alpert, Hollis. *Broadway*. New York: Arcade, 1991.

Astaire, Fred. *Steps in Time*. New York: Harper & Brothers, 1959.

Atkinson, Brooks. *Broadway*. New York: Macmillan, 1974.

Barrios, Richard. *A Song in the Dark: The Birth of the Musical Film*. New York: Oxford University Press, 1995.

Bergreen, Laurence. *As Thousands Cheer: The Life of Irving Berlin*. New York: Viking, 1990.

Black, Shirley Temple. *Child Star*. New York: McGraw-Hill, 1988.

Bordman, Gerald. *American Musical Theatre: A Chronicle*. New York: Oxford University Press, 1986.

———. *Jerome Kern*. New York: Oxford University Press, 1980.

Burton, Humphrey. *Leonard Bernstein*. New York: Doubleday, 1994.

Croce, Arlene. *The Fred Astaire–Ginger Rogers Book*. New York: Galahad Books, 1972.

Easton, Carol. *No Intermissions: The Life of Agnes de Mille*. Boston: Little, Brown, 1996.

Epstein, Helen. *Joe Papp: An American Life.* Boston: Little, Brown, 1994.

Fields, Armond, and L. Marc Fields. *From the Bowery to Broadway: Lew Fields and the Roots of American Popular Theater.* New York: Oxford University Press, 1993.

Fordin, Hugh. *Getting to Know Him: A Biography of Oscar Hammerstein II.* New York: Random House, 1977; 1996.

——. *The World of Entertainment: The Freed Unit at MGM.* Garden City, N.Y.: Doubleday, 1975.

Furia, Philip. *Ira Gershwin: The Art of the Lyricist.* New York: Oxford University Press, 1996.

Goldman, Herbert G. *Jolson: Legend Comes to Life.* New York: Oxford University Press, 1988.

Gordon, Eric A. *Mark the Music: The Life and Work of Marc Blitzstein.* New York: St. Martin's Press, 1989.

Gottfried, Martin. *All His Jazz: The Life and Death of Bob Fosse.* New York: Bantam, 1990.

Green, Stanley. *The Great Clowns of Broadway.* New York: Oxford University Press, 1984.

Harvey, Stephen. *Directed by Vincente Minnelli.* New York: Harper & Row, 1989.

Hay, Peter. *MGM: When the Lion Roars.* Atlanta: Turner Publishing, 1991.

Hirsch, Foster. *Harold Prince and the American Musical Theater.* Cambridge: Cambridge University Press, 1989.

Houseman, John. *Run-through.* New York: Simon & Schuster, 1972.

Ilson, Carol. *Harold Prince: From Pajama Game to Phantom of the Opera and Beyond.* New York: Limelight Editions, 1989.

Ison, Stephen. *Walt Disney's "Snow White and the Seven Dwarfs": An Art in Its Making.* New York: Hyperion, 1994.

Jablonski, Edward. *Alan Jay Lerner: A Biography.* New York: Henry Holt, 1996.

Jablonski, Edward, and Lawrence D. Stewart. *The Gershwin Years.* New York: Doubleday, 1973.

Johnson, James Weldon. *Black Manhattan.* Repr. Salem, N.H.: Ayer, 1990.

Kahn, E. J. Jr. *The Merry Partners: The Age and Stage of Harrigan and Hart.* New York: Random House, 1955.

Kimball, Robert, ed. *The Complete Lyrics of Cole Porter.* New York: Knopf, 1983.

——, ed. *The Complete Lyrics of Ira Gershwin.* New York: Knopf, 1994.

Kimball, Robert, and William Bolcom. *Reminiscing with Sissle and Blake.* New York: Viking Press, 1973.

Kimball, Robert, and Alfred Simon. *The Gershwins.* New York: Atheneum, 1975.

Kissel, Howard. *David Merrick: Abominable Showman.* New York: Applause, 1993.

Kobal, John. *Gotta Sing, Gotta Dance: A History of Movie Musicals.* New York: Exeter Books, 1971.

Kreuger, Miles. *Show Boat: The Story of a Classic Musical.* New York: Oxford University Press, 1977.

Lahr, John. *Automatic Vaudeville.* New York: Limelight Editions, 1985.

Lawrence, Vera Brodsky. *Strong on Music: The New York Music Scene in the Days of George Templeton Strong, 1836–1875,* vol. 1. New York: Oxford University Press, 1988.

Lerner, Alan Jay. *The Musical Theatre: A Celebration.* New York: McGraw-Hill, 1986.

Mandelbaum, Ken. *A Chorus Line and the Musicals of Michael Bennett.* New York: St. Martin's Press, 1989.

McNamara, Brooks. *The Shuberts of Broadway.* New York: Oxford University Press, 1990.

Merman, Ethel, and George Eells. *Merman.* New York: Simon & Schuster, 1978.

Meyerson, Harold, and Ernie Harburg. *Who Put the Rainbow in the Wizard of Oz?* Ann Arbor: University of Michigan Press, 1993.

Mielziner, Jo. *Designing for the Theatre.* New York: Bramhall House, 1965.

Minnelli, Vincente, with Hector Arce. *I Remember It Well.* Garden City, N.Y.: Doubleday, 1974.

Mordden, Ethan. *Rodgers and Hammerstein.* New York: Harry N. Abrams, 1993.

Nolan, Frederick. *Lorenz Hart: A Poet on Broadway.* New York: Oxford University Press, 1994.

Prince, Harold. *Contradictions: Notes on Twenty-Six Years in the Theater.* New York: Dodd, Mead & Co., 1974.

Rich, Frank, and Lisa Aronson. *The Theatre Art of Boris Aronson.* New York: Alfred A. Knopf, 1987.

Riis, Thomas L. *Just before Jazz: Black Musical Theater in New York, 1890–1915.* Washington, D.C.: Smithsonian Institution Press, 1989.

Rodgers, Richard. *Musical Stages.* New York: Random House, 1975.

Rogers, Ginger. *Ginger, My Story.* New York: HarperCollins, 1991.

Rosenberg, Deena. *Fascinating Rhythm: The Collaboration of George and Ira Gershwin.* New York: Dutton, 1991.

Schickel, Richard. *The Disney Version: The Life, Times, Art and Commerce of Walt Disney.* New York: Simon & Schuster, 1985.

Sennett, Ted. *Hollywood Musicals.* New York: Harry N. Abrams, 1981.

Snyder, Robert W. *The Voice of the City: Vaudeville and Popular Culture in New York.* New York: Oxford University Press, 1989.

Taylor, William R., ed. *Inventing Times Square: Commerce and Culture at the Crossroads of the World.* New York: Russell Sage Foundation, 1991.

Thomas, Tony, and Jim Terry. *The Busby Berkeley Book.* Greenwich, Conn.: New York Graphic Society, 1973.

Toll, Robert C. *On with the Show: The First Century of Show Business in America.* New York: Oxford University Press, 1976.

Wilk, Max. *O.K.! The Story of Oklahoma!* New York, Grove Press, 1993.

Zadan, Craig. *Sondheim & Co.* 2d ed. New York: Harper & Row, 1989.

Ziegfeld, Richard, and Paulette Ziegfeld. *The Ziegfeld Touch.* New York: Harry N. Abrams, 1993.

——. *Blacking Up: The Minstrel Show in Nineteenth Century America.* New York: Oxford University Press, 1974.

RECORDINGS AND THE AMERICAN MUSICAL:
A SELECTED DISCOGRAPHY

Recordings were a significant component of the research conducted for this text. This discography offers a complete listing of the recordings consulted, along with basic discographical information. Many of the cited sources are LPs that have yet to be issued on compact disc. Wherever possible, we have included compact discs that are currently available; however, knowing well the vagaries of the recording industry, even those issued in that format may now be deleted from the catalog. At present, the most complete available discographical source for data on original cast and film soundtrack recordings is the excellent *Show Music on Record* (Smithsonian Institution Press, 1992) by Jack Raymond. The authors would also like to thank Mr. Raymond for his advice and encouragement throughout the development of this project.

ANTHOLOGIES

Many anthologies—good, bad, or indifferent— have been issued over the years that convey the recorded high points of the American musical. For charting the major milestones of the American musical stage, *American Musical Theater: Shows, Songs, Stars* (CD/Smithsonian RD-036) offers eighty-four classic performances ranging from Eugene Cowles singing "Gypsy Love Song" from Victor Herbert's *The Fortune Teller* to Zero Mostel and company performing "Sunrise, Sunset" from *Fiddler on the Roof.* The accompanying text provides a historical-critical overview and a show-by-show and featured-song commentary. Also of great merit is the multivolume *Original Cast!* (CD/Metropolitan Opera Guild), which has a number of rare items folded in with more familiar materials and excellent program notes. Recorded anthologies of film musicals tend to be grouped in collections devoted solely to the

Hollywood studios that originally produced them These are discussed below in the discographical entries for chapters 3 and 4. Currently, the only collection to extensively anthologize recordings that document both musical theater and musical film is *Star Spangled Rhythm* (CD/Smithsonian RD 111), which serves as a companion to this text.

SETTING THE STAGE

Aside from the performances themselves, the most fascinating aspect of early American musical theater recordings is what was—and was not—preserved on cylinder and 78-rpm discs. What *does* exist can be heard on the exhaustive 12-CD collection *Music of the New York Stage* (Pearl CD GEMM CDS 9050-2; 9053-8; 9056-8; 9059-61). Present are vintage recordings by many well-remembered (and forgotten) personalities, including Weber and Fields, Bert Williams, Lillian Russell, Nora Bayes, and George M. Cohan, as well as original cast performances of works by Cohan, Williams, Victor Herbert, Irving Berlin, and Jerome Kern. Of the modern reinterpretations of pre-1905 musical theater, *I Wants to Be an Actor Lady* (CD/New World CD-221), performed by students (including a young Kim Criswell) of the University of Cincinnati Conservatory of Music, is authentic, fresh, and highly recommended.

Victor Herbert

An excellent sampling of period recordings of Herbert's rapturous music is displayed on *The Early Victor Herbert: From the Gay Nineties to the First World War* (LP/Smithsonian R017), which features the composer himself conducting selections from *The Fortune Teller, Babes in Toyland, Mademoiselle Modiste, Naughty*

Marietta, and *Sweethearts,* along with rare original cast recordings from *The Fortune Teller* and *Sweethearts.* The Smithsonian's 1980 reconstruction of *Naughty Marietta* (LP/Smithsonian N 026), with carillon-voiced Judy Blazer in the title role, remains the most complete and winningly performed example of Herbert's rich musical style.

George M. Cohan

Cohan's Stars-and-Stripes repertoire receives elaborate treatment in the original cast recording of the biomusical *George M!* (CD/Columbia CK 03200), although Joel Grey's performance owes more to his own brand of powerhouse delivery than to Cohan's homey *Sprechgesang,* at least as evidenced in the latter's extant recordings of Cohan on *A Tribute to George M. Cohan* (LP/Folkways RF-604).

Bert Williams

During the first two decades of the twentieth century, Bert Williams had a prolific recording career, which is meticulously documented on the LP *'Nobody' and Other Songs by Bert Williams* (LP/Folkways RBFA-602).

Sophie Tucker

When it comes to Sophie Tucker's recordings, earlier is definitely better, particularly as evidenced in one of her first efforts, a gutsy version on a 1911 Edison cylinder of her signature tune, "Some of These Days" (preserved on *American Popular Song: Six Decades of Songwriters and Singers,* CD/Smithsonian R031). The best anthology of Tucker's recording career is *Follow a Star* (CD/ASV 5046), a collection consisting of a variety of her early recordings.

CURTAIN UP

Florenz Ziegfeld and the Brothers Shubert

Several excellent LPs preserve the star power and catchy tunes of the Ziegfeld and Shubert revues. Overall, the most diverting is *Follies, Scandals, and Other Diversions from Ziegfeld to the Shuberts* (LP/New World 215), a tasty assemblage of 78s by performers from various *Follies* and *Passing Shows.* An archival reconstruction of the *Ziegfeld Follies of 1919* (LP/Smithsonian R 009) offers seventeen selections from the score, including John Steel's "A Pretty Girl Is Like a Melody" and Eddie Cantor's "You'd Be Surprised."

Fanny Brice

Fanny Brice's twin talents as a comic and chanteuse are showcased in *Fanny Brice Sings the Songs She Made Famous* (LP/Audio Fidelity AFLP 707). Among the gems are the familiar "My Man" and "Second Hand Rose," along with the raucous monologue "Mrs. Cohen at the Beach." On compact disc, an abbreviated slice of Brice makes up half of the contents of *Makin' Whoopee: Fanny Brice and Eddie Cantor* (CD/ProArte CDD-460).

Eddie Cantor

A Centennial Celebration: The Best of Eddie Cantor (CD/BMG 66033) preserves Cantor's frenetic vaudeville style in a progression of sides originally recorded for Victor in the 1910s and 1920s. Included among the rediscoveries are his standards "If You Knew Susie" and "Makin' Whoopee." Cantor also shines in *Whoopee!* (LP/Smithsonian R O12), an archival reassembly that includes some hot sounds from George Olsen's Band (the show's pit orchestra) and Ruth Etting, the latter offering the definitive rendition of "Love Me or Leave Me."

Al Jolson

Of the many reissues of Jolson material, *Stage Highlights* (CD/Pearl 9748) best represents his musical comedy songs, including his hit from *Robinson Crusoe, Jr.,* "Where Did Robinson Crusoe Go with Friday on Saturday Night?" Jolson's screen debut in *The Jazz Singer* has also been issued in LP format (LP/Soundtrak 102).

Eubie Blake and Noble Sissle

Shuffle Along (LP/New World 260) is a remarkable archival reconstruction of various 78s of material from the show performed by original cast members Noble Sissle, Miller and Lyles, Gertrude Saunders, and the composer himself. (Strangely enough, one of the few songs not recorded by a member of the original cast was the perennial "I'm Just Wild about Harry.") Other pre–*Shuffle Along* acoustic recordings by Sissle and Blake from their vaudeville days are contained on an LP bearing the composer's name (LP/Eubie Blake Music 4). A sparkling retrospective of the Sissle-Blake oeuvre is provided with *Eubie!* (LP/Warner Bros. HS-3267), the 1978 Broadway revue that introduced Gregory Hines to Broadway.

Irving Berlin and Jerome Kern

Because of the longevity of their careers, both Irving Berlin and Jerome Kern are extensively documented on decades of recordings, although performances of their early works by original cast members prove maddeningly elusive. Aside from the *Ziegfeld Follies of 1919* LP mentioned above, the most treasurable collection of the earliest Berlin is on *Irving Berlin, 1909–1939* (LP/JJA 19744), which includes an enticing array of 78s. The respective original London casts of *Watch Your Step* (1915) and *Stop! Look! Listen!* (retitled *Follow the Crowd* in the West End) made a number of 78s of numbers from each score, but none of them have been extensively reissued in any modern format (LP or compact disc) to date. Of more recent vintage, the 1960s recital *All by Myself,* volume 1 (LP/Monmouth 6809) with singers Annette Sanders and Steve Clayton re-creates the early material with great charm and authenticity. Several Berlin songs of the Tin Pan Alley era are among the multiple delights of *Unsung Berlin* (CD/Varese Sarabande VSD2-5632), a two-CD set of rediscovered Berlin material (featuring, among many other performers, his granddaughter Mary Ellin Lerner singing the 1914 swinger "If You Don't Want My Peaches, You'd Better Stop Shaking My Tree").

Similarly, early Kern can be savored in both compilations of period recordings and in more recent re-creations. His contributions to the Princess Theatre shows receive glowing performances by the 1918 English cast of *Oh, Boy!* (known as *Oh, Joy!* in London), which are reassembled on the British LP *Jerome Kern in London, 1914–23* (LP/World Records SHB-34). Hearing costars Beatrice Lillie and Tom Powers's charmingly effortless duet on "Till the Clouds Roll By" brings us closest to what the Kern musicals of this period must have sounded like. The LP also features recordings by the 1921 London cast of *Sally*, with American expatriate Dorothy Dickson in the Marilyn Miller role. Dickson is also heard in another Miller role in a reissue of recordings by the 1926 London cast of *Sunny* (LP/World Records SH-240). A number of Kern's pre–*Show Boat* efforts have received excellent revivals both in the theater and/or on recordings. The first of these is the fine 1959 off-Broadway production of *Leave It to Jane* (CD/Stet 15017XP), with Kathleen Murray radiating warmth in the title role. The Goodspeed Opera House–Broadway revival of *Very Good Eddie* (DRG CD/DRG-6100) has much to recommend it, most notably its atmospherically spare, violin-wrapped orchestrations. *Sitting Pretty*, the sixth and final (and least-known) Kern-Bolton-Wodehouse collaboration, gets a full-dress reconstruction in a 1989 recording (CD/New World 80387-2) guided by historian/musicologist John McGlinn, whose immaculate taste and affection for the material make it a very special achievement, indeed.

These scores and their recordings are a mere prelude to the wealth of riches to be found in *Show Boat*, easily one of the most frequently recorded of American musicals. Of the many recordings of excerpts available, the leading candidates are a 1932 collection (CD/CBS A-55) featuring original cast member Helen Morgan and London cast member Paul Robeson and the 1946 revival cast (CD/SONY 5330), which includes Kern's final composition, the song "Nobody Else but Me." John McGlinn's three-CD recording (CD/Angel CDS 7 49108 2), including all the music composed for the work in its many incarnations, is a brilliant accomplishment. The cast recording (CD/Quality RSPD 257) of Harold Prince and Garth Drabinsky's 1994 rethinking of the show is superb throughout, particularly in performances by Elaine Stritch, Lonette McKee, and Gretha Boston.

LIGHT THE LIGHTS

A constellation of the stars who rose to fame during the early years of the talkies made contemporary recordings of their film hits. Of the many compilations that exist, *Stars of the Silver Screen, 1929–1932* (LP/RCA Victor LPV-538) functions as a first-class primer in both performance styles and in examples of classic film songs. A selection of Victor 78s made by movie musical legends, the collection spotlights, among others, Jeanette MacDonald ("Dream Lover"), Maurice Chevalier ("Louise"), and Charles King ("Broadway Melody").

Busby Berkeley

The sounds of the Warner Bros.–Busby Berkeley musical are marvelously recalled in the sumptuous-sounding (and looking) collection, *The Busby Berkeley Musicals* (CD/Turner-Rhino 72169). With its informative program notes and parade of key musical moments from such films *Gold Diggers of 1933*, *Footlight Parade*, *42nd Street*, *Dames*, *In Caliente*, and *Wonder Bar*, this package is a definite must.

Fred Astaire and Ginger Rogers

Although ideally Astaire and Rogers should be *seen* as well as *heard*, virtually all of the musical moments from their films have found their way onto LPs. The finest overall sound quality can be found on two albums on the British EMI label, the first of which pairs the soundtracks of *Swing Time* and *The Gay Divorcee* (LP/EMI EMTC-101) and the second of which teams the soundtracks of *Top Hat* and *Shall We Dance* (LP/EMI EMTC-102). Equally enjoyable, if inferior sonically, are issues of the soundtracks of *Flying Down to Rio* (LP/CIF 3004), *Roberta* (LP/CIF 3001), *Carefree* (LP/CIF 3004), and *The Story of Vernon and Irene Castle* (LP/Caliban 6000). The songs from Astaire and Rogers's 1949 reunion, *The Barkleys of Broadway*, have also been issued in LP format (LP/MGM2-SES-51).

Shirley Temple

The English Conifer label has issued a highly listenable collection of the musical highlights of Shirley Temple's career on the compact disc *Shirley Temple: Little Miss Wonderful* (CD/Conifer CDHD-141). Included are the standbys "On the Good Ship Lollipop" and "Animal Crackers in My Soup" as well as the charming rediscovery "I Like to Walk in the Rain."

Mickey Rooney and Judy Garland

Splendidly remastered soundtrack recordings of songs from the Mickey Rooney–Judy Garland film collaborations *Babes in Arms*, *Strike Up the Band*, *Babes on Broadway*, and *Girl Crazy* are heard in the collection *Mickey and Judy: The Judy Garland & Mickey Rooney Collection* (CD/Turner-Rhino R2 71921). The package includes extensive notes and virtually *all* of the songs in each film and also tosses in a number of alternate takes and deleted numbers. Of special merit are Rooney and Garland's spin on the Gershwin score for *Girl Crazy*—most notably their rambunctious version of "Could You Use Me?" Another tour de force by young Garland is given brilliant focus in the reissue of *The Wizard of Oz* soundtrack (CD/Turner-Rhino R2 71964). Like the *Mickey and Judy* set described above, this edition of *Wizard* includes everything recorded for the 1939 film, including the swinging discard, "The Jitterbug," and a touching reprise of "Over the Rainbow" that was cut from the final print. Historian John Fricke's program notes combine solid historical data with a real ardor for the subject. Two other classic examples of Garland on screen can be savored on the soundtracks of *Meet Me in St. Louis* (CD/MGM 305123) and *A Star Is Born* (CD/Columbia CK-44389).

Ethel Waters

Two of Ethel Waters's hits from *As Thousands Cheer* ("Heat Wave," "Harlem on My Mind") are included on CD/CBS A-2792. "Supper Time" was not recorded until late in her career (LP/Mercury 20051). Waters is also featured in two numbers ("Hottentot Potentate," "Thief in the Night") on *At Home Abroad* (LP/Smithsonian R 024). *Cabin in the Sky* offered Waters her best musical comedy role. Her 78s of four songs from the score ("Taking a Chance on Love," "Love Turned the Light Out," "Cabin in the Sky," "Honey in the Honeycomb"), along with the original overture, have been reissued on compact disc (CD/AEI 117), as has the soundtrack of the film version (CD/Turner-Rhino R272245).

Lena Horne

Aside from her many LPs of popular songs and her two original cast recordings (*Jamaica*: CD/BMG 09026-68041-2; *A Lady and Her Music*: LP/Qwest 2QW-3597), Lena Horne can be heard on commercially issued soundtracks of the MGM musicals *Panama Hattie* (on *Cole Porter in Hollywood, 1929–1956*, LP/JJA 19767), *Cabin in the Sky* (see "Ethel Waters"), *As Thousands Cheer* (LP/Hollywood Soundstage 409), *Till the Clouds Roll By* (CD/Sandy Hook CDSH 2080), *Ziegfeld Follies* (CD/Turner-Rhino 71959), and *Words and Music* (CD/MCA MCAD-5949). The soundtrack of *Stormy Weather*, which also stars Bill Robinson, has been remastered and issued on compact disc (CD/Fox 11007).

George and Ira Gershwin

There are several options to sample the George and Ira Gershwin theater scores. For starters, try the archival reconstructions (with original Broadway and London casts) of *Lady, Be Good!* (LP/Smithsonian R-008), *Oh, Kay!* (LP/Smithsonian R-011), and *Funny Face* (LP/Smithsonian R-019) to hear the youthful Fred and Adele Astaire and the glorious Gertrude Lawrence. A long-term collaboration between Roxbury Recordings (fronted by the

late Mrs. Ira Gershwin) and the Library of Congress resulted in comprehensive recordings of *Lady, Be Good!* (CD/Elektra Nonesuch 79308-2), *Oh, Kay!* (CD/Nonesuch 79361-2), *Strike Up the Band* (1927 version, CD/Elektra Nonesuch 979273-2), *Girl Crazy* (CD/Elektra Nonesuch 9 79250-2), and *Pardon My English* (CD/Elektra Nonesuch 79338-2). If the choice of soloists occasionally leaves more than a bit to be desired, Tommy Krasker's restorations/approximations of the original orchestrations are "delishious," to borrow a word from one of Ira's lyrics. Gershwin musicologist Michael Tilson Thomas supervises and conducts complete recorded versions of *Of Thee I Sing* and *Let 'Em Eat Cake* (CD/CBS M2K 42522), with Maureen McGovern, Larry Kert, and Jack Gilford in the leads. Multiple recordings exist of the *Porgy and Bess* score. Essential to every show music collection is the recording featuring original cast members Todd Duncan and Anne Brown (CD/MCA MCAD-10520), which preserves fourteen selections from the opera. The most complete and intensely theatrical version of *Porgy* is the 1976 Houston Grand Opera production (CD/RCA RCD3-2109), starring Donnie Ray Albert and the extraordinary Clamma Dale. The four-CD archival collection *I Got Rhythm: The Music of George Gershwin* (CD/Smithsonian RD 107) provides an extensive overview of the composer's work. For this study, of particular interest is volume 2 of the set, which spotlights 22 cuts featuring original cast and original soundtrack performances. *Crazy for You* (CD/Angel 54618) is a high-spirited reworking of the score for *Girl Crazy*, with the bonus of added Gershwin tunes from other sources. Ira after George is heard to best advantage in the various recordings of *Lady in the Dark*. Gertrude Lawrence's Victor set (LP/LPV-503), made during the Broadway run, is definitive, although the radio soundtrack release on the AEI label (CD/AEI-CD 003) preserves six songs from the score with a fair amount of Moss Hart's script. Hart also wrote the screenplay for Ira's last hurrah, the 1955 Judy Garland remake of *A Star Is Born* (CD/Columbia CK-44389).

Richard Rodgers and Lorenz Hart

Rodgers and Hart in Hollywood, volume 1 (LP/JJA 19766), contains treasurable soundtracks from such early films as *Masters of Melody* (a 1930 short featuring the songwriters themselves performing their own works), *The Hot Heiress* (1930), *Love Me Tonight* (1932), *The Phantom President* (1932, starring George M. Cohan), *Hallelujah, I'm a Bum* (1933), and *Mississippi* (1935). Their theatrical collaborations can be appreciated through a selection of studio re-creations and revivals. The 1943 production of *A Connecticut Yankee* (LP/AEI 1138) is distinguished by Vivienne Segal's authoritative performance as temptress Morgan LeFay. The George Abbott–supervised 1983 Broadway revival of *On Your Toes* (CD/TER 2-1063) boasts a vibrant cast and complete orchestral renditions of Rodgers's ballets "La Princesse Zenobia" and "Slaughter on Tenth Avenue." A 1989 concert version of *Babes in Arms* (CD/New World NW-386-2) also includes its ballet ("Peter's Journey") along with fresh interpretations of its hit parade score. The 1950s Goddard Leiberson–supervised Columbia studio cast recordings of *The Boys from Syracuse* (CD/Columbia SK 53329, with Portia Nelson and Jack Cassidy) and *Pal Joey* (CD/Columbia CK 4364, with Vivienne Segal and Harold Lang) still outshine all other comers, although the 1995 revival of the latter, starring Patti LuPone and Peter Gallagher (CD/DRG 94763), is notable for its use of the original Hans Spialek orchestrations. A 1967 revival of *By Jupiter* yielded a zestful recording (LP/RCA Victor LSO-1137) of Rodgers and Hart's final score.

Marc Blitzstein

The 1938 Musicraft 78s of Marc Blitzstein's *The Cradle Will Rock* represent the first American original cast album of a complete Broadway score. These have been reissued on LP (LP/American Legacy T-1001). A 1985 London revival (CD/TER 1105) features superior sound and Patti LuPone's dramatic rendition of "The Nickel under the Foot." *No for an Answer* (1941), something of a companion piece to *Cradle*, includes a very young Carol Channing in its cast recording (LP/AEI 1140). Blitzstein's final two Broadway scores are also covered on LPs: *Regina*, a 1949 operatic adaptation of the play *The Little Foxes*, is preserved in its entirety by the cast of the 1958 New York City Opera production (LP/Columbia-Odyssey Y3 35236); *Juno*, a musical version of O'Casey's *Juno and the Paycock*, features Shirley Booth heading the 1959 Broadway cast (LP/Columbia OS-2013).

Cole Porter

From This Moment On: The Songs of Cole Porter (CD/Smithsonian RD 047) offers a cavalcade of Porteriana, highlighted by a number of original cast excerpts. Porter's Hollywood legacy is best served by soundtrack recordings from *Born to Dance* (LP/CIF3001), *Broadway Melody of 1940* (LP/CIF 3002), *The Pirate* (CD/Sony AK 48608), and *High Society* (CD/Capitol 93787). Porter's early stage musicals exist only in recorded excerpts, with the exception of his 1929 show *Fifty Million Frenchmen*. It has been preserved in toto in a handsome 1991 recording (CD/New World 80417-2) featuring a large, talented cast of young and seasoned professionals. The Smithsonian label has reissued assemblies of 78s documenting the Broadway productions of *Anything Goes* (LP/Smithsonian R 007), *Red, Hot and Blue!*, *Leave It to Me!*, and *Let's Face It!* (all on LP/Smithsonian R 016). The remainder of Porter's scores for Ethel Merman can be found, respectively, on *Red, Hot, and Blue!* (CD/AEI 1142) and *Panama Hattie* (CD/MCA 10521), both consisting of 78s reissues, and *Something for the Boys* (CD/AEI CD-004), a transcription of a wartime Armed Forces Radio broadcast. Porter himself is heard in rare demo recordings of his scores for *Jubilee* and *Can-Can* on the valuable reissue *Cole Sings Porter* (CD/Koch 7171). His 1940s and 1950s Broadway shows are all best served by their original cast recordings, particularly the masterful *Kiss Me, Kate* (CD/Columbia CK 4140) and the unjustly obscure *Out of This World* (CD/SONY SK 48223). Porter's only original television musical, *Aladdin*, is preserved in a

recording by members of its video cast (CD/SONY SK 48205).

Walt Disney

A bountiful assembly of songs from the soundtrack of Disney films is offered in the two-volume *The Disney Collection* (CD/Disneyland CD-002/003). The soundtrack of *Snow White and the Seven Dwarfs* (CD/Disneyland 004), which includes the deleted song "Music in My Soup," was issued during the film's fiftieth anniversary year. Disney Studios has maintained an ongoing commitment to the musical over the years in live-action and/or animated features. Deserving of special mention are the soundtrack recordings of *Pinocchio* (LP/Disneyland WDL-4002), *Mary Poppins* (CD/Disney CD-016), *The Little Mermaid* (CD/Disney CD-018), and *Beauty and the Beast* (CD/Disney 606812).

George Abbott

Besides the scores for *On Your Toes*, *The Boys from Syracuse*, and *Pal Joey* listed above under *Rodgers and Hart*, the other Abbott-directed musicals with cast albums that demonstrate his energetic, down-to-brass-tacks staging approach include *The Pajama Game* (CD/Columbia CK-32606), *Damn Yankees* (CD//RCA 3948-2-RG), *Fiorello!* (CD/Angel 65023), *Once upon a Mattress* (CD/MCA 10768), and *Flora, the Red Menace* (CD/BMG 09026-60821-2).

THE HEIGHTS

Richard Rodgers and Oscar Hammerstein

The 1940s ushered in the great era of the original cast recording and the original soundtrack—first on 78s, and then on LP. The Rodgers and Hammerstein legacy is, for the most part, best conveyed through recordings by their original Broadway companies—*Oklahoma!* (CD/MCA MCAD-10046), *Carousel* (CD/MCA MCAD-10048), *Allegro* (CD/BMG 52758), *South Pacific* (CD/CK32604), *The King and I* (CD/MCA

MCAD-10049), *Me and Juliet* (LP/RCA LOC-1012), *Pipe Dream* (CD/BMG 09026-61481-2), *Flower Drum Song* (CD/Columbia CK-2009), and *The Sound of Music* (CD/Columbia CK-32601). Only the last named is superseded by the soundtrack of its film version (CD/RCA PCD1-2005), a rare instance of Hollywood improving upon the stage original. In addition, there are recordings of the TV musical *Cinderella* performed by casts from both its 1957 (CD/Columbia CK-2005) and 1965 (CD/Sony 53538) productions.

Alfred Drake

Drake's best role came in 1948's *Kiss Me, Kate* (see "Cole Porter"), which shows off his virile baritone and flair for high comedy. He recorded twice his Tony-winning portrayal of Hajj the beggar in *Kismet*. The 1965 revival cast (CD/RCA 68040) has the advantage of rich stereo sound. However, the original 1953 cast album (CD/Columbia CK-32605) capitalizes on the tongue-in-cheek sensibilities of the show and offers a better cast. *Kean* (LP/Columbia KOS-2120) is notable for Drake's striking turn as Shakespearean actor Edmund Kean, although the lushly orchestrated score is undistinguished. Drake's final recorded effort, a stage adaptation of the film *Gigi* (CD/RCA 68070), finds him in fine fettle in the role originally created in the film by Maurice Chevalier.

Mary Martin

Martin's career can be expressed primarily in two phases: the saucy temptress of the late 1930s and early 1940s and the lovable tomboy-at-heart that more or less became her permanent onstage persona in the mid-1940s. Early Martin gets an excellent display in *Mary Martin: The Decca Years, 1938–1946* (CD/KOCH 3-790-2), which includes a version of her first showstopper, "My Heart Belongs to Daddy," as well as selections from the musicals *One Touch of Venus* ("Speak Low") and *Lute Song* ("Mountain High, Valley Low"). The albums of selections from *One Touch of Venus* (LP/Decca

79122) and *Lute Song* (LP/Decca DL 8030) reveal an actress in states of transition—in fine voice but curiously remote in personality. Her best show album performances are contained in *South Pacific* (see "Richard Rodgers and Oscar Hammerstein"), *Peter Pan* (CD/BMG 3762-2-RG), and *The Sound of Music* (see "Richard Rodgers and Oscar Hammerstein"), all of which give ample outlets for her immense good cheer and hearty professionalism.

Ethel Merman

The best of Merman's earliest show music recordings can be found above listed under the entry on Cole Porter. Merman recorded three separate albums devoted to the score of *Annie Get Your Gun*. The last (LP/London XPS-905) is the least impressive, with its soupy orchestrations and substandard supporting cast. The Decca 1946 cast album (CD/MCA MCAD-10047) is classic Merman, although she is in fine voice in the more vividly theatrical 1966 revival recording (CD/RCA 1124-2-RC). Her contract with Decca kept her from appearing on the RCA cast recording of *Call Me Madam* (LP/RCA LOC-1000), where she was supplanted, if not precisely replaced, by RCA contractee Dinah Shore. Merman's studio recording of the show (CD/MCA 10521) is game but disappointing—only she, and not her fellow singers (Dick Haymes, Eileen Barton), seems to be having a good time. The show's 1954 film soundtrack (Stet DS-25001) is easily the best of the lot. If there was no other Merman show recording, the cast album of *Gypsy* (CD/Columbia CK-32607) would be more than enough to show the depth and breadth of her considerable talents as an actress, singer, and all-out entertainer.

Dorothy Fields

Fields's five-decade career as a lyricist is extensively archived on sound recordings, beginning with *Blackbirds of 1928* (LP/Columbia OL-6770). *Swing Time* (listed under "Fred Astaire and Ginger Rogers") is a felicitous demonstration of her work with Kern, and her ability to portray the Merman persona is evident in *Stars*

in Your Eyes (CD/AEI 1142). Her finest overall work for the theater was done for *A Tree Grows in Brooklyn* (CD/SONY SK 48014), although both *Sweet Charity* (CD/Columbia CK-2900) and *Seesaw* (CD/DRG CDRG-6108) contain some delightful material that expresses her characteristic big-city tender cynicism.

Alan Jay Lerner and Frederick Loewe

Lerner and Loewe's first work to be committed to an original cast recording is *Brigadoon* (CD/BMG 1001-2 RG). The recording still has merit, although it has been surpassed in quality and completeness by several subsequent recordings—most notably, a 1957 album with Jack Cassidy and Shirley Jones (LP/Columbia OS-2540). Lively moments and beautiful music abound in the cast recording of *Paint Your Wagon* (CD/BMG 60243-2-RG), although, aside from star James Barton, the cast seems second-rate. Goddard Lieberson's cast recording of *My Fair Lady* (CD/Columbia CK-5090) is a timeless triumph, with Rex Harrison, Julie Andrews, and Stanley Holloway delivering at the peak of their powers. Lerner sings "Come to the Ball," a number deleted from *My Fair Lady*, on *American Songbooks: Alan Jay Lerner* (CD/Smithsonian RD 048-8). Liberated from Lerner's muddled script, the original cast album of *Camelot* (CD/Columbia CK-32602) offers a delightful collection of songs and performances. Post-Loewe Lerner is a mixed lot, although the cast recordings of *On a Clear Day You Can See Forever* (CD/BMG 60820) and *Carmelina* (CD/OC 8019) are well worth investigation.

Julie Andrews

Aside from her appearances in *My Fair Lady* and *Camelot*, Andrews's finest musical moments can be traced to her fresh-as-a-mountain-spring appearances in the films *Mary Poppins* (see "Walt Disney") and *The Sound of Music* (see "Richard Rodgers and Oscar Hammerstein"). Worth hearing also is her Broadway debut at the age of nineteen in *The Boy Friend* (CD/RCA 60056-RG). Her triumphant performances in the film

(LP/MGM MG-1-5407) and stage version (CD/Phillips 446 919-2) of *Victor/Victoria* are highly enjoyable in their respective recordings, as is her 1992 recording of *The King and I* (Phillips 438 007-2).

Vincente Minnelli, Gene Kelly, and the Hollywood Musical

Many of the major contributors to the MGM musical are celebrated in the mammoth six-CD collection *That's Entertainment* (CD/Turner-Rhino 72182). This compendium traces the evolution of the MGM musical from its first incarnations through the glory days of the Arthur Freed Unit. The past decade has produced a major reissue on compact disc format of soundtracks from classic MGM film musicals. These include *Meet Me in St. Louis* (CD/MGM 305123), *An American in Paris* (CD/CBS AK-45391), *Singin' in the Rain* (CD/CBS AK-45394), and *Gigi* (CD/CBS AK-45395).

Leonard Bernstein

The original Broadway production of *On the Town* did not have a cast album, although stars Nancy Walker, Betty Comden, and Adolph Green did make 78 singles of their numbers (LP/Decca DL 8030). In 1960 Bernstein presided over a dazzling recording for Columbia (CD/Columbia CK-2038), which reunited original casters Walker, Comden, Green, and Cris Alexander, with the composer himself making an uncredited vocal appearance. Although *Wonderful Town* has two recordings with Rosalind Russell in the lead—with the Broadway company (CD/MCA MCAD-10050) and with the 1958 TV cast (CD/SONY 48021)—the former has the edge, particularly because of Edith (Edie) Adams's deft performance as Eileen. The 1956 cast recording of *Candide* (CD/CBS MK-38732) is an unequaled classic, although the 1982 New York City Opera production (CD/New World 3402/341-2) is more complete and splendidly sung. *West Side Story* is freshest in its performance by the Broadway company (CD/Columbia CK-32603). Also worthy of note is *Leonard Bernstein Revisited* (LP/Painted Smiles PS 1377), which includes songs dropped from the score of *Wonderful Town* and several selections from Bernstein's final stage musical, *1600 Pennsylvania Avenue.*

Betty Comden and Adolph Green

Along with their musicals written with Leonard Bernstein and Jule Styne, Comden and Green have written two splendidly theatrical scores with Cy Coleman: *On the Twentieth Century* (CD/SONY SK 35330) and *The Will Rogers Follies* (CD/Columbia CK 48606). But their work sounds best in their own hands, as their duo-revue, *A Party with Comden and Green*, attests. The show has been recorded twice: first in a 1958 performance on Capitol (now available on CD/Angel 64773) and in a more complete 1977 version (CD/DRG CD-2-5177).

Jule Styne

Jule Styne's Broadway brashness is conveyed in a variety of cast recordings, beginning with the turn-of-the-century romp *High Button Shoes* (LP/RCA LSO-1107). A parade of star vehicles follows: Carol Channing in *Gentlemen Prefer Blondes* (CD/SONY SK 48013), Bert Lahr and Dolores Gray in *Two on the Aisle* (LP/Decca DL 8040), Mary Martin in *Peter Pan* (see "Mary Martin"), Judy Holliday in *Bells Are Ringing* (CD/Columbia CK-2006), and his crowning achievement, Ethel Merman in *Gypsy* (see "Ethel Merman"). The 1960s and 1970s found Styne, for the most part, abandoning the marvel of *Gypsy* for a return to formula, albeit tuneful and enjoyable. From this late period of his work, his finest efforts are *Funny Girl* (CD/Capitol CDP-746634), *Hallelujah, Baby!* (CD/SONY SK 48218), and *Darling of the Day* (LP/RCA LSO-1149).

Chita Rivera

Chita Rivera's fiery brilliance as a dancer has often obscured her skillful way with a theater song. Virtually all of the significant milestones in her career have been recorded, including her earliest efforts as a supporting player in the now campy 1950s musicals *Seventh Heaven* (LP/Decca DL 9001) and *Mr. Wonderful* (CD/MCAD-10303). The original cast recording of *West Side Story* (see "Leonard Bernstein") preserves, among others, her vibrant rendition of "America," while the cast album of *Bye Bye Birdie* (CD/Columbia CK-2025) reveals her comic talents. Both *Bajour* (CD/Columbia SK 48208) and *Zenda* (LP/Blue Pear BP 1007) offer Rivera amusing but unchallenging material; however, her performances of the fine Kander-Ebb songs on the cast recordings of *The Rink* (CD/Polydor 823124-2) and *Kiss of the Spider Woman* (CD/BMG 09026-61579-2) reveal an artist at the summit of her powers.

Frank Loesser

Aside from *Where's Charley?*, which exists only in a recording by its 1958 British cast (CD/Angel ZDM 7243 5 65072 2 8), virtually all of Frank Loesser's stage musicals received original cast recordings. The 1950 Broadway production of *Guys and Dolls* (CD/MCA MCAD-10301) is still a charmer, although the cast recording of the 1992 Broadway revival (CD/BMG 09026-61317-2) is splendid throughout, particularly in Faith Prince's Miss Adelaide and Nathan Lane's Nathan Detroit. Loesser's expansive score for *The Most Happy Fella* (CD/Columbia S2K 48010) is passionately performed by its original cast, headed by Robert Weede and Jo Sullivan (Loesser). The ethereal *Greenwillow*, one of Loesser's rare theatrical failures, is happily back in the bins (at this writing), thanks to a current reissue of its 1960 RCA cast recording (CD/DRG 19006). Robert Morse's guilefully guileless performance on the original cast recording *How to Succeed . . .* (CD/RCA 60352-2-RG) makes the most of Loesser's cynical satire of urban big business.

Barbara Cook

Barbara Cook's Broadway career can be traced through the legacy of her cast recordings (only her appearance in 1965's *Something More*

went unrecorded). The chirping winsomeness of *Flahooley* (CD/Angel ZDM 7 64764 2 1) and *Plain and Fancy* (CD/Angel ZDM 7 64762 2) is supplanted by the more mature pleasures of *Candide* (see "Leonard Bernstein"), *The Music Man* (CD/Angel ZD 7 64663 2), *The Gay Life* (CD/Angel ZDM 7 64763 2), *She Loves Me* (CD/Polydor 831968-2), and *The Grass Harp* (CD/Painted Smiles PSCD-102).

"SIDE BY SIDE BY SIDE"

Jerry Herman

One of the rarest of original cast recordings is Herman's promising 1960 revue *Parade* (LP/KAPP 7005). The score for *Milk and Honey* (CD/BMG 09026-61997-2) is intensely romantic and lovely in the voices of Robert Weede and Mimi Benzell and touchingly comic in the gamboling of Molly Picon. There is really only one Dolly—Carol Channing. It's intriguing to compare her performance on the 1964 original cast album (CD/RCA 3814-2-RG) with that heard on the thirtieth anniversary revival cast recording (CD/Varese Sarabande VSD 5557). Angela Lansbury brims with good cheer (and talent) on the cast recording of *Mame* (CD/Columbia CK-3000), ably abetted by Beatrice Arthur and Jane Connell. *Dear World* (CD/SONY 48220) offers Lansbury's brilliant take on the role of the Madwoman of Chaillot, and Herman's lovely tunes glimmering amid a miasma of bloated orchestrations. *Mack and Mabel*, with its spectacular cast and splendid score, clearly deserved a more felicitous fate; however, its cast album (CD/MCA 10523) is a gem from start to finish. The wildly popular *La Cage aux Folles* (CD/RCA RCD1-4824) is musically uneven, although George Hearn is hilarious and touching as the show's hero/heroine.

Gower Champion

In addition to *Hello, Dolly!* and *Mack and Mabel* (see "Jerry Herman"), there are three other original cast recordings that are essential to studying Champion's magic touch in shaping a musical: the youthful *Bye Bye Birdie* (CD/Columbia CK-2025), the wistful *Carnival!* (CD/Polydor 837195-2), and his pull-the-stops-out grand finale, *42nd Street* (CD/RCA RCD1-3891).

Bob Fosse
Fosse's sexy, jazzy style is first evidenced in "From This Moment On," on the soundtrack to the 1953 film version of *Kiss Me, Kate* (CD/CBS AK-46196) and the original cast recording of *The Pajama Game* (see "George Abbott"). Virtually all of his collaborations with Gwen Verdon have been recorded, from the traditional musical comedy exercises in *Damn Yankees* (see "George Abbott"), *New Girl in Town* (CD/BMG 09026-61996-2), and *Redhead* (CD/BMG 09026-61995-2) to the adventurous, experimental natures of *Sweet Charity* (see "Dorothy Fields") and *Chicago* (CD/Bay Cities BCD-3003). Minus the sight of Fosse's corybantic staging style, the score of *Pippin* (CD/Motown MCDO-6186) seems fairly ordinary. However, the soundtrack of his film version of *Cabaret* (LP/ABC 752) is a gritty, tinseled classic.

Joseph Papp
Papp's first production of a musical—*Hair*—sprouts a sunburst of flower power in the 1967 original Public Theater cast recording (LP/RCA LSO-1143). Papp's second musical with Galt MacDermot as composer is the Latin jazz and blues-flavored *Two Gentlemen of Verona* (LP/ABC BCSY-1001), with Raul Julia and Jonelle Allen as standouts in a cast that recalls the youthfulness (if not the innocence) of *Babes in Arms*. The original cast album of *A Chorus Line* (CD/Columbia CK-33581), like the show itself, is a milestone, ranking as one of the greatest of all show albums.

Michael Bennett
Bennett appeared in the chorus of two middling 1960s musicals, *Here's Love* (LP/Columbia KOS-2400) and *Bajour* (CD/SONY SK 48208). His debut as a Broadway choreographer is documented via some vigorous, Copland-esque dance music on a live performance recording of *A Joyful Noise* (LP/Blue Pear BP 1018). Along with his work for *Company* and *Follies* (see "Harold Prince"), essential clues to Bennett's skill is manifested in the cast albums of *Promises, Promises* (LP/United Artists 9902), *Coco* (LP/Paramount PMS-1002), *Seesaw* (see "Dorothy Fields"), *A Chorus Line* (listed under "Joseph Papp"), *Ballroom* (LP/Columbia JS 35762), and *Dreamgirls* (CD/Geffen 2007 2).

Geoffrey Holder
Holder's first significant appearance in a Broadway musical was in the legendary failure *House of Flowers* (CD/CBS A-2320), with its ravishing, Caribbean-flavored score by Harold Arlen and Truman Capote. Even without Holder's opulent visual decor, Charlie Smalls's score for *The Wiz* (LP/Atlantic SD-18137) is galvanic and brimming with vitality, from the insinuating "Ease on Down the Road" to the Wicked Witch's humorous tirade "Don't Nobody Bring Me No Bad News."

Gregory Hines
The cast album of the revue *Eubie!* (see "Eubie Blake and Noble Sissle") represents Hines's dynamic debut as a musical comedy comer. *Sophisticated Ladies* (LP/RCA CBL2-4053) gives him a chance to refine his image, as he croons the sleek, moody Duke Ellington ballads "Sophisticated Lady" and "Something to Live For." The star-making *Jelly's Last Jam* (CD/Mercury P2-10846) is a veritable showcase for both Hines and the music of Jelly Roll Morton.

Stephen Sondheim
Stephen Sondheim's theater compositions have been scrupulously documented on recordings, beginning with his lyrics for *West Side Story* (see "Leonard Bernstein") and *Gypsy* (see "Ethel Merman"). Songs from an early effort, the unproduced *Saturday Night*, are found on *A Stephen Sondheim Evening* (CD/RCA

61174). *A Funny Thing Happened on the Way to the Forum* (CD/Bay Cities BCD-3002) and *Anyone Can Whistle* (CD/Columbia CK-2480) are audacious, melodic, and wildly funny. He would like to forget his collaboration with Richard Rodgers on 1965's *Do I Hear a Waltz?* (CD/SONY 48206), although the score is wistfully engaging. His collaborations with Harold Prince are beautifully captured on their original cast recordings: *Company* (CD/CBS CK-3550), *A Little Night Music* (CD/Columbia CK-32265), *Pacific Overtures* (CD/RCA RCD1-4407), *Sweeney Todd* (CD/RCA 3379-2-RC), and *Merrily We Roll Along* (CD/RCA RCD1-5840). Sondheim enthusiasts still shake their fists at Capitol Records for their abbreviated cast album of *Follies* (CD/Angel ZDM 7 64666 2). A more extended treatment of the score (with an unrepeatably starry cast) is available on a 1983 concert version (CD/RCA RCD2-7128).

Sondheim's work in the last decade has been both innovative and remote. His partnership with James Lapine has yielded some challenging material, as evidenced in *Sunday in the Park with George* (CD/RCA RCD1-5042), *Into the Woods* (CD/RCA 6796-2 RC), and *Passion* (CD/Angel CDQ 7243 5 55251 23).

Harold Prince
(See listings under "Jerome Kern," "George Abbott," and "Stephen Sondheim"). The 1966 Broadway production of *Cabaret* (CD/CK-3040) marked Prince's striking personal use of the idea of the concept musical. Among the other important musicals stamped with his distinctive style are *She Loves Me* (see "Barbara Cook"), *Zorba* (CD/Angel ZDM 7 64665 2), *Kiss of the Spider Woman* (CD/RCA 09026-61579-2), and two works by British composer Andrew Lloyd Webber: *Evita* (CD/MCA D2-11007) and *The Phantom of the Opera* (CD/Polydor 831273-2).

SOURCE NOTES FOR SONG LYRICS

PHOTOGRAPHY CREDITS

The appearance of Mr. Fred Astaire has been contributed through a special license with Mrs. Fred Astaire, Beverly Hills, California. All rights reserved.

Sheet music for "Top Hat, White Tie, and Tails," "Some Day My Prince Will Come," "There's No Business Like Show Business," and "You're Just in Love" is courtesy of The Estate of Irving Berlin.

Image on p. 82 is © Turner Entertainment Company. All rights reserved.

INDEX